Library of Congress Cataloging-in-Publication Data

Cuyvers, Luc, 1954–
    Sea power : a global journey / text and
  photography by Luc Cuyvers.
        p.   cm.
    Includes bibliographical references.
    ISBN 1-55750-145-9. —ISBN 1-55750-146-7 (pbk.)
    1. Shipping. 2. Sea power. 3. Ocean travel. 1. Title.
    HE571.C89   1993
387.5—dc20   93-4470

Printed in the United States of America on acid-free paper ♾

9 8 7 6 5 4 3 2

First printing

Page i: A view from the foremast of the Portuguese naval training ship *Sagres.*

Page iii: Odysseus and the Sirens, as painted on a vase of the fifth century B.C. The Greeks left us many accounts and illustrations, providing the first complete record of the maritime doings of the ancient Mediterranean.

Page vi: Portuguese sailors climb the rigging of the Portuguese naval training ship *Sagres.*

Page x—xi: Hong Kong's *Star Ferry.* Still one of the most scenic, and cheapest, rides in the world.

To my parents

with deep appreciation for the many years

of support and encouragement

Contents

Acknowledgments

One of the nice things about writing a book, as opposed to making a television program, is that you can do it by yourself. All you need is a pen and paper, or preferably a word processor, something to write about, and off you go. At least, that's how it works in theory. In practice it is often a different matter. This book couldn't have been done without the help of a lot of people, to whom I am deeply indebted. It is impossible to mention all, but I'll do my best.

Getting aboard the several ships that are featured in this book was a major challenge. For one thing, there was the matter of working out schedules. Some shipping lines operate like veritable bus services, but most don't, and joining their ships within well-defined time limits proved to be a brainteaser. There also was the matter of permissions. Oil tanker companies, for instance, are not keen on taking along writers. As far as I can tell they have nothing to hide, but after getting a bum wrap from the press for many years, they'd rather not deal with it. So back came the negative replies from Exxon, Mobil, Shell, and others.

Nonetheless, I did eventually get on a tanker, courtesy of the Troodos Shipping Company, which kindly allowed me to sail along on the *Crown,* one of its Greek-flagged vessels. Meeting up with the ship, and her unpredictable schedule, took a couple tries but it finally worked and was well worth the effort. Of the many people at Troodos, I would like to thank Captain Richard Gunns, Captain Roger Holt and Captain George Fragiadakis in particular for allowing me aboard. As for the *Crown* herself, I'll never forget the hospitality I received from her officers and crew. A special thank you goes to Captain Kostas Papagiannakis and Chief Officer Kanaris Antonopoulos for sharing so much about their work, and to Chief Steward Petros Viazis for the punctual (10:00 A.M. and 3:00 P.M.) frappés.

Getting aboard the *OOCL Envoy* for the trip described in chapter two was easier, because most container vessels stick meticulously to a schedule. Nonetheless, if it weren't for the kind cooperation from Hong Kong–based Orient Overseas Container Line (OOCL), I wouldn't have been able to join her trans-Pacific crossing. Thank you Jaemi Frankenberger and Stanley Chen for making the trip possible. I am also indebted to the officers and crew of the *Envoy,* and in particular to Martin Weir, her indelible master. Thank you also Terrance, Andy, Simon, and Bee for showing me around and sharing what life at sea is all about.

It didn't take a great deal of foresight to plan the Caribbean trip aboard the *Majesty of the Seas* for the middle of January, yet it wouldn't have been possible without the kind cooperation of the people at Royal Caribbean Cruises, Ltd., where Jim Lida in particular was extremely generous with his time and assistance. Special thanks also go to the officers and crew of the *Majesty,* who introduce some 2,500 landlubbers a week to a different kind of sea power. I am particularly indebted to Captain Eigil Eriksen, Staff Captain Gunnar Liland, Chief Engineer Tormod Isaksen, Hotel Manager Barry Jones, Cruise Director Jeffrey Arpin, and Executive Chef Werner Zürcher for generously allowing me a look behind the scenes.

A book on sea power wouldn't be complete without naval vessels, and I was particularly fortunate to be permitted aboard the USS *Ranger* and the USS *Valley Forge,* as they were diverted from Operation Southern Watch in the Persian Gulf to Operation Restore Hope off Somalia. I am indebted to Rear Admiral Kendell Pease, the U.S. Navy's Chief of Information, and Commander Charles Quigley, Assistant Chief of Information, for allowing me to join this fascinating trip. Many thanks also to Lieutenant Jim Fallin for working out the details, and to Fred Rainbow, Editor-in-Chief of *Proceedings,* for putting in a good word on my behalf.

Visitors sometimes feel out of place aboard ships that have been away for months on end, but that certainly was not my experience aboard the *Ranger* and the *Valley Forge.* In fact, the officers and crew of both vessels actually went out of their way to make me feel welcome, for which I am grateful. Aboard the *Ranger,* I was fortunate to spend some time with Rear Admiral William Hancock, Commander, Cruiser Destroyer Group One; Captain Dennis McGinn, Commanding Officer; and Commander Frank Bossio, Executive Officer. Lieutenant Rod Hill, the ship's public affairs officer, meanwhile, helped me figure out which way was forward and aft in a matter of days.

Due to unforeseen circumstances I remained on the *Valley Forge* longer than expected, but it wasn't a delay I will ever regret. I am grateful to Captain Billy Cornett, II, Commanding Officer; Lieutenant Commander Alvin Smith, Executive Officer; and Master Chief George Luiz for extending the welcome mat for several days. And thank you to all other officers and crew who so generously gave of their time to provide insight into the workings of an Aegis cruiser.

The most northerly excursion described in this book was made possible through the kind cooperation of Norsk Hydro A.S., operator of the North Sea's massive Oseberg oil field. Making sure I got the most out of a relatively short trip were Ove Lunde, public relations manager; Øivind Berg, senior training officer; and Eigill Nysæther, chief geologist. Many thanks are also due Svein Vaksdal, platform manager of the Oseberg Field Center, and Eirl Marholm, shipment manager at the Mongstad Base, who arranged passage aboard a supply vessel. Both Captain Ollbjørn Austnes and First Officer Per Gunnar Vasdal of the *Far Sky* made the short trip to the platform extremely pleasant and interesting.

The final voyage would not have been possible without the cooperation of series co-producer NHK, where Executive Producer Masao Ogasawara and Producer Syunya Hirano coordinated our request to join the Japan Marine Science and Technology Center research vessel *Yokosuka.* It is thanks to their tireless efforts that Jamstec allowed me and a camera crew to join the *Yokosuka* on one of her trips to the Japan Trench. At Jamstec I am indebted to Dr. Hiroshi Hotta, Director of the Deep Sea Research Department, Tadaaki Soejima, Manager of Public Relations, and Katsumi Sakakura for their invaluable support and assistance. Many thanks go also to the officers and the crew of the R.V. *Yokosuka,* headed by Captain Hiroshi Hyōdo, who treated this gaijin with a great deal of consideration.

Because this book was tied to a television series, there was naturally a bit of inter-action between the two, from which both benefitted, I hope. As far as the television side of the equation is concerned, I am indebted to Glenn Tolbert for developing the Sea Power series idea and then sticking with it long enough to get it into production. A special thank you goes to Executive Producer Leo Eaton of Maryland Public Televi-sion for inviting me to be a part of the project, and then managing to keep me at it until the very end.

Producers David Clark, Nigel Turner, and Glenn Tolbert, along with their Asso-ciate Producers Gabrielle Davidson, Sarah Kerruish, and Cynthia Coppage, thought-fully allowed me to share their research materials and to tag along on some of their shoots, for which I am grateful. I would also like to thank Line Producer Robert Maier for his excellent organizational support and researcher Brian Noell for helping locate research materials and reference sources. Assistant Producers Anna Maria Vavloukis, Victoria Brown, Kim Johnson, and Michelle Schiller also generously gave me the benefit of their time and help in the preparation of the manuscript. At our Lis-bon base, Associate Producer Alice Milheiro helped greatly with the research for the sections on the Portuguese discoveries, which benefitted greatly from her skills.

I was fortunate to be teamed up with an Associate Producer whose boundless energy in no small part made this book, and the film we produced, a reality. Melanie Pefinis was a great travel and work companion, who somehow made me forget it probably took Odysseus less time to get home than this series to be made. I admire her poise and energy, because I know working with me sometimes isn't all that easy. For that, I am inclined to forgive being dragged to countless vegetarian restaurants throughout the world. Mind you, I said *inclined.*

Finally, special thanks are due to the staff at the Naval Institute Press for making this book look the way it does. I would like to acknowledge designer Karen White in particular for a job extremely well done, and editor Mary Yates for making my writ-ing look much better than it actually is. It was a pleasure working with all. Thank you also Kristine Dahl of International Creative Management for locating a publish-ing group that was willing to go the extra mile.

The sound track album of music by Michael Whalen from the Sea Power series is available on the *Narada Cinema* label at fine record stores everywhere and can be ordered directly from Narada by calling (800) 966-3690.

Introduction

There are a wealth of sea power books on the market, most of them displaying a massive warship on the cover. This book departs from tradition, although not out of a mere desire to be different. Its cover shows what it shows for a good reason: sea power is about far more than warships and naval battles.

To understand what sea power means, we have to go back some hundred years, to when Alfred Thayer Mahan, then a little-known American naval historian, published two books on the subject: *The Influence of Sea Power upon History, 1660–1783* and *The Influence of Sea Power upon the French Revolution and Empire, 1790–1812*. In the first he coined a definition of sea power that is as relevant today as it was one hundred years ago. *Sea power* refers not just to military power at sea, Mahan said, but to a much wider set of activities. The sea is a highway, and sea power is about controlling this highway—something that calls not only for a vast naval presence, but also for a large trading fleet as well as overseas bases and colonies. In his view, these were the ingredients not only of sea power but of world power. Mahan never doubted that national greatness was linked to sea power.

To test this theory Mahan examined Britain's ascent as a world power during the seventeenth and eighteenth centuries, and argued that this rise was directly related to the country's command of the sea. If other nations wished to contest that hegemony, he continued, they too would require a powerful navy, along with bases and a merchant fleet, to make an effective bid for command of the sea.

In retrospect, it is a debatable thesis, but one hundred years ago it struck a responsive chord. The governments of Britain, Germany, Japan, and, later, the United States hailed Mahan's work as the most important review conducted of the nature of sea power, and they began to implement his recommendations. Before long they were involved in a naval arms race that would lead to confrontations among them all. Mahan did not just interpret history. He made it.

SEA POWER: *A Global Journey*

To be fair, Mahan was not the first historian to emphasize the importance of sea power. "Whosoever commands the seas commands the trade of the world; whosoever commands the trade of the world commands the riches of the world, and consequently the world itself." These words, written by Sir Walter Raleigh in 1616, are in many ways no more than a variation on this theme. And some of the ancient historians said much the same thing, suggesting that Mahan's concept of sea power is probably as old as history itself.

Whoever introduced the term, it is generally accepted that Mahan popularized it as no one else ever had, and that he deserves some credit for that. His writing and lectures fostered a level of maritime awareness that would be difficult to match today. In fact, his broad-based concept of sea power appears to have been all but forgotten. To most people "sea power" conjures up images of big battleships and massive aircraft carriers. Yet as Mahan pointed out, naval power is only part of the story. Sea power is about using and controlling the sea in pursuit of broad geopolitical goals. Today, just as one hundred years ago, that ability, or the lack thereof, shapes the fate of nations.

Take seaborne trade, for instance. It is easy to see how the maritime trade of the past shaped history. After all, those nations that expanded their horizons and boldly ventured out to sea often dominated the world. Sea trade continues to shape our world as well, although it is no longer as readily recognized. Now that most ports are located miles from urban centers and are inaccessible for the most part, we have lost touch with the world of sea trade. But it continues to affect us as strongly as ever. We often hear about the rise of the Pacific Rim nations, for instance, and its effects on Western economies. One factor in particular is responsible for that rise: sea power.

Commercial shipping has effectively paved over the oceans, enabling Asian nations to project their economic might into Western markets with unparalleled ease and efficiency. Shipping costs, once so high that they naturally limited international trade, have become virtually negligible, creating a global marketplace and propelling new powers to its forefront. Trade wars between East and West, unemployment in traditionally strong industries—these issues become much clearer if we examine them from a maritime perspective.

The trade in essential materials such as oil continues to affect world politics as well, as the Gulf War confirmed. And navies throughout the world continue to maintain the missions Mahan so clearly delineated: presence, protection, and, when needed, the projection of force. Missions that first and foremost support the sea's role as a highway, as a system that connects all nations and nourishes their economies—the planet's lifeblood.

Much of what is described in the first four chapters of this book parallels what Mahan had to say about sea power, conveying a sense of unfaltering continuity. From our first hesitant steps at sea, the need for seaborne communication has shaped our world and our destinies, and it continues to do so, though our terrestrial orientation often keeps us from realizing it. But this sense of continuity also helps put modern issues in perspective. Oil, considered indispensable in modern times, is just one of many commodities that once played a vital role; the wars we fight today have been fought before and undoubtedly will be fought again; and sea power will always be an essential component of world power. On a planet covered mostly by water, there is no alternative.

Despite this pervading sense of continuity, it would be untrue to say that nothing has changed. Twentieth-century developments have altered the fundamental nature of sea power. Nations now rely on the ocean for much more than trade and defense. They increasingly depend on its resources. In his theory of sea power Mahan emphasized the importance of colonies and their riches, but he never mentioned marine resources. Of course, he could not have known that this great highway, as he called it, would one day be a source of essential materials, not merely a means of carrying them from one side of the world to the other.

Over the past fifty years the extraction of marine minerals has become a vital component of sea power. Determining the ownership of these riches has caused major revisions in the law of the sea, revisions that affect all other components of sea power. And these revisions are not yet complete. There remain many disagreements among nations when it comes to dividing the mineral wealth off their coasts. Some of these disputes could lead to regional conflicts, as a brief glance at the participants and their longstanding dislikes makes clear. Even traditional friends have had heated exchanges over the sharing of the last major mine on earth.

Mahan did not include knowledge in his overview either, which is somewhat surprising. If sea power, as he contended, is about trade, defense, and possession—about using the sea—then knowing how best to use it would seem to be a vital component. This was as true hundreds of years ago, when that knowledge was needed to discover the best routes to distant trading regions, as it is now, when ocean information may be needed to detect enemy submarines.

Today we need this information for more than the pursuit of national goals, however. For the sea is the planet's lifeblood in more than an economic or political sense. It also is its lifeblood in a literal sense. Without a healthy ocean, there cannot be a healthy planet. For this reason the concept of sea power must be broadened to include the ability to preserve and protect the oceans, rather than just the ability to use and control them.

These are some of the issues explored here. Given the vast scope of the topic, this book represents no more than a broad survey, which may disappoint some people. But the intent never was to provide an exhaustive treatment of the subject. Instead, the book seeks to correct some misconceptions about the nature and importance of sea power. Mahan was right when he argued that the sea played an important role in the affairs of nations. And he was right when he emphasized that nations ignore this role at their peril.

When published one hundred years ago, Mahan's work helped people better understand the world in which they lived. Without being so pretentious as to imply a comparison, it is hoped that this broad survey of sea power will also deepen our understanding of the pervading role of the sea in our lives—not as a barrier, as something that separates us, but as a medium that connects us, individually as well as collectively, emotionally as well as pragmatically.

The Great Highway

Ten days out of Kharg Island in the Persian Gulf, the Greek oil tanker *Crown* arrives off Suez, drops anchor, and waits her turn to pass through the Suez Canal. It doesn't take me long to figure out why they also call it the Marlboro Canal. Though we're waiting a good ten miles from the port, a little boat is soon spotted making her way to the *Crown*. Half an hour later there is another one, and then two more. The first carries someone from the Harbour Authority, the second a state agent, the third the company's shipping agents, and the fourth one of the canal's chief pilots. After they conduct their business, they all leave, each with a white plastic bag tucked under his arm.

Intrigued, I walk into Captain Kostas Papagiannakis's office, where the Egyptian chief pilot is rummaging through some papers. "Coming in I noticed you have a little list to starboard," he finally says, "but according to this paper it should be a list to port." The captain responds with some comment about very good eyesight, which the pilot gracefully acknowledges before dismissing the list as "nothing serious."

This ritual goes on a while longer, with each small problem being grandly dismissed, until the conversation turns to small talk. But the pilot doesn't leave quite yet. He waits until the captain gets up, disappears for a moment, and returns with the white plastic bag. In it are four cartons of Marlboro cigarettes, presumably the number due one of the canal's chief pilots. Obviously overwhelmed by this generosity, the pilot mutters something along the lines of this not being needed, and could the captain perhaps spare one more carton for the boy at the office? "They always want one more for the 'boy,'" Captain Kostas later explains, his eyes rolling.

Above: The *Crown* anchored off Suez. Her cargo of 135,000 tons of Iranian crude is less than full capacity, but it allows her to meet the Suez Canal's depth restrictions.

Left: A tanker, in ballast, leaves the Suez Canal and heads toward the Persian Gulf for another cargo.

The Suez Canal. A view from the bridge.

Right: Egypt. It was here that documented sea power began.

This practiced bit of extortion takes place on every ship in every port in the world, of course, but the Egyptians seem to have raised it to an art. In the course of Kostas's last transit through the canal, no fewer than thirteen pilots and officials managed to come aboard. No fewer than fifty cartons of cigarettes changed hands in the process—that and about $300,000 worth of transit dues. The Marlboro Canal indeed, although the Golden Cow Canal wouldn't be an inappropriate nickname either.

For the *Crown* there isn't much to do but wait until the National Iranian Tanker Company, which has chartered the vessel, decides to pay these dues so that we can head on to Port Said. True to the vagaries of the Middle East, there's no way of knowing. It could be tomorrow, or a week from now. Last time, the *Crown* was held up eight days, which strikes me as a distinctly unpleasant prospect, for there isn't much to do here but watch other ships—presumably blessed with promptly paying charterers—sail in and out of the canal.

Judged by Western logic, anchoring out here doesn't make much sense, for the *Crown* costs her charterers at least $20,000 a day. But from what I can gather, the National Iranian Tanker Company hasn't found a buyer for the *Crown*'s cargo yet. Or perhaps the company is scouting for a better deal. I assume that while we're waiting off Suez, someone in Tehran is hard at work trying to get rid of 135,000 tons of Iranian heavy crude at a reasonable price. Until that takes place, it doesn't matter where we wait.

One hundred and thirty-five thousand tons of oil may seem like a lot, but in reality it represents no more than a trickle in the vast flow that fuels our lives and economies. Every day, nearly nine million tons of oil are pumped up from deep beneath the earth's surface, most of it to be refined and promptly consumed. On this trip the *Crown* carries no more than 1.5 percent of this daily flow, less than one twenty-five thousandth of annual production—a drop in the proverbial bucket. Figures that deal with oil—whether they relate to production, consumption, transport, or even pollution—have become so large that they sometimes sound meaningless. They simply join a long list of superlatives.

There is a good reason for this. Oil has become so pervasive in our lives that we have come to take it for granted. Not only does it fuel virtually all of our vehicles—ships, planes, trains, and of course cars; along with natural gas, it also produces most of our heat and electricity. Agriculture too depends on oil, because it is used in the production of fertilizers, and it would be hard to imagine a world without plastics and other synthetic chemicals made—you guessed it—from oil.

Of course, it has not always been this way. It was coal that fueled the Industrial Revolution of the nineteenth century, and even as recently as fifty years ago coal remained the world's dominant energy source. But nothing could stop oil's inexorable march to the top after World War II. Discoveries of new reserves, especially in the Middle East, and more efficient production techniques lowered the price of oil, while the price of coal at best remained the same. During the 1940s the situation was reversed. The share of oil rose rapidly, while that of coal began to drop. Today oil, along with natural gas, supplies about 60 percent of our energy needs, with coal providing about 27 percent—a distant second. Novel technologies such as nuclear energy and the modern solar alternatives lag far behind. Naturally these figures change from one place to another, but there is no escaping the fact that without oil, virtually every country in the world would come to a grinding halt.

It is no surprise, then, that oil plays such an important role in global politics. Changes in supply and demand can cause massive changes in economic conditions, as the past twenty years have shown time after time. In times of conflict that quest for oil becomes even more important. Hints of the strategic importance of oil began to emerge during World War I, when the internal combustion engine, powering such things as tanks, made its appearance on the battlefield. World War II began with immediate moves by both sides to secure or protect strategic reserves. And Saddam Hussein's 1990 attempt to claim the oil riches of Kuwait was no more than a variation on the theme. Had he succeeded, Saddam would have found himself ruler of the world's leading oil producer, a position that would have secured him the money and the power necessary to dominate the Arab world. No wonder the West reacted—not, as its leaders wanted us to believe, because the 1990s heralded the beginning of a New World Order, but simply because none of them wanted an unreliable despot to control the world's richest oil stake.

Most people are vaguely aware that it takes a major effort to get oil from the Persian Gulf, or anywhere else for that matter, to a nearby gas station. The industry generally divides this process into three distinct stages. The *upstream* stage consists of exploration and production: the task of finding the oil and then bringing it to the surface. *Downstream* refers to refining and distribution: the process of producing various fuels and other products from crude oil and then delivering them to the market. Connecting these two stages is the *midstream* portion, a link consisting of pipelines as well as tankers like the *Crown.*

Since many of the major production regions are located thousands of miles from the principal consumer markets, this midstream portion has developed into a major industry in its own right. In fact, on any given day millions of tons of oil and oil products are making their way across the oceans, mostly from offshore terminals scattered around the Middle East to Japan, Europe, and North America. Taken on a yearly

basis, well over a billion tons of oil move at sea at one point or another. And servicing that steady flow of oil is a fleet of 6,153 tankers totaling 253 million tons of deadweight tonnage—again, a figure that would seem meaningless were it not for the fact that it amounts to just about one-third of the entire world merchant fleet. Put another way, of everything that is moving at sea at any one time, more than one-third, by weight, is oil. Make no mistake about it; this is by far the world's most important seaborne trade, economically as well as politically.

At 173,864 dead-weight tons (dwt) and over 200,000 tons displacement, the *Crown* just makes it as what is known in the industry as a VLCC, or very large crude carrier. Thirty years ago she would have been by far the largest ship in the world, but today she is no more than average. In fact, she is a somewhat awkward size—too large to pass through the canal fully loaded, too small to justify the long trip around Africa. She and her sister ship started life in Japan as the *Shoho Maru 1* and *Shoho Maru 2*, shuttling oil from the Persian Gulf to the Japanese market. There are no canals to be negotiated on that run—only the Straits of Malacca, which can handle ships of that size.

In 1987 both ships were bought by the Troodos Shipping Company, which owns thirty-two tankers worldwide. Actually, the company doesn't like to refer to itself as the owner. Each ship is owned by a separate little company based in Liberia or somewhere like that. Troodos sees itself as being the manager of the fleet, something it does from offices in Piraeus, London, and New York. Its job is to keep the ships busy carrying oil from producing regions to wherever it may be needed.

After the purchase, the *Shoho Maru 1* became the *Leni* and her sister became the *Crown*. Since last year both ships have been deployed on a long-term charter to the Iranians, running oil from Kharg Island to Europe. As far as Troodos is concerned, it is a good deal because it keeps the ships occupied at a time when there is still a lot of overcapacity in the tanker trades. But for the crew aboard, it is a bit of a guessing game. With the Iranians in charge of cargo and destination, nothing is certain.

As the ship's delay off Suez stretches into its fourth day, I am decidedly unimpressed with the bungler in Tehran responsible for selling this cargo. Admittedly, the oil shortages of the past have long faded from memory, but as far as I can tell, no tanker around us has waited longer than a day before disappearing into the canal. I guess it's a good thing that the canal's draft restrictions allow the *Crown* to be only partially loaded; I hate to think how long it would take them to sell a full cargo.

Chief steward Petros Viazis does little to cheer me up when he estimates that we'll be here a while longer. "Seven to ten days," he explains, adding that another Greek tanker chartered by the Iranians went through yesterday; why should they send two ships through in less than a week? "So we just wait," he goes on. "Waiting is a seaman's life."

I pray that Petros is wrong, and for once my prayers are answered. That evening Captain Kostas informs me that the dues have been paid and we'll be joining the northbound convoy early the next morning. But first there are a few more visitors; another chief pilot and port authority representative are supposedly making their way to the *Crown*, and would I care to sit in. Officials chasing Marlboros are a sure sign that we will be off the next morning, but I decline the honor. I've seen the ritual before. Later Kostas tells me that they didn't show up till after midnight. No wonder; with twenty-one ships scheduled for the northbound convoy, presumably there were quite a few rounds to be made.

As we glide through the canal the next morning, one of our pilots tells me a bit more about the traffic. First I want to know how many ships pass through each day. "On the average there are about forty," he replies, "twenty northbound and the same number southbound. But sometimes there are thirty each way." He also explains that the convoys are split into two groups: first the tankers, along with the bulk carriers, the

The *Crown* was built in Japan, which remains one of the principal supertanker building nations.

Left: The anchorage at Suez is always crowded. Ships sail through in convoys, one northbound and one southbound each day.

Below: Thursday morning, day five. The canal dues have finally been paid, and the *Crown* proceeds toward the entrance at Suez.

Suez Canal pilot Ahmed Kassem, *right*, keeps a watchful eye as the *Crown* glides through the canal.

largest container ships, and the car carriers, all spaced about a mile apart, and then the smaller ships. The northbound contingent gets to sail through in one leg. The others have to wait midway, since the canal isn't wide enough to let ships pass one another.

I continue the conversation with Ahmed Kassem, one of the pilots who boards at Ismailia. Mr. Kassem has brought along fresh dates and guavas from his garden, which he readily shares, and while munching on these he describes the difficulties of navigating the canal. "Usually it's fine weather like this," he explains, pointing at the deep blue sky overhead, "but in spring we can have sudden sandstorms. Sixty-mile winds, no visibility. It can be difficult. But experience tells you how each ship will react." He also explains that all Suez Canal pilots have to have a master's license and a year's worth of training before they are allowed to guide a ship through. They then start piloting the smallest ships, moving up five thousand tons each year. Since he is now on a ship of almost two hundred thousand tons, Mr. Kassem has obviously been doing this for a while. I ask him whether he has seen many changes. "Oh, yes," he laughs. "When I began, the canal was only half as wide, and the maximum draft was thirty-four feet. Today it can handle fifty-three-foot drafts, in two years fifty-six feet, and there are plans to deepen it to sixty-seven feet."

With her fifty-two-foot draft, the *Crown* doesn't have much room for error, but we pass through uneventfully, only stirring up a bit of bottom muck once or twice. It is dark by the time we reach Port Said. The canal actually runs a couple of miles into the Mediterranean, but the pilots decide that we should be able to handle that bit by ourselves, leaving the bridge to Captain Kostas, second officer Georgios Halkos, and the helmsman.

We are supposed to anchor in the North Anchorage about twelve miles north of Port Said, and the maneuvering involved gives me a firsthand look at what is involved in handling a vessel of this size. "This isn't a car," Kostas explains between giving orders to the helmsman. "It takes between four and five miles to bring the ship from sea speed to a stop. Just from dead slow, moving no more than a few knots, to a stop takes about half an hour." It doesn't sound that complicated, but when it is pitch black outside, with the local continent of fishing vessels acting as if they had the right-of-way, it can be tricky. To Kostas and his crew, it is no more than a routine maneuver, however. By 10:00 P.M. we are safely anchored and awaiting further instructions.

No one aboard is expecting these "further instructions" anytime soon, and I prepare for a leisurely few days of observing the traffic, this time at the other end of the canal. "Last week the *Leni* waited here ten days," Petros tells me, shrugging his shoulders. "So maybe we wait ten days as well; maybe longer."

With this gloomy prediction in mind I begin to devise ingenious plans for getting off the ship, perhaps by feigning some critical illness, but there is no need. The following day instructions arrive from Tehran to heave anchor and proceed to Taranto, Italy's southern oil terminal. For the Greek officers aboard this is not the most welcome news; they were half-expecting to head into Pachi near Athens, and thus a chance to see friends and family. "When I signed on they told me this ship goes to Pachi every twenty-five days," Petros sighs. "I've seen Pachi once in the last six months. This time Italy, next time America. . . . We never know," he adds stoically. "It is a seaman's life."

 As the Egyptian coast fades in the distance, it becomes easier to realize that we are sailing through waters that, in a very real sense, witnessed the birth of sea power—of documented sea power, that is. We can never be certain where in the world people first went out to sea to trade, but we know that they first left records of it in ancient Egypt, reflecting how important this business was to them too. In and around the Suez Canal it was a bit difficult to make that association, but here, a few miles out at sea, the coast begins to look like any other coast—with a bit of imagination perhaps even like the coast seen by those courageous souls who ventured out to sea thousands of years ago.

Egypt's earliest sailors did not venture this far, however. They stuck to the relative safety of the Nile, which formed a natural highway for the country's commerce. At first people just paddled their papyrus rafts up and down the great river, but during the fourth millennium B.C. sails began appearing on Egyptian craft, making the downwind part of the trip a bit easier.

A thousand years or so later another important development took place: shipwrights began using wood to build their hulls, producing a boat that, unlike a papyrus raft, could take a bit of wave action and keep both crew and cargo relatively dry. In retrospect it seems like a long time for wood to be recognized as a superior boat-building material, but trees were scarce in the Nile delta, explaining the long delay. At any rate, with a wooden hull it became possible to leave the safety of the Nile and venture into open waters. And within a few hundred years Egyptian mariners were doing so, fanning out all over the eastern Mediterranean in search of new markets. International sea trade had begun.

Since Egypt lacked a good supply of timber, it is no surprise that its first documented foreign trading voyage was sent out to obtain wood for the construction of ships, temples, and other buildings. This took place around 2650 B.C., during the reign of Pharaoh Snefru, founder of the Fourth Dynasty. Among many achievements his scribes listed the "bringing of forty ships filled with cedar logs." We know that these ships went to Byblos, near present-day Beirut in Lebanon—at that time the site of magnificent cedar forests (which have now all but vanished). And they all made it back. In fact, one of the invoices still exists.

Before long the Egyptians had also learned to use their ships for less peaceful ventures. Just fifty years after Snefru's trading voyage to Byblos, Pharaoh Sahure sent a fleet of transports to raid the Syrian coast, an expedition that reportedly returned with many prisoners. To commemorate the event Sahure ordered a depiction of it to be carved into the walls of his pyramid. It is the first record of such a trip, but it would by no means be the last. For the next thousand years Egyptian ships regularly made the trip to the eastern Mediterranean seaboard, alternating peaceful commercial ventures with well-prepared military campaigns.

In addition to visiting the Levant, the Egyptians also sailed north to Crete and Cyprus, and south to what their scribes called the Land of Punt. Located along the East African coast, in present-day Somalia, this was by far the Egyptians' most ambitious trade destination. In fact, as a glance at any map reveals, this was not just a matter of sending out ships and waiting for them to return. Before they could even sail, the ships had to be brought to the Red Sea, a trip that required the transport of wood down the Nile and then overland, across 150 miles of desert, to the Gulf of Suez.

FIG. 1.—Egyptian ship of the Punt Expedition. About 1600 B.C. *From Dêr-el-Bahari.*

One of the ships of Queen Hatshepsut's expedition to Punt heads back toward Egypt. "Never was the like brought back to any monarch since the world began," the inscriptions claim.

There the ships were assembled and then proceeded on the long and dangerous voyage down the length of the Red Sea into the Gulf of Aden. Sometime in the twentieth century B.C. Pharaoh Sesostris I had a canal dug from the Nile to the Red Sea, but even then the voyage to Punt remained a daunting one, especially considering the technology of that time.

What did Punt have to offer that was important enough for the Egyptians to go to all that trouble? Not building materials such as wood or limestone, but rather exotic goods and luxury items. Things like incense, myrrh, and frankincense, which were burned in large quantities during religious ceremonies. Or gold and ivory, from which jewelry could be made. And exotic woods—ebony and cinnamon, for instance, which were not known to grow in Egypt. Many of these goods had made their way to Egypt before, passing from one trader to another on the long overland route, but with each exchange their prices rose, reaching virtually unheard-of levels by the time they arrived at their destination. To ensure that the profits would flow to them, rather than to some obscure middleman, the pharaohs decided to seek a sea route to Punt, creating one of the first great maritime state enterprises in the process.

The most famous of these expeditions was sent out around 1500 B.C. by Queen Hatshepsut. By that time Sesostris's canal had silted up, so people again had to resort to the laborious trek through the desert, but apparently it was worth the effort. Hatshepsut's five ships made it to Punt and back, laden with riches, as a marvelous series of reliefs in her temple at Deir al-Bahri reveals. These depictions show the five ships and their crews, as well as people loading and unloading different kinds of wood and incense, skins, ivory, cattle, monkeys, dogs, and a few human passengers. "Never was the like brought back to any monarch since the world began," one of the inscriptions boasts.

It would be a long time before another Egyptian ruler would be able to make a similar claim. After Hatshepsut's reign, interest in these great maritime expeditions began to wane, as it had several times before. Never a seafaring people in the first place, the Egyptians were content to let others haul the cargoes. And there were plenty of takers. Some of the southern trade shifted to the Persian Gulf, to reach

Egypt via Mesopotamia and the ports of the Levant. To the north, the Minoans of Crete were well placed to service the trade routes between Egypt and the rest of the Mediterranean. To some extent both parties benefited from this arrangement, because the Minoans were far more capable sailors than the Egyptians, but there is little doubt that Egypt thereby lost some of its international presence and prominence.

A poignant illustration of the relationship between Egypt's standing and its maritime capabilities is found in the story of Wenamon, a priest who was sent to Byblos to buy wood around 1100 B.C. Wenamon wrote an account of his voyage, presumably to justify why it took him so long to return (and to return with neither money nor wood). And what a story it is! Either this priest turned trader was very good at making up excuses, or else he had encountered more than his share of problems. He lost his ship, was robbed, cannily managed to recover some of the money (though from the wrong people), was cheated out of his money again, was pursued by pirates, and escaped death on several occasions. That may not even be all, because the rest of the journal is lost.

Wenamon indicated that at least some of his troubles were caused by the sorry state of Egypt's merchant fleet. The country had hardly any ships of its own, relying instead on foreign ships to carry its trade. And that, Wenamon's journal seems to imply, is something too vital to trust to foreigners. Moreover, Egypt obviously no longer had the international stature it had once enjoyed. Gone forever were the days when Pharaoh Snefru's forty ships got the wood and the respect due the most powerful state in the world. There is more to this story than the unique glimpse it offers into the life of a trader of three thousand years ago. Hidden within is a message: merchant marines are vital to the well-being of a strong nation. Alfred Thayer Mahan could not have put it any better.

At a sea speed of 13 knots, the final leg of the *Crown's* trip should take no more than three days. The ship can actually handle 16 knots, but there is obviously no need to hurry. Besides, running at that speed, the ship's massive engines would consume one hundred tons of fuel a day, chief engineer Eleftherios Karavokirou tells me. Going a few knots slower cuts that by about 40 percent. Before the energy crisis no one minded paying the extra fuel costs, he adds. Speed was essential. Today, in contrast, the emphasis is on making the most economical passage.

Built in 1976, the *Crown* is separated by just ninety years from the *Gluckhauf*, the prototype of modern tankers, which made her maiden voyage in 1886. It would take many Gluckhaufs to transport what the *Crown* is carrying on this trip, but setting size considerations aside for a moment, the two ships share some basic design elements. Most important, they carry oil in bulk in separate tanks.

It would be hard to imagine anything else nowadays, but in the nineteenth century oil was transported from America to Europe in barrels or tins, which were loaded and unloaded one by one. American entrepreneurs took care of production and transportation from the oil fields of western Pennsylvania to places like Pittsburgh, where the light fractions were distilled off—the rest was either burned or simply thrown away—and then carried on to the ports of New York or Philadelphia. It was up to European shipowners to come and get it there, and to carry it safely (and economically) across the Atlantic.

At first, shipowners simply used the same barrels in which the oil had been carried on land. But no matter how well made and sealed, the wooden barrels always leaked during transportation. On land that could be disregarded as a messy inconvenience, but at sea, in the confined space of a ship's hold, the volatile gases released by the leaking oil could be very dangerous. Not surprisingly, oil shipments quickly

The painting never stops aboard a super-tanker.

Previous page: The *Crown* at night, waiting off Port Said.

gained a bad reputation. In fact, the first full cargo of oil to be shipped across the Atlantic left Philadelphia with a replacement crew scraped together from local bars, because the original crew had deserted. Even so, Captain Charles Bryant brought his ship, the brig *Elizabeth Watts*, and her historic 1,329-barrel cargo safely into London fifty-two days later.

From then on oil shipments across the Atlantic grew slowly but steadily. In 1864 a total of some 750,000 barrels (about 100,000 tons) was carried across, most of it in small ships. By 1870 the figure had grown threefold. It doubled again during the next ten years and reached the one-million-ton mark during the mid-1880s. Virtually all of this oil was still carried in barrels, but by then shippers were looking for more efficient ways of transporting the cargo.

The most logical approach, it seemed, was to replace the leaky barrels with much larger containers, from which the oil could be pumped rather than having to be hand-carried. On a few occasions the ship's cargo hold was directly filled with oil, creating a floating tank of sorts, but this was not very successful. In fact, several of the vessels sent out like this disappeared without a trace, probably because their hulls could not withstand the stresses caused by the oil moving around.

A better alternative appeared in the form of separate metal tanks installed within the hull, but this too was far from perfect. Ships built this way had a longer life than their predecessors, but many eventually succumbed to fires. After some time their metal tanks began to leak, and since the dead spaces between the tanks could not be cleaned or repaired properly, all it took was one spark to set the ship afire. No wonder few sailors volunteered for tanker duty.

At first, shipowners saw few incentives to invest in safer designs. For one thing, the flow of oil moving from America to Europe did not amount to much, especially considering that it was distributed among about thirty or forty different ports in Britain and on the Continent. In addition, the transport from western Pennsylvania to the East Coast—most of it by train—remained an uncertain affair, never quite guaranteeing the steady flow of oil new ships would require to break even. And finally, there were plenty of small tramp ships operating across the Atlantic, taking—along with other cargo—a few barrels to one port and a few to the next.

This situation changed when the world's first oil pipeline, linking Pennsylvania with the East Coast, was completed in 1879. Suddenly, far greater amounts of oil reached the ports along the eastern seaboard, where refineries were built to handle the increased flow of crude. Along with the refineries came storage tanks, ensuring shippers a guaranteed supply of oil products. And last but not least, the pipeline reduced the price of oil, opening new markets. Exports, in turn, rose rapidly, from one million tons in 1884 to nearly twice that much in 1889.

Carrying this much oil in barrels or tins no longer made economic sense, and many shipowners converted their vessels so that they could carry oil in bulk. Several new sailing tankers also appeared, and some oil shippers began to give serious consideration to steam-powered ships. One of these, built for the German oil importer Heinrich Riedemann, would become the prototype. He called her the *Gluckhauf*—which can be roughly translated as *Prosperity*.

Unfortunately, the *Gluckhauf* taxed Riedemann's prosperity quite heavily. To begin with, construction took much longer than expected because of several problems that had to be resolved. Over the previous twenty years it had become clear, for instance, that the cargo tanks had to be filled as full as possible; otherwise the movement of the ship would cause the oil to slop and surge around, reducing stability. At the same time, it was known that the tanks could not be filled to capacity, because oil expands or contracts depending on the temperature. If it could not escape, the expanding oil could easily rupture the tanks or even the hull. Some kind of gas-release system was needed as well, and leaks had to be avoided at all costs, requiring the best in tank construction. And naturally, the ship's coal-fired engines had to be located as far as possible from the cargo.

The *Gluckhauf* attempted to address these problems. To prevent the oil from slopping around, her cargo space was divided by one longitudinal and several transverse bulkheads, creating sixteen internal tanks. Each of these tanks, in turn, was connected to a separate overflow, in case the oil expanded during transit, and to a ventilation system that removed volatile gases. The ship's engine was placed at the stern, where its coal-fired boilers would least interfere with the cargo, and to load and unload the cargo there was a central pumping system, which allowed for rapid transfers.

Together these advances made for a very efficient tanker, but the new ship did not sit well with longshoremen, who feared for their jobs. In fact, upon her first arrival in New York, the port's longshoremen persuaded coal merchants not to bunker her. As a result, the *Gluckhauf* had to sail up to St. John's to refuel before she could head back to Germany. The longshoremen had a point, of course, for the twenty-seven hundred tons of kerosene taken on would normally have required over eighteen thousand barrels—enough to fill three sailing vessels and to keep many dockworkers busy for a month. The *Gluckhauf,* in contrast, did the whole thing in less than three days.

But the longshoremen were fighting a losing battle. Oil exporters were interested in efficiency, not in job opportunities for waterfront labor, and the *Gluckhauf* exceeded their expectations. By 1890, just four years later, more than fifty vessels like her were sailing the North Atlantic. Their combined carrying capacity was nearly two hundred thousand tons—just about as much as the capacity of the thousand sailing vessels that had handled the flow of oil between Europe and America ten years earlier.

The *Gluckhauf*, however, did not live up to her name. In March 1893, after several years of sailing between New York and Germany, she ran aground in a dense fog off Long Island. It was her last voyage; the ship had to be given up as a total loss. Thus ended the career of this small pioneer, though not her legacy. Even ships like the *Crown* retain many of the design features she introduced more than a hundred years ago.

Of course, there have been many changes in that hundred years. First and foremost, there are the differences in size. At more than 170,000 dwt, the *Crown* could easily

Valves on the *Crown*'s deck.

carry sixty times the *Gluckhauf*'s cargo. The engines too have become far more economical and reliable. So have the manning levels. The *Crown*'s thirty-three-man crew is large by modern standards; the more recent additions to the tanker fleet usually carry a crew half that size. In fact, some of the most highly automated vessels make do with a crew of barely ten. That does not leave much room for day-to-day maintenance, but it cuts down on manning costs, traditionally a considerable chunk of a vessel's operating budget.

Earlier in the trip chief officer Kanaris Antonopoulos showed me around the ship, giving me a better idea of the changes that have taken place. The *Crown* has twenty tanks: six center tanks and twelve wing tanks, along with two slop tanks. Unlike the *Gluckhauf*'s tanks, they are reinforced by a honeycomb web frame, which strengthens the hull and is actually the only way ships this size can survive the pounding they get at sea. "And even then," Kanaris adds, "we have to be very careful during loading and discharging, making sure all the tanks get filled or emptied gradually. Otherwise the entire structure could be stressed and weakened beyond the breaking point."

Loading is always done by means of shoreside pumps or simply by using gravity, but to discharge, the *Crown* uses her own pumps. Kanaris points out three of them, each capable of handling thirty-five hundred tons an hour. There is also a stripping pump, which is used to suck up the last bits of oil from the tank bottom. The system allows for very efficient operations, with the *Crown* needing no more than a day to load and two at most to discharge and ballast. The rest of the time is spent at sea or, as in our case, waiting at both ends of the Suez Canal.

As we continue the tour, I gradually become aware how many of the ship's systems were introduced in response to specific accidents. During the 1970s, for instance, there were several explosions aboard the new generation of supertankers, leading to many casualties and losses. Since the accidents were obviously caused by the buildup of explosive vapors, the tanks are now covered by a blanket of inert gases. As we walk along the superstructure, Kanaris points out the inert-gas system next to the chimney stack, which filters and purifies the exhaust until there is virtually no oxygen left, and then pumps it into each tank.

"A few years ago there was an explosion on one of our own ships off Genoa," Kanaris explains. "Several people were killed and the ship sank, so we aren't certain what caused the explosion, but the surveyors believe that air from the ballast tank somehow seeped into one of the cargo tanks. From then on the company decided to install a second inert-gas system to keep the ballast tanks oxygen-free as well. There's no room for a single mistake."

As we walk on, Kanaris continues his account of tanker developments. "Three center is now used as a ballast tank. Before, the ballast water was taken into the cargo tanks and then pumped out before arrival, but that led to heavy pollution. So now we have segregated ballast tanks, and whatever water we take into the cargo tanks is pumped out ashore. There are no operational discharges from this vessel." Kanaris and his colleagues take this no-pollution mandate seriously. "Not only is it the law," he says. "The sea is also our home. And you don't pollute your home."

Of course, sometimes that home is devastated by a big tanker running aground. I get a reminder of this when we enter the steering-gear compartment, located right above the rudder. "You remember the *Amoco Cadiz*?" Kanaris asks. I nod. Who could forget? The *Amoco Cadiz*, 230,000 dwt, ran hard aground off Brittany in March 1978. Pounded by the waves, she broke up, covering the coastline with 220,000 tons of oil. "As you know, the accident was caused by a steering-gear failure," Kanaris continues. "The steering-gear system broke down because of a leak in these pipes. So now we have a double-steering-gear engine, and also a rudder-arresting system that can be kicked in if both others malfunction. Even the grating on which you stand was installed after the *Amoco Cadiz*, because the person who was trying to repair the pipes while the ship was in heavy seas was constantly getting knocked down and couldn't do his work."

Everywhere we turn there is something that reminds Kanaris of an emergency somewhere, showing a macabre sort of evolution at work. "We installed this sprinkler in the paint room just last week," he says as he takes me into a small storage room on the main deck. "I imagine that somewhere in the last few months a ship was affected because of a fire that started in the paint room. So we responded. Every accident teaches us a lesson, and we can't afford to ignore it."

There are even some lessons from the *Exxon Valdez* oil spill, which took place in March 1989 half a world away. In response to the grounding and the public outcry that followed, the U.S. Congress implemented the Oil Pollution Act of 1990, also known as OPA. OPA stipulates that by the first decade of the next century all tankers calling at American ports must have a double hull. Whether this really is the best way to prevent oil pollution accidents remains a matter of considerable debate, but for the *Crown* it is a moot point. Since she is single-hulled, she will soon be prohibited from entering U.S. ports. The legislation may even shorten her life. Construction standards are becoming stricter by the day, and one day it will simply be uneconomical for her to comply.

There is another outcome of the *Exxon Valdez* incident that affects everyone aboard the *Crown*. Courtesy of Captain Joseph Hazelwood, who appears to have drunk a few beers before leaving Valdez, alcohol is strictly prohibited aboard all Troodos vessels and many other tankers as well. Throughout the ship are little posters showing a Troodos tanker inside a bottle, with a big slash across it. "This is an alcohol-free ship," it says, as if anyone aboard could forget. The policy is strictly enforced. Pointing at the poster, Captain Kostas jokes that it is easier to put the ship in a bottle than to put a bottle in the ship. "But I fully support the policy," he adds. "Emergencies can happen at any time, and I feel much more secure knowing that no one aboard the ship has had anything to drink."

 Sunday morning finds us just south of Crete on what promises to be another glorious day. To our right Crete's coastal mountains rise majestically out of the sea; to our left there are miles and miles of deep blue Mediterranean. A few dolphins frolic near the ship. It would feel timeless were it not for the two hundred thousand tons of oil and steel barging through the middle of it. Even so, the view from the bridge wing reminds me that this area too was once a center of sea power.

Unfortunately, we do not know much about Crete's early inhabitants. We do not even know what they called themselves. Presumably it was something more definite than "People of the Isles of the Midst of the Sea," as the Egyptians referred to them, but since we cannot decipher their writing, we have no idea. So instead we named them after the legendary King Minos—the one with the labyrinth and the nasty habit of feeding young men and maidens to a creature half man, half bull.

As recently as a hundred years ago Minos and his Minoans were thought to be no more than a figment of the Greeks' rich mythology. But in 1900 the British archaeologist Arthur Evans uncovered the remains of a spectacular palace at Knossos, not far from the city of Heraklion on Crete's north shore, proving that Crete had once been the site of a highly advanced—and, until then, totally unknown—civilization.

As the work progressed, more pieces of the Minoan puzzle began to fall into place. Perhaps most important, the excavation revealed Crete as the source of the beautifully decorated pottery that had previously been found all over the eastern Mediterranean. At the same time, plenty of non-Minoan objects were found as well, suggesting that these people had been great traders. Of course, being an island nation, they had no choice but to turn to the sea if they wanted to obtain something. But they apparently did so with a vengeance, becoming the first sea power worthy of that designation.

The copper deposits of Skouriotissa, Cyprus. Located near the Troodos Massif in Central Cyprus, they have been mined since times immemorial.

The pottery's distribution, along with a good deal of educated guesswork, has revealed that the Minoans ranged widely over the eastern and central Mediterranean. We know that they went south to Egypt, because the Egyptians wrote about them. Being located just south of the Cyclades and mainland Greece, the Minoans obviously conducted a healthy trade with those regions too. East they went as far as the countries of the Levant and Asia Minor, and west to Sardinia and possibly the coast of Spain. In some of these areas they established colonies and trading posts to facilitate the flow of commerce.

Aside from this, information is scant. We know hardly anything about Minoan ships, for instance. There are a few representations of ships on seals and in wall paintings, but most of them are not quite detailed enough to allow us to make anything but a few generalizations. As to a navy or naval vessels, again we cannot be certain. Thucydides, one of ancient Greece's most reliable historians, mentions that "Minos was the first to whom tradition ascribes the possession of a navy," but there is little evidence to confirm this assertion. Presumably there were naval vessels of some sort, because Minoan traders would have made tempting targets for pirates, and Minos's unwalled cities must have required some first line of defense. But nothing remains except for one small potsherd showing warriors with spears aboard what is probably a ship.

As most of what we know about the trading activities of the Minoans depends on their pottery, it is tempting to imagine their ships sailing all over the Mediterranean filled to the gunwales with pots of various shapes and sizes. But they carried much more than that, of course—everything from wine and food to ordinary utensils. And what they brought back is just as interesting. Manufactured goods and, above all, raw materials: precious metals, grains, and papyrus from Egypt; tin from Asia Minor; copper from Greece, Sardinia, and Cyprus; obsidian from the Cyclades; and blocks of porphyry from Greece. These were the resources the Minoans needed to make their highly sought-after products, the materials on which their economy depended. We do not usually see these materials in museums; exhibited are the finished products, not what it took to make them. But that trade in raw materials was just as important as the movement of the consumer goods the Minoans fashioned from them.

Among the most important of these raw-material cargoes were copper and tin, the ingredients of bronze. During the second millennium B.C., when the Minoans were active, people had already been using copper for thousands of year. But unfortunately, copper was quite soft. It was fine for utensils such as cups or plates, as well as for ornaments and even some tools; but as soon as it was put under strain—by trying to hammer it into a sharp edge, for instance—it began to yield. People naturally had no clue why this happened, yet one way or another they figured out that by adding tin, an even softer metal, they could obtain a metal—or rather, an alloy—that was much stronger than either.

That discovery, made around five thousand years ago, changed the world. It is no coincidence that we refer to this period in history as the Bronze Age, for bronze had a dramatic impact on all kinds of activities. Bronze tools were far more durable than the stone or copper implements they replaced. Plowing, which had once taken days, could now been done in a matter of hours. Bronze axes could fell far larger trees. And bronze made for far more lethal weapons—or better armor, for that matter. These may seem like ordinary changes, but they were not. In many ways they enabled people to lead more productive lives and to create more advanced things, be they ships or shovels.

It is no surprise, then, that tin joined copper as one of the key commodities traded over the ancient world. People like the Minoans, who had few metal resources of their own, had to go get them. The copper they obtained from mainland Greece and Cyprus; the tin, most likely, came from Asia Minor and ports in the Levant, which in turn obtained it from sources much further east, probably in Afghanistan. To facilitate the transport, the metals were molded into sixty- or seventy-pound ingots at smelting sites along the eastern Mediterranean seaboard and in Cyprus. Most of them were shaped in the form of ox-hides so that they could be easily picked up by the corners.

It is doubtful that ships specialized in carrying just tin or copper; instead, they transported the ingots along with a number of other goods. But there is no doubt that it was an important cargo. Just about every Bronze Age wreck found thus far has revealed hide-shaped copper or tin ingots among its sunken cargo—proof that they were in continuous demand wherever the ships went.

It is tempting to look for similarities between the bronze trade of thousands of years ago and the oil trade of today. Here, after all, are two materials that dramatically changed their world.Like oil today, bronze was found only in certain areas and thus had to be transported from production to consumption sites.Like oil, it was much sought after, by rich and poor alike. Just as no nation today can do much without a steady oil supply, nations then relied on bronze as the backbone of their economies. And much as we refer to that period as the Bronze Age, historians two thousand years from now may refer to our era as the Oil Age—a wasteful time when people managed to consume, in no more than a few hundred years, the fossil fuels accumulated over millions of years.

It is tempting to draw such a parallel, but probably a bit far-fetched. For one thing, we know far too little about that era, not to mention the geopolitics of the bronze trade. Did people go to war over bronze? Did they hoard supplies? Did some become immensely rich and powerful by controlling the trade? One would assume so, but it is difficult to say with certainty. For a period of about five hundred years, from 1500 to 1000 B.C., little precise information exists about what was happening in the eastern Mediterranean. Once again, the principal trading clues are potsherds, though no longer from Crete; the Minoans disappeared from the scene around 1500 B.C. Instead, the pottery comes from their neighbors to the north, the Mycenaean Greeks.

The Mycenaeans are believed to have taken over from Crete as the region's greatest sea power, but we know even less about their maritime exploits. Not a single detailed picture of a Mycenaean ship has yet been found, for instance. A few small-scale models of boats have been recovered from tombs, but most of our information comes from the literary record, which pays little attention to the ordinary ships that sailed back and forth across the eastern Mediterranean. Instead, the literature glorifies the deeds of warriors such as Agamemnon, Achilles, and Odysseus—mighty men who sailed forth to sack Troy. From these stories we learn what Mycenaean ships looked like, and how they were built and sailed, though it should be remembered that the great poet Homer was compiling them a leisurely five hundred years after the fact. But maritime technology did not change dramatically in those days. It is safe to assume that, aside from a few obvious exaggerations, these descriptions have a basis in fact.

From about 1200 to 1000 B.C. the picture becomes ever cloudier. This was a period of great demographic change, when the ancient world thoroughly altered its political map. The Mycenaeans disappeared, driven out by invaders from the north. In Asia Minor the ruling Hittites too were displaced, as were the peoples of the Levant. For some time mysterious peoples like the Tjeker, the Weshesh, and the Peleset dominated certain regions. Yet eventually the situation settled down, new boundaries were set, and the vibrant trade of earlier days resumed.

A different economic picture emerged from this upheaval. The focus of Mediterranean sea power shifted east once more, from the Mycenaean Greeks to the people of Canaan, in present-day Lebanon. They called themselves Sidonians, after their principal city, but to us they are better known as the Phoenicians. Excellent mariners and traders, they managed to control much of the region's sea trade from about 1000 to 600 B.C.

It should come as no surprise to learn that we don't know much about these people either—not because we cannot decipher their writing or because there are no pictures of their ships or trade, but because the Phoenicians were notoriously tight-lipped, and far more interested in short-term profits than in long-term recognition. Trade secrets were just as tightly guarded then as proprietary information is today. And the Phoenicians excelled at keeping others guessing. They are even known to have spread deliberate falsehoods, to prevent competitors from heading in a certain direction and possibly breaking one of their trade monopolies.

Whatever those competitors thought or wrote about them—much of it not very nice—the Phoenicians changed the geopolitical map of the Mediterranean by being the first to venture into its western reaches. Like the Minoans and Mycenaeans before them, they established colonies and trading posts along the way, first in Cyprus and then further west, in Sardinia and along the North African coast. Eventually they reached the Strait of Gibraltar, sailed through it, and founded the city of Tartessos, not far from present-day Cádiz. There they found silver as well as tin, which was brought in by local traders from the north. Though bronze had lost some of its critical importance to iron, tin and copper remained very much in demand. The Phoenicians managed to control the trade of both, growing very rich and powerful in the process.

Other Phoenicians reportedly were active in the Red Sea. The Bible talks about the ships of King Solomon going to Ophir (probably located in India) to obtain gold and exotic products. It mentions matter-of-factly that the ships were manned by Phoenicians, as if any sensible ruler would naturally rely on Phoenician sailors for such a dangerous mission. And there is more. Other sources, though less reliable, tell of one Phoenician contingent going all the way around Africa, and another ending up in, or at least near, America. It does not really matter whether any of this is true. What is interesting is that these stories were making the rounds in the first place, as if no one would have been surprised if the Phoenicians had indeed pulled off such a feat and come back to tell the story.

Starting in the seventh century B.C., the Phoenicians' influence began to wane. In the eastern Mediterranean their dominance of the trade routes collapsed when the Assyrians moved in and overwhelmed their ports one by one. This caused many Phoenicians to move further west. It was a group of Phoenicians, for instance, who founded Carthage, which would later challenge Rome for Mediterranean supremacy. Others continued to operate profitably from Sardinia, Sicily, and other sites in the western Mediterranean for many years to come.

To some extent the Troodos name that I run into all over the *Crown* is a reminder of that time when bronze ruled the world. Indeed, the Troodos massif in central Cyprus was one of the most important copper-producing regions in the ancient world. At one point thousands upon thousands of laborers toiled in its mines, making Cyprus the center of a vibrant trade. But these riches did little for the island's independence. For nearly thirty-five hundred years Cyprus was under almost uninterrupted foreign domination, beginning with the Egyptians under Thutmose III around 1500 B.C. and ending with the British in 1960.

Growing up in the Troodos mountains during the 1930s was Lukas Haji Ioannou. Young Lukas, it is still recalled in his native village, was very good at numbers, so he went into trading. That eventually got him into chartering ships, and from there it was but a short step to owning them. He named his shipping company after the mountains he had come to love as a boy, and then continued to expand it. By the 1970s the Troodos Shipping Company had become a fixture in the international tanker world. For a short time Lukas Haji Ioannou was even the largest independent shipowner in the world.

Except for the *Crown*, the *Leni*, and perhaps one or two other ships, all of the Troodos fleet is registered in Cyprus. With several equally energetic shipowners operating out of the country, the Cypriot fleet grew rapidly, becoming an increasingly important component of the national economy. In fact, as of late 1991 the island's shipping register included more than two thousand ships totaling a little over 20 million gross register tons (grt)—the seventh largest merchant fleet in the world. About 130 of these ships were tankers, giving Cyprus a disproportionate 5 percent of the world's total tanker tonnage.

Cyprus is not the only country that seems—to the uninitiated, at least—to possess a surprisingly large tanker fleet. There are others: Liberia, Panama, Greece, Norway, the Bahamas, Malta, even places like Vanuatu, the former New Hebrides. Their tankers are home-ported in places the average oil consumer has never heard of: Monrovia, Valletta, Kristiansund, Balboa, or Piraeus. Even Luxembourg has a few tankers under its flag, without so much as a port to host them.

Flags and nationalities are a bit deceptive in the oil transport business. In the beginning, in the days of the *Gluckhauf* and her successors, things were simple enough. It was up to the Europeans to go and get the oil in America, and consequently they built and owned most of the vessels. In 1900, for instance, the world's tanker fleet consisted of 109 vessels. Sixty-one of them were under the British flag; and of the rest, all but a few were under other European flags. Taken together the fleet totaled about five hundred thousand tons—just 1.5 percent of the world's merchant fleet.

Between 1900 and 1920 the situation began to change. Oil began to find new uses. By 1920 the automobile had grown from a toy for rich eccentrics into something a lot of people could afford—a transformation due in no small part to Henry Ford's assembly lines. Especially in America, car sales soared, from a total of eight thousand cars in 1900 to more than eight million in 1920. They all needed oil, of course, keeping a growing tanker fleet, much of it owned by the oil companies themselves, increasingly busy.

As a result, traditional oil routes changed. Oil traffic no longer flowed primarily across the Atlantic. Instead, much of it now moved to and within the United States: from the new Gulf Coast fields to the East Coast, from West Coast sites to the East Coast via the Panama Canal, and from new fields in Mexico and Venezuela to the Atlantic seaboard. Smaller amounts went from the West Coast to Japan, and from Southeast Asia and the Middle East to Europe, but none of these quite compared with the volumes carried in the intra-American trades.

Since the U.S. government insisted that all the oil carried between American

First officer Kanaris Antonopoulos (right) teaches Georgios Manousakis, one of the cadets aboard the *Crown*, the ropes of supertanker operations.

ports had to be carried in American vessels, the United States had by far the largest oil tanker fleet in the world during the early 1920s. The traditional European tanker fleets fell far behind; in fact, much of Britain's tonnage had been sunk during World War I, and whatever was left of the German fleet had been either seized or transferred, most of it to the American flag. In 1923 the world tanker fleet amounted to 7.7 million dwt—fifteen times the size of the fleet at the turn of the century. America controlled almost 50 percent of the total, and England just over 30 percent. The total fleet carried about fifty million tons of oil that year, about ten times the amount carried in 1900.

Proportionately, this was the largest American tanker share ever, but the situation would not last long. Nearly a quarter of the U.S. fleet was laid up after the war because there simply was not enough work. The oil companies found it harder to keep their ships busy, not to mention to make a profit, and one by one they began moving away from owning tankers, barges, and whatever else was needed to move oil at sea. They kept some, just in case, but were happy to leave most of the transport, and the inherent risks, to independent shipowners, as had been the case fifty years earlier.

What was needed, then, was a sufficient number of shipowners who were willing to seize the resulting opportunity and to face the uncertainties of the tanker trades. And that is where Norway, the first of the great tanker nations, came into the picture. Encouraged by the demand for tankers and by extremely easy credit terms, Norwegian shipowners began to order large numbers of ships. Between 1920 and 1932, a period of just twelve years, their tanker fleet increased almost twelvefold, from just 200,000 tons to more than 2.3 million tons. Some shipowners became very powerful—people like Wilh Wilhelmsen, for instance, whose family had been in the shipping business for more than a hundred years. At one point he controlled 40 percent of the fleet. Another was Earling Naess, a former whaler who, like many of his colleagues, had switched from chasing oil to carrying it.

Thus was born the independent tanker sector, a group of vessel owners who specialized in the carriage of oil—the midstream portion of the oil business—even though they had no involvement in the up- or downstream sectors. Like the oil companies, they had their ups and downs. Norwegian owners, for instance, made good money during the 1920s and continued to expand and reinvest until they owned almost 20 percent of the world tanker fleet. But their plans came to a grinding halt during the early 1930s—the Depression years. With international trade in a slump, they too were forced to begin laying up their vessels, quickly dissipating the profits they had made earlier.

By 1938, in the wake of the Depression, the tanker fleet had grown to some seventeen hundred vessels totaling 16 million dwt—twice the size of the fleet just fifteen years earlier. But within a year the world was at war again, and many of these ships ended up at the bottom of the Atlantic or Pacific, committing America to another massive building program. Yet this time the additions did not lead to overcapacity. In fact, since the recovery of Europe and Japan was based on oil rather than coal, they were barely sufficient to meet demand. In America too, oil consumption grew massively as the many years of rationing finally came to an end.

As the flow of oil increased after the war, independent owners moved in to claim their share of the growing transport market. New faces appeared on the tanker scene, most notably the Greeks. Like the Norwegians before them, Greek shipowners such as Aristotle Onassis and Stavros Niarchos expanded their fleets by borrowing heavily, using long-term charters with reputable oil companies as their loan guarantees. They then began ordering their vessels, not just one at a time but in blocks, thereby lowering construction costs. Lower costs, in turn, led to greater profits, and with oil consumption growing at astonishing rates, there was plenty of profit to be made.

Vlassios Voidilas, the *Crown*'s chief cook.

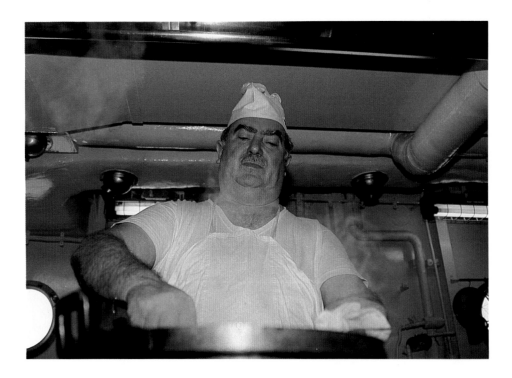

Unlike the Norwegians, Greek shipowners did not feel any great commitment to their national flag. Their shaky government was a little too greedy, targeting the maritime industry as a source of much-needed state revenue. As a result, many Greek shipowners operated out of places like London and New York, or even (like Onassis) Monte Carlo. They also registered their ships elsewhere, primarily in Panama and Liberia, both countries whose laws for ship registration and taxation were rather accommodating (or "convenient"—hence the term *flag of convenience*). Even so, aside from a strange flag and a home port they had probably never visited, these vessels remained Greek to the core, owned and manned by Greeks, many of them from the same island as the owner.

Putting registration aside for a moment, the Greek fleet grew from virtually nothing after the war to 13 million dwt by 1965 and to double that in the course of the next five years. In less than twenty years Greek shipowners had come to control the largest tanker fleet in the world—some 17 percent of the world's total, which then stood at 158 million dwt. The Norwegian fleet continued to grow too, from 3 million dwt in 1947 to 14 million dwt in 1965 and 17 million dwt in 1970—some 11 percent of all tankers. Still very large at that time (22 million dwt) was the British fleet, favored by oil companies as well as by British shipowners. The United States at the time possessed a tanker fleet of some 9 million dwt, though it also controlled a fleet at least as large under the Liberian and Panamanian flags.

All this explains the strange composition of the world tanker fleet. In 1991 it consisted of 6,153 vessels, totaling more than 253 million dwt. Liberia continued to head the list, with 486 ships totaling nearly 53 million dwt, some 50 percent of it owned by American companies (many of which refer to it, somewhat self-servingly, as a "flag of necessity"). Next came Panama with 599 tankers and 26.7 million dwt, followed by Norway (229 ships, 21.8 million dwt) and Greece (307 ships, 18.2 million dwt). The Bahamas was in fifth place, with 195 tankers totaling 16.6 million dwt, followed closely by the United States, with 235 ships and 16.4 million dwt—a seemingly respectable number that in fact includes a disproportionately large number of older ships, serving the U.S. domestic trades. Japan, Cyprus, Singapore, and the former Soviet Union rounded out the top ten tanker fleets.

Disregarding nationality and turning instead to effective ownership, it appears that American companies control the largest tanker fleet in the world, followed by Japan and Greece. One evening I ask Captain Kostas to explain Greece's predominant position in the world of shipping. "It is because of the Greek owners," he replies. "They take risks. And they are very clever." There is no argument about that. The Greeks themselves like to refer to this as the "Greek maritime genius." But there is obviously something else, something I begin to sense after only a few days aboard the *Crown*. Morale is high on this ship. There is always a bit of Greek music floating around. People are generally in a good mood, even after the hoped-for call at Pachi fails to materialize. "We're like a big family," Kostas explains. "We talk to one another, work out any problems. It's not easy being on a ship for so long, but we make the best of it."

Perhaps this level of comfort with life at sea should come as no surprise. After all, the Greeks have been at the business of shipping longer than almost anyone else. It was their forebears, the Mycenaean Greeks, who controlled much of the Mediterranean trade more than three thousand years ago. And their successors, who drove them out around 1000 B.C., would match that achievement. By the eighth century B.C. they had formed a loose alliance of independent city-states in and around the Aegean Sea, an alliance strong enough to begin claiming a dominant role in the affairs of the ancient world.

One could be forgiven for assuming that, once again, what we know about these people is based on the pottery they left behind, but fortunately this is not the case. These Greeks were prolific writers, and they left us a wealth of material, from business ledgers and admiralty cases to historical accounts and adventure stories. They also liked to depict their everyday activities in paintings, particularly on vases and plates, giving us a visual record to go with the writings. And if that were not enough, a few wrecks of their merchant ships have been found, some of them veritable time capsules. There is more than enough, in other words, for us to get a decent glimpse at the maritime doings of that era.

From all this information it has become clear that Greek trade routes penetrated deep into the Black Sea, and south and west into the Mediterranean, in search of everything from luxuries to raw materials. Of course, this did not sit well with other traders, who began to feel squeezed out of profitable trade routes. The Phoenicians in particular objected, and there were frequent clashes between Greek and Phoenician city-states. The most serious of these occurred in 480 B.C. at Salamis, where a Phoenician contingent sided with a strong Persian fleet intent on invading Greece. Against strong odds the Greeks prevailed, greatly strengthening their political and commercial position.

In the wake of this victory Athens reached the zenith of its power, dominating the other Greek city-states as it never would again. Piraeus thrived as well. During the sailing season goods from all over the Mediterranean flowed into the port, to be unloaded along its quays. "The wares of the whole world find their way to us," the Athenian leader Pericles is known to have said, and he was not exaggerating. Incense from Arabia, carpets from North Africa, timber from Macedonia, dried fruits from Asia Minor, pork and cheese from Italy, and slaves from all over were unloaded on a daily basis. If it existed in the known world, there was a good chance that it could be had in Piraeus.

Amid this massive flow of materials were three key commodities. The first was olive oil, used for cooking as well as lighting. Athens had plenty of it. In fact, olive oil was one of its main export products. Second came wine, of which the Greeks consumed copious amounts. It too could be found nearby in adequate supplies. But third, and most important, was grain—the main staple of the Greek diet. Its supply was a different matter altogether. Athens had long outgrown its local supply, so most of its grain had to be imported from wheat-producing regions in South Russia, Egypt, and Sicily—all of them many hundreds of miles away.

Many traders in Piraeus specialized in grain imports, teaming up with ship captains and bankers to outfit a voyage. Usually only one round trip could be fit into a season. The problem was not that it took so long to get to Egypt—the reliable north winds saw to that. But getting back, beating against the same winds in heavy ships, took forever. The trip north toward the Black Sea took about the same amount of time, though in reverse order: returning was a snap compared with getting there.

When the ships returned to Piraeus several months later, wholesalers came aboard to check the cargo and bid on it. Regulations existed to make sure that no single dealer could buy too much and thus corner the market. By law only one-third of the grain could be transshipped for destinations beyond Athens; the rest stayed right there. Clearly, the Athenian government thought it unwise to leave such an important trade just to merchants.

By the fifth century B.C. grain had become by far the largest business in Athens. A city of three hundred thousand in its heyday, it needed to import as much as sixty thousand tons of grain each year. If that flow faltered, there was trouble, and the Athenians did everything they could to prevent that. Sometimes, especially when pirates were a menace, the grain ships would sail in convoys, accompanied part or even all of the way by triremes—the Greeks' fast war galleys. But they did not always succeed. During the Peloponnesian War, for instance, Sparta, Athens' archenemy, destroyed a fleet of triremes that had been sent out to protect a grain shipment from South Russia. Within weeks Athens had been starved into submission.

As the *Crown* ploughs on toward Taranto, following the route of these ancient grain ships, it becomes clear that there are quite a few similarities between the grain trade of classical times and the oil trade of today. In many ways grain was the oil of its day. It was the backbone of the Athenian economy and, like oil, it had to be moved long distances from production sites. Disruptions, then as now, could affect the political picture, as Athens' stunning defeat in the Peloponnesian War showed. Rumors of a bad harvest in Egypt or Sicily could send prices skyrocketing. Some people made fortunes during such times. One of Egypt's fourth-century (B.C.) governors, for instance, held back on the country's grain exports during a serious shortage and subsequently sent ships wherever grain was needed the most and the highest prices were paid.

What may be different about oil is that it has also been used to achieve political ends. A first warning of what was to come emerged in 1951 when the Iranian government, under Prime Minister Mohammed Mossadegh, nationalized the assets of the Anglo-Iranian Oil Company, also known as British Petroleum or BP—one of the so-called seven sisters. Though the other major oil companies promptly boycotted Iranian oil, BP in the end lost its exclusive "right" to it. But all the oil majors had clearly been served warning that the Middle East was no longer the stable area they had thought it was.

Two years later a new crisis rocked the oil market, this time brought about by Egypt's president Gamal Abdel Nasser. Unlike Iran, Egypt did not have major oil fields to nationalize, but on its territory was the Suez Canal—then, as now, the major oil highway to Europe. But the canal was controlled by the Anglo-French Suez Canal Company, which collected the tolls. Egypt saw none of the revenues. No wonder the canal

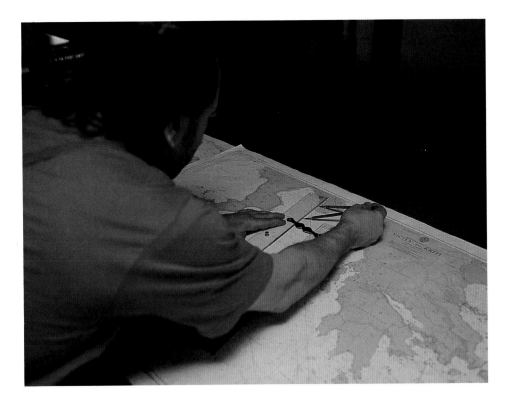

Second officer Georgios Halkos marks up the *Crown*'s position as we begin to approach southern Italy. Like many Greek sailors, he is a veteran of the tanker war.

Following page: Heading toward Taranto, the *Crown* follows the route of the ancient grain ships.

became a symbol of colonialism. To Nasser, who harbored ambitions of a pan-Arabian empire dominated by Egypt, that hated control had to be broken.

When Egypt's financing request for the construction of the Aswan Dam on the Nile was rejected by the West, Nasser made his move. Within a week his troops had occupied the Canal Zone, effectively nationalizing the canal. Several months of feverish diplomatic efforts followed in an attempt to work out a solution, but to no avail. France and Britain then decided to retake the canal by force, but their joint military operation turned into a failure. Before they could occupy the Canal Zone, Nasser scuttled dozens of ships at both entrances to the canal, effectively closing it. At the same time, Syria sabotaged the pipelines transporting Iraqi crude to the eastern Mediterranean. For the first time in peacetime the West knew what it felt like to have its oil flow interrupted.

Supplies became tight, and Western European nations had to implement conservation measures. Belgium banned driving on Sundays; France limited oil sales; Britain introduced rationing. The oil companies worked feverishly to maintain an adequate flow of oil, rerouting tankers around the Cape of Good Hope, securing supplies wherever they were available, and generally cooperating to minimize the effects on Western economies. They largely succeeded, and eventually the crisis was resolved, but it was another heavy blow to the British, who this time lost their majority share in the Suez Canal.

By April 1957 the canal had been sufficiently cleared for tankers to pass through, but things would never be quite the same. More than ever before, Western Europe realized how vitally dependent it was on the Middle East. Unfortunately, that realization did not persuade Western nations to curb their appetite for oil. Despite the warnings, they continued to shift from coal to oil, growing more vulnerable in the process and setting the stage for additional trouble.

Within ten years an even more serious crisis erupted. On 5 June 1967 the Six-Day War broke out between Israel and its Arab neighbors. It was a total victory for the Israelis; in fact, their forces needed only three days to effectively neutralize—or rather destroy—most of Egypt's army. But Israel's military victory did not spell good news for the West. The day after fighting began, Arab oil ministers jointly decided to ban oil

Third engineer Georgios Meggulis, hard at work in the ship's workshop.

exports to all nations "friendly" to Israel. Being friendly did not mean rendering active support; just recognizing the country was considered sufficient, and within days the oil tap was shut off, initially to the United States and Britain.

When the Suez Canal and the pipelines from Iraq and Saudi Arabia were closed as well, a decided sense of déjà vu began to prevail, but in reality this crisis went a step beyond. This was no longer just a matter of transportation logistics, as had been the case during the first Suez crisis. Here the flow of oil had actually been cut off (albeit selectively) by the producers, and a tremendous effort was mounted to reorganize normal flow patterns and divert supplies from one place to another.

Eventually this massive scramble paid off. As the industry succeeded in redistributing oil to where it was needed, the Arabs' enthusiasm for the embargo—and for the much-reduced revenues that came with it—began to wane. Within a few months the situation had returned to normal, and Western nations could breathe a collective sigh of relief. But once more the lessons of the crisis were soon forgotten. Before long everyone was at it again, gobbling up oil in amounts that once would have been considered absurd.

Naturally, this situation could not last forever. By the early 1970s the demand for oil had begun to catch up with supply. The years of surplus, brought about by the exploitation of the Middle East's incredible oil wealth, were coming to a close. There were several consequences. First, as buyers had to scramble to fill their orders, the price of oil began to increase, from a little over $1 a barrel in 1969 to $2 and then $3. Second, the Arab oil producers now had far more clout than ever before. With little spare capacity, they could begin to force price increases by themselves, rather than leaving that task to the oil majors. And their oil became a far more important pawn in global strategies. Everyone realized that it would be much harder now to circumvent an embargo like the one enforced in 1967. Just how difficult, the West found out six years later, when the Yom Kippur War broke out—the most intense of all Arab-Israeli conflicts.

Unlike the Six-Day War, the Yom Kippur War went very badly for Israel. The attack by Egypt and Syria on Israel's holiest holiday took the country by surprise, and its armies were driven back. Moreover, they ran out of supplies much more rapidly than expected. Unless the West intervened, Israel faced a devastating defeat. But intervention, the West was warned, would invite retaliation in the form of another oil embargo. And this time, a massive oil shortage could hardly be avoided.

Despite these unpleasant prospects, the United States sent in supplies to Israel. Almost overnight the United States' overseas supply of oil was cut off, sending the price of oil sky-high and triggering shortages at gas pumps throughout the industrialized world. Though the embargo was lifted after several months, prices continued to rise for the rest of the decade, from $1.90 a barrel in 1972 to more than $35.00 a barrel in 1980. The results were devastating. The end of the era of cheap oil brought about the biggest recession since the 1930s. No one would ever again look at oil as just another commodity.

In many ways the *Crown* is a reminder of what happened in the Middle East during those twenty years of crisis. It is no coincidence that shortly after the first show of Arab muscle, tankers became the largest moving objects ever built.

It all began in 1956, during the first Suez Canal crisis. Though the closure was relatively short-lived, it made clear that the canal was too vulnerable as the principal oil highway to Europe. So were pipelines, for that matter, as the sabotage of Iraqi lines to the eastern Mediterranean had shown. Oil companies came to the conclusion that there was only one reliable alternative: the all-sea route around the Cape of Good Hope. But rerouting ships around the cape was easier said than done. From the Red Sea to Western Europe via the Suez Canal was about four thousand miles; around the cape, that trip jumped to more than ten thousand miles. To do that practically and economically would require not only more tankers, but also larger ones.

At this time the largest tankers measured about 50,000 dwt, which many operators considered to be a ceiling. Of course, larger passenger ships had been built, but these were not carrying oil slopping around in tanks. Moreover, tanker owners generally assumed that larger tankers would be uneconomical. Purchase prices would increase, fuel bills would rise—in short, larger ships did not seem to make practical sense.

The Suez Canal crisis and the forced detour around Africa changed the economic picture, creating a demand for larger ships. Japanese yards quickly seized the opportunity. Taking advantage of better steels and superior building techniques, they produced the first 100,000-dwt tanker in 1959. The industry hailed it with all manner of superlatives: a mammoth tanker, the ultimate in shipbuilding technology, it seemed. But the Japanese yards were not about to stop there. In 1965 they delivered the first "giant" 150,000-tonner, one year later the first 170,000-dwt ship, and yet another year later the first VLCC—a then-unbelievable 200,000 dwt in size.

The second Suez Canal crisis in 1967, which led to a much longer closure, provided even more incentives to increase tanker sizes. In 1968 ships larger than 300,000 dwt, the so-called ultra large crude carriers (ULCC), came into operation. By the time the *Batillus* and the *Bellamiya*, the first half-million-ton ships, entered the scene in 1976, the shipping industry had run out of superlatives. By now there was talk of million-ton ships, so why even bother?

As it turned out, things never went that far. The recession and the dramatically reduced demand for oil during the 1970s saw to that. But in the meantime, the tanker industry had effectively circumvented the effects imposed by both Suez Canal closures and even one of the embargoes. The fleet of supertankers that came into existence in the wake of these crises enabled Western countries to continue increasing their imports of oil despite the closure of their main shortcut, and to shuttle supplies from one country to another.

No one, however, escaped the global effects of the 1973 oil embargo, least of all the tanker industry. To handle the massive increase in oil consumption and to maintain the flow in times of crisis, the fleet had grown to unprecedented size, reaching a total of 230 million dwt in 1973—ten times the size of the fleet just thirty years earlier.

Now it had to pay the price for that expansion. Faced with rapidly increasing prices, oil consumption stagnated and even began to fall back. Ironically, in some places coal made a comeback. Priced out of the market by the low pre-crisis price of oil, coal now became an attractive energy source again, at least from a cost perspective.

Meanwhile, the tankers ordered during the boom times continued to be delivered, creating a massive glut. By late 1974, 35 percent of the fleet was laid up. Many new tankers went straight from delivery into lay-up, without so much as a single commercial voyage. Rows of tankers laid up, side by side, in Norwegian fjords became a familiar sight. Those who predicted that the slump would be short-lived were wrong, *very* wrong. By 1978, with the fleet reaching an all-time high of 350 million dwt, there was still a 30 percent oversupply of tanker capacity. By 1982 the figure had grown to 60 percent.

These were difficult times for the tanker industry. Everyone had to cut back, but the delivery of unwanted ships cut deep into the pockets of even the most powerful tanker operators. It took well into the 1980s for the balance between tanker supply and demand to be restored somewhat, partly as a result of increased oil consumption caused by falling prices. But no one returned to the half-million-ton megaships; they were scrapped after no more than a few years of service. By then the enthusiasm had turned a bit sour anyway. Supertankers had the nasty tendency to do strange things: disappear, for instance, or explode at sea, or collide under mysterious circumstances. Not to mention the mess that was created when one of them went aground. The tanker world's love affair with giant ships was relatively short-lived. It was probably all for the best.

 There is an account written by the Greek historian Lucian that reminds me of the early reactions to supertankers. Lucian was writing in the second century A.D., and one day a large Roman grain ship, probably blown off course, wound up in Piraeus—reason enough for him to walk the five miles from Athens to the port to check it out.

With a few obvious modifications, Lucian's description could have fit one of the shipping trades of the early 1960s. "What a size the ship was," he wrote. After detailing the vessel's length, beam, draft, crew, and so on, he concluded, obviously overawed, "Everything was incredible. . . . And it all depends for its safety on one little old man who turns those great steering oars with a tiller that is no more than a stick. They pointed him out to me," he continued, "a wooly haired little fellow, half bald; Heron was his name, I think."

No one aboard the *Crown* fits the description of Heron, and the steering mechanism is a bit more sophisticated these days, but there are similarities. As many shipowners do today, the Romans often crewed their merchant ships with other nationalities. A race of farmers and soldiers, they never took a great liking to ships. But that did not prevent them from dominating the Mediterranean as no one ever had before.

To get to that point, the Romans had to conquer dramatic odds. For starters, they had to contend with the powerful Carthaginians, heirs to Phoenicia's maritime legacy, as they began to expand their territory in the third century B.C. The Carthaginians had a powerful navy; the Romans had none, but they proceeded to build one and, despite their lack of experience at sea, inflicted one defeat after another. Of course, the Romans lost massive numbers of men and ships too, in battles as well as in terrible storms, but they always rebounded, starting anew if need be. Against such initiative and resourcefulness Carthage was powerless, and over the course of the Punic Wars it was wiped off the map.

Next the Romans turned their attention to the eastern Mediterranean, then the trading domain of small states like Rhodes and the two major powers in the region, Egypt

Jason and the Argonauts, as seen on a Roman tomb relief. Roman artists enjoyed depicting stories from Greek mythology, providing us in this case with a look at their shipbuilding techniques.

and Macedonia. Here too the Romans moved rapidly, sending in fleets of galleys wherever needed and, more important, merchant traders, who set up a free-trade port on the island of Delos. To do away with the constant problem of piracy in the region, they organized a simultaneous attack on pirate bases all over the Mediterranean. Within a matter of weeks the area had been swept clean of pirates from east to west.

After the empire was reunited under Octavian, later known as Caesar Augustus, the Romans controlled all of the Mediterranean. They could rightly call it Mare Nostrum—Our Sea. In fact, not only the sea but virtually its entire littoral fell under Roman domination, leading to a phenomenal expansion of trade. As before in Athens, grain was the key commodity, though the scale of imports increased vastly. By the time of Augustus, Rome had grown into a city of a million people, and in some years as much as two hundred thousand tons of grain had to be brought in. To handle such amounts the Romans built very large ships, like the one Lucian described. They are estimated to have carried as much as a thousand tons of grain each, perhaps even more. These were the largest ships ever built in the West, and they would remain so for at least another thousand years, long after Rome's demise.

Naturally, most everything else had to be imported as well, including wine and olive oil—still among the most important commodities—which came from Gaul, Greece, and Spain. The trade in raw materials was important too: metals like tin, lead, iron, and copper, and building materials to satisfy the Romans' insatiable demand for

To handle the massive grain ships, the Romans built a new port at Ostia, near the Tiber's mouth. Mosaic pavements at Ostia's ruins still reflect its maritime ties.

grand public structures. Luxuries did extremely well: aromatics like myrrh from East Africa and frankincense from South Arabia, spices from India, and even silks that came all the way from China more than eight thousand miles away.

Rome initially had no problem paying for these materials. Essentials such as grain were collected as taxes in kind from North Africa; the others were paid for from taxes imposed on other provinces. The key problem was transportation: getting all these goods to the Imperial City. Even though they preferred not to go to sea, the Romans understood the vital importance of a strong merchant fleet. So they relied on Greeks, Syrians, and others, and provided plenty of incentives. Freed slaves who invested in merchant ships were given full citizenship. This was a smart move. It cost the state nothing, and enticed many freedmen to enter the shipping business, where their energies were needed most.

Historians have often remarked that Rome became the ancient world's greatest sea power more or less in spite of itself. While true, the Romans certainly understood how essential control of the sea was to their empire. In fact, Mahan could probably have proven his thesis using their example: the Romans controlled the resources they needed and the fleets to transport them; they had the means to protect the trade from pirates and other marauders—to keep the sea lanes open, in other words; and if need be those means could be used in support of their expansionist policy.

Like all of its predecessors, this empire in time too came crashing down—a downfall preceded, not surprisingly, by a decline in the naval capabilities that had helped it into being. Yet in a very real sense the Romans brought to its conclusion a process started by the Minoans and Mycenaeans, and later the Greeks. Sea power gave them the ability to acquire territories that provided resources, people, money, and power. Despite their terrestrial orientation, they were truly the first to use and control the sea fully to obtain the ultimate prize: world power.

The evening before reaching Taranto, I am on the bridge with second officer Georgios Halkos. Like several of his colleagues, Georgios was in the Persian Gulf during the Iran-Iraq War, the so-called tanker war, and I ask him what it was like. Initially he is a bit hesitant. "You know, I'm not particularly fond of that period," he tells me. But he keeps talking anyway, telling a story that is almost impossible to picture under this peaceful Mediterranean night sky.

"It wasn't until 1983, two years into the war, that Iran and Iraq began targeting the tankers," Georgios begins. "At first it was one ship, then the other side retaliated, and soon the situation ran out of hand. Because of the dangers, the Iranians had two tanker routes: one from Kharg Island to Larak in the Strait of Hormuz, which was more or less outside the range of Iraqi aircraft. There, other tankers picked up the cargo to carry it on to the West. Tankers sailing with Iraqi cargoes, on the other hand, were exposed throughout the entire Persian Gulf."

The tanker industry took no sides, so ships would sail for Iran one time, for Iraq the next. When Georgios arrived on his first trip into the war zone in 1985, things were in full swing. Three times his ship was hit by missiles—twice by the Iranians and once by the Iraqis. "There were a few precautions we took," he tells me. "First we plugged the scuppers and flooded the deck with water. Not good for rust on the deck, but who cared? Second, depending on the route, we only slept on that side of the ship where we didn't expect an attack. For instance, if we were sailing from Kharg to Larak with a full cargo, the Iraqis would come from starboard, so we slept on the port side. On the return trip, we would switch. And finally, we never allowed people to be in the engine room when we were in the most dangerous areas. Since all of the missiles that hit us exploded in the engine room, we probably saved a lot of lives."

It is strange listening to Georgios's account. Safety regulations aboard tankers are

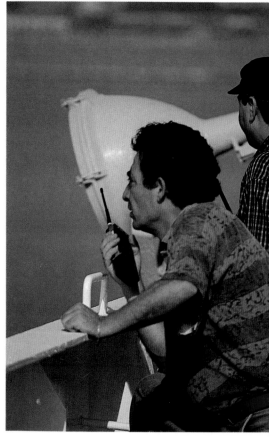

Above: Captain Kostas Papagiannakis, keeping a watchful eye while the ship maneuvers inside Taranto harbor.

Left: Taranto. Four Italian tugs push the *Crown* toward the mooring site.

the strictest in the industry. No Smoking, Safety First, Keep Doors Closed, Don't Blow Up the Ship—there are warning signs all over the *Crown*, for like any tanker she is a floating bomb. Yet during the war there people were, sailing around on the biggest sitting duck in the world while Iraqi and Iranian pilots shot Exocets at them. Many tankers were lost in the process, but there were plenty of replacements. After all, hundreds of tankers were still laid up throughout the world. For many companies, going into the Gulf was simply a matter of economic survival.

Outside, a quarter moon has risen, casting a silvery glow over the water and much of the ship. Georgios's story has set me thinking. The risks people took during the tanker war confirms how well the movement of oil illustrates what Mahan had to say about sea power. Oil is vital and strategic; much of it moves across the sea at one point or another, and if need be, that flow must be protected. Mahan, of course, could not have foreseen the eventual importance of oil. When he was formulating his theories,

Above: Italian tug at Taranto.

Right: Taranto. A hose is nudged toward the ship. Once connected, it will transport the oil from the *Crown* to the tank farm on shore.

Following page: Italian longshoremen connect a hose to the *Crown*'s valves so that the oil can be pumped out and sent to shore.

he was probably thinking about coal, which fueled everything from steam locomotives to steel mills, or about iron and other ores, needed to produce steel for heavy machinery and weapons of war. Sea power, and by implication global power, requires access to these materials, he said, and the ships to carry them as well as the ships to protect them.

I guess it has always been like that. Here, after all, on this last leg of the *Crown's* voyage, we are tracing the route of the ancient Roman grain ships from Egypt to Rome. Though more than two thousand years apart, we are not really doing anything different. They were carrying fuel for men, we are carrying fuel for machines. The grain was just as important to Rome as oil is to the industrialized world. And just like us, they had to master and control the sea to obtain it. For that is what sea power, as Mahan rightly observed, is mostly about.

A day later we arrive in Taranto. Escorted by four tugs, the *Crown* is carefully nudged to her mooring site. Tomorrow morning she'll be connected to hoses that will transport her cargo to the tank farm on shore. Then the 135,000 tons of crude will be refined into gasoline—about 65,000 tons of it, enough to keep the average car running for sixty thousand years. But long before the oil ever gets to a gas pump in southern Italy, the *Crown* will have turned back to Kharg Island, ready to bring another cargo to the West.

That evening part of the crew gets to go ashore. I walk around with Kanaris, who seems intent on taking a look at just about every shop window. He tells me that this is the first time in seven months he has had a chance to walk around like this. Chief officers, he explains, are responsible for loading and unloading, which precludes shore leave. But since we won't start discharging until tomorrow, this is his chance to go ashore and remind himself what the real world looks like.

We run into the others and decide to remind ourselves what alcohol tastes like. But far too soon it is time to return to the *Crown*. As the launch takes us back to the massive ship moored in the distance, Petros sits down next to me and lights up a cigarette. "Thirty-five days at sea and four hours ashore," he finally says, not addressing anyone in particular. "And then we'll do it all over. Thirty-five days at sea, a couple hours ashore." He glances at me, making sure it has sunk in. It has, my dear Petros: "It is a seaman's life."

The Riches of the East

From a distance the place looks a bit like a massive Lego yard, with thousands upon thousands of brightly colored boxes neatly stacked in rows and an endless stream of trucks and trailers flowing in between. But Hong Kong International Terminals, also known as HIT, is anything but a playground. More than 90 percent of the colony's trade moves through the massive container yard, making it the hub of Hong Kong's vibrant economy. Not that you would ever notice, for HIT lies somewhat secluded at Kwai Chung on the western edge of Kowloon. Besides, a double chain-link security fence discourages any sightseeing. There are no viewing areas for the inquisitive here; this place is all business.

Once it has reached HIT, it is impossible to guess where a container came from. Many were packed—or stuffed, as it is called in shipping parlance—in HIT's Container Freight Station a few hours earlier. Some arrived by truck from Canton or from the Shenzen Special Economic Zone just across the border. Others reached Hong Kong on top of rusty Chinese freighters from one of the mainland ports. In true Hong Kong fashion, they were then transferred in the middle of the harbor onto a barge—the way it has always been done here. And increasing numbers were brought to Kwai Chung aboard smaller containerships, called feeders, from the Philippines, Indonesia, or Thailand—places that do not yet qualify for their own major container services.

Figuring out the containers' destination is a bit easier; almost all of them arrive at Kwai Chung to be loaded onto the massive container vessels that connect East and West. Some of them head toward the Indian Ocean and the Suez Canal, to unload their cargoes of consumer goods in European ports. The others move East, across the North Pacific to North

Above: The *Envoy* arriving in Hong Kong. Voyage 7—12,425 miles in thirty-five days—is just a few miles short of completion.

Left: The *Envoy* enters Nagoya Bay.

41

Hong Kong harbor, with Kowloon and the New Territories. Despite the progress of containerization, a lot of cargo is still transferred in the middle of the harbor, the way it has always been done there.

The *Envoy*'s stack, with OOCL's distinctive red plum blossom.

Right: As the *Envoy* ties up, one of her colleagues, the *OOCL Fortune,* sets out on her transpacific crossing.

America. Virtually all are capable of carrying thousands of boxes, crammed with the modern equivalent of the riches of Cathay: Walkmans, videocassette recorders, auto parts, textiles, foodstuffs, toys, and just about everything in between.

At Berth 9 one of these carriers, the *OOCL Envoy*, is docking. The ship is medium-sized—about 850 feet overall—with a freshly painted light gray hull, trim upper works, and a yellow funnel with a red plum blossom. Along the hull the OOCL logo, painted in big red letters, identifies the ship as part of the Orient Overseas Container Line, one of the largest container carriers in the world. As containerships go, the *Envoy* is nice-looking, even with her boxes stacked three and four high on deck. She shows few of the angular lines and towering superstructures of the newest generation of carriers. Then again, she is about thirteen years old, well into middle age in this business.

As she moves closer to the berth, the *Envoy* is about to complete Voyage 7—a 12,425-mile round trip that took her to Kaohsiung in Taiwan, Nagoya and Yokohama in Japan, Seattle and Vancouver in North America, and then back to Hong Kong via Kobe and Kaohsiung. But there will not be much of a break; tomorrow morning she will leave on Voyage 8, repeating the itinerary—a trip I will be joining as far as Seattle.

I am not the only one waiting along the berth. So are a number of longshoremen, and many trucks, their diesel engines idling as the ship is nudged closer to the quay. As always, the unloading takes place with remarkable efficiency. The moment the ship is tied up, the giant gantry cranes swing into action, and within minutes the first containers have been plucked off the deck and deposited onto a waiting trailer. The system never ceases to amaze me. To the uninitiated eye it may seem confusing; after all, with ten ships being loaded and unloaded at the same time, it may be hard to discern any "system" at all. But this is actually a highly synchronized effort, involving not only trucks and cranes but also a number of strange-looking vehicles lumbering up and down the yard, some of the most advanced computer technology in existence, and the people who make it all possible, from longshoremen to crane operators, truck drivers, and many more. When they work in synchrony, a crane can handle from twenty to twenty-five containers per hour. If one of them hiccups, however, the whole system stalls, though never for long.

As soon as the gangway is lowered, I climb aboard to get installed. In the officers' mess I briefly meet Captain Martin Weir, an affable Scot who has been in command of the *Envoy* for the last seven months, ever since she was deployed on this route. He has just been informed by company representatives that he will have a passenger, but that's no problem. In fact, as the only Westerner aboard, he may enjoy the company. The rest of the crew, he quickly explains, is either Chinese or Filipino. Since there will be plenty of time to meet them later, I head back into town for some last-minute shopping. High on the list are some snacks; a quick look at the number of woks stacked in the galley gives me the impression that there might not be much Western fare on this voyage.

By the time I get back and clear security at the gate, it is dark. A fog has set in, and the floodlights on top of the cranes and around the terminal give the setting an eerie, futuristic glow. Meanwhile, the loading and unloading continues unabated. Three cranes are hovering over the ship. Two of them are loading by now, but one is still unloading. They often work that way, to prevent stressing the vessel's hull.

The next morning the cranes are still at it. They should have finished by now, but it was pouring all night. Not that this should stop them, but at one point the entire operation had to be halted for the simple reason that no one could see a thing in the downpour. There are not many things that will bring HIT to a halt, but this is one of them. The *South China Post* later reports that the rains were Hong Kong's worst since the mid-1960s, so a one-and-a-half-hour interruption is not that bad.

A foggy departure.

Because of the delay, the *Envoy's* departure has been pushed back, but at 11:00 the last containers have been stacked on deck, everything has been securely lashed, and ship is ready to go. Unfortunately, the weather has gotten even worse. Aside from the steady rain, the fog has grown more dense, limiting visibility to no more than a few hundred feet. No problem, though. The tugs pull the ship away from her berth and nudge her into Voyage 8 and the busiest harbor in the world.

This is not the departure I had envisaged, with the ship gliding majestically against the backdrop of Hong Kong's skyline. No skyline to be seen anywhere—in fact, we can barely see the bow of the ship. Tension on the bridge is high, for this is, after all, Hong Kong, where few, if any, barges bother to keep a radio or radar watch. Rules of the Road? Not here. But the *Envoy* isn't going to let them get away with it. Through the fog we notice a dredging barge leisurely making her way into the channel and into our path. Five deafening blasts of the horn make it clear that we are heading that way too, have little room to maneuver, and are much bigger. Five more blasts, and the barge slowly veers away, probably indignant at our nerve.

It goes on like this for an hour or so, with the *Envoy* slowly snaking her way through the channel and the plotting radar working overtime. Hundreds of ships are anchored in the harbor, occasionally emerging ghostlike from the fog off starboard. When we reach the Lamma Channel the weather clears somewhat. The pilot is let off, and Captain Weir orders increased speed. Gradually the ship gains momentum, and soon the last of Hong Kong's islands disappear from view. A course due east is set for Kaohsiung, where we will pick up some more of the riches of the East, twentieth-century style, before heading on.

The riches of Cathay have always tantalized the West. Even during Greek times, more than twenty-five centuries ago, there was a caravan trade with India, which introduced the West to some of its marvels: things like sugar from sugarcane, cotton, and spices. A trickle at first, this trade from East to West grew rapidly. By Roman times it had developed into a major enterprise. The Romans actually became obsessed with Eastern luxuries. Chinese silk was coveted by men and women alike, provided they could afford it. Spices too were always in demand. The Romans gained an appreciation for Indian pepper in particular, turning it from a luxury into a virtual necessity in less than a hundred years. By the end of the first century A.D. Rome even had special warehouses to store the precious commodity. Along with pepper came other spices such as ginger and cinnamon, also from India, and occasionally such things as cloves and nutmeg, from a mysterious region even further to the East. Like pepper, these were not used simply to spice up food. They were worked into medicines or cosmetics just as readily, explaining the enormous demand.

Pearls were also immensely popular, as they still are, of course. Back in Roman times only natural pearls were available, most of which came from the Persian Gulf and Ceylon. Rounded pearls were immensely expensive, but that did not deter Roman socialites. In fact, just like silk, they became a status symbol, and staggering amounts were paid for them. Vitellius, one of Rome's most successful military commanders, once financed an entire campaign by selling just one of his mother's pearls, it was said. Pliny the Elder found the pearl craze rather distasteful. "Women glory in hanging these on their fingers, or hanging two or three for a single earring," he grumbled; they are entranced by the "mere rattling together of the pearls."

Pliny may not have understood the obsession, but he expressed a real concern. The fabulous sums being paid for pearls and other Eastern luxuries were depleting the Roman treasury. As early as the first century, laws had to be implemented to restrict the exchange of Roman money for these goods. But that did not stop the tide of imports for long. By the second century much higher taxes had to be imposed to pay for them, stifling trade and initiative. The infatuation with the riches of Cathay was not the only reason for Rome's gradual weakening, but it certainly contributed to the Empire's ultimate decline.

Between Rome and China lay some ten thousand miles that had to be covered one at a time, explaining the phenomenal markup in prices. Actually, there were two routes by which Eastern goods reached the Imperial City. Some reached Rome via complex overland trails, later collectively known as the Silk Road, which ran all the way from China to the ports of the Levant. It was an arduous route, crossing lifeless deserts, desolate mountains, and just about everything in between. Along the way lurked untold dangers: robbers of every nationality, preying on the rich caravans; wild animals; death by accident or starvation. Massive detours were common, but even so, year after year, caravans set out on the long trek to the East, for the profits that could be made in this trade were phenomenal.

A somewhat more reliable route went by sea. Chinese junks and Indian vessels brought Eastern wares to ports along the Indian Malabar (or West) Coast, and there Greek, Syrian, Egyptian, and other "Western" vessels traded wine, corals, glass, and (preferably) Roman coin for them. Their holds filled, the ships returned. At first, Western sailors hugged the coast of India, Persia, and South Arabia before proceeding up the Red Sea toward Egypt, but during the first or second century B.C. they figured out how to sail directly across the Arabian Sea, using the seasonal monsoon winds. It made for a rougher but much faster trip. The final destination was either Berenice or Myus Hormus, along the northeastern coast of the Red Sea. From there the goods were carried overland to the Nile and shipped onward again to Alexandria, the western terminal of the sea route to the East.

Little was known about the overland route to China until about a thousand years later, when European travelers such as Willem van Ruysbroeck and Marco Polo voyaged that way and described their adventures. Of the sea route to the East, on the other hand, we know much more, thanks to the *Periplus of the Erythraean Sea*, a mariners' guide to the Red Sea and Indian Ocean, written sometime during the first century A.D. Presumably there were quite a few of these guides at that time, but this is the only one that has survived.

The *Periplus* offered a detailed description of the sea route to India, providing information not only about winds, currents, and anchorages but also about trade products and the people who lived along the way. Like a modern-day pilot, it was filled with good advice. The Arabian coast of the Red Sea is dangerous, it cautioned, "for it is without harbors, with bad anchorages, foul, inaccessible because of breakers and rocks, and terrible in every way." Not that there seemed to be any reason to stop there; the land was inhabited by "rascally men speaking two languages, who live in villages and nomadic camps, by whom those sailing off the middle course are plundered." Move on "as fast as possible," the *Periplus* wisely concluded.

Further south things improved. Muza, near modern-day Mocha in Yemen, "crowded with Arab shipowners and seafaring men," was a safe stop, as was much of the South Arabian coast, the fabled Arabia Felix. Beyond, across the Persian Gulf, was Persia, whose inhabitants ("a villainous lot") kept it off the list of recommended stopovers. Much better to cut straight across the Arabian Sea to India, the *Periplus* advised. Be careful on the approach to Barygaza (modern-day Broach in India), it warned, for "there is a great force in the rush of the sea at the new moon."

The *Periplus* was quite accurate up to the Indian Malabar Coast, but beyond that it got a little vague, referring to the land of the "Horse-faces and the Long-faces" and another land, much further to the east, inhabited by "peaceable, flat-faced men" who manufactured silk. Getting there is a little difficult, it explained, because of the "great cold" or because of "some divine influence of the gods."

Chinese descriptions of this part of the voyage are of no help, either. It is known that Han-dynasty junks were traveling to Ceylon and India during this era, but the only descriptions that have survived were written by imaginative people who had probably never set foot on a ship. The region would not remain unknown to the West for long, however. Within a hundred years a courageous Greek sailor, known only as Alexander, figured out that there were monsoon winds on the other side of India as well, in the Bay of Bengal, and sailed boldly beyond the confines of the *Periplus*. On his first trip he got as far as the Malay Peninsula, pioneering direct trade with Malaya and Indonesia On his second voyage he went even further, around the peninsula to Indochina and perhaps even Canton. Chinese records mention that several enterprising traders followed in Alexander's footsteps. Unfortunately, their visits abruptly stopped during the early fourth century A.D. It would be more than a thousand years before a Westerner would set foot in this part of the world again.

Western traders disappeared from China not just because of the hardships involved; they were forced out of the trade. As Rome's influence at one end of the Silk Road and that of the open-minded Han dynasty on the other began to wane during the third century, others stepped in to claim their share of the lucrative commerce between East and West. During the fifth century, for instance, the Persians began to dominate the trade, diverting its western terminals from the Red Sea to the Persian Gulf, which they controlled. Unfortunately, little is known about their ships and travels, as Persian artists and writers showed little interest in describing them.

Though they grew very rich in the trade, the Persians would be forced out of it as well. During the seventh century the growth of Islam created a new power in the Middle East. By A.D. 650 Muslim armies had conquered and converted Egypt, Syria, Iraq, and much of the powerful Persian Empire, gaining access to the Mediterranean and the Persian Gulf. During the next hundred years they pushed into Spain and

الق ر آن ثم وبعل ل ش اطير لا أها ور خارف ج لا ها وق ال ا ز ك واب ها بسم الله مجرا ها
وم رس ا ها ت ة نفس نفش المغ م ین او عبا د الله ل الك س ین ق ل اما انا

An illustration from the *Maqamat* (Assemblies) of Al-Hariri, showing a passenger vessel in Iraq. This is one of very few images showing what thirteenth-century Arab ships looked like.

northern Africa in the West, and as far as the border of India in the East. Nothing then stood between the Arabs and exclusive access to the riches of Cathay—nothing, that is, except for the dangers of the route.

Despite these dangers, Arab traders quickly seized the opportunity. They preferred to deal with rare, high-value goods, and that was what the Eastern trade was all about. The caliphate government hardly interfered in their activities, leaving risk and gain to the private sector. It did impose high taxes, but these were simply added to the price. There was never a shortage of buyers anyway. The key problem was transportation: getting to the East to buy the goods and returning with them safely, preferably by ship.

Few Arabs felt comfortable at sea. "Trust it little and fear it much," wrote one Arab scholar in response to a question posed by the caliph of Baghdad. "Man at sea is but an insect on a splinter, now engulfed, then scared to death." This apprehension never totally vanished, but it did not stop the Arabs from turning to the sea as they never had before. First they focused on the trip to India, which coastal Arabs had been sailing since the days of the *Periplus*, if not before. Then they began to move beyond, first to Malaya and Indonesia, and later to China, where they arrived in 787. T'ang-dynasty officials welcomed them and allowed them to establish settlements in the capital at Changan and in Khanfu, today's Canton. By the end of the century the Arabs had reached Korea, and some may even have ventured as far as Japan.

For much of the ninth century Arab merchants sailed this route regularly, and with this increased frequency of travel came more information about the trip to China. Some of these accounts worked themselves up in the Persian Gulf's shoreside cafes into stories of tempest-tossed seas and mysterious lands—fairy tales, really, such as the *Seven Voyages of Sinbad the Sailor*. Others were more to the point, providing straightforward descriptions of what was to be seen on the voyage and what it took to get there. One of the best of these is told in the *Adventures of Sulayman the Merchant*. We don't know whether Sulayman was a real person, but it doesn't matter. Many merchants probably contributed stories to the book, turning it into a fascinating narrative of the sea voyage from Siraf in the Persian Gulf to Canton.

Sulayman's account makes clear that Arab ships made the trip in four legs, each one lasting about a month. The first went from the Persian Gulf to Quilon or Kulam Mali on the Indian Malabar Coast. The ships usually left in the fall so that they could take advantage of the northeast monsoon. After stocking up with food and water they crossed the Bay of Bengal to the Malay Peninsula. From there they followed the Strait of Malacca and then turned north along the coast of Indochina to Sander Fulat, off the Vietnamese coast. The final leg went across the South China Sea to the island of Hainan, and from there along the coast to Khanfu. Along with time spent provisioning, the outbound voyage usually took about six months.

The next six months were spent in China, trading and stowing the ships with ceramics, spices, silks, and things like camphor and musk. In the fall the merchants left again, retracing their route as far as the Malabar Coast and then heading to South Arabia. The first breezes of the southwest monsoon in the spring then allowed them to set course for their ports in the Persian Gulf, returning there about a year and half after having left. This gave them another six months or so to sell the cargo, buy new goods, and repair the ships before setting out on another trip.

Extending over a distance of some eight thousand miles, this was by far the longest regular sea trade route ever, and it would continue to be so for many hundreds of years. Even more remarkable, it was maintained by ships that were quite fragile. Few, if any, pictures exist to show what the dhows of that time really looked like, but there are plenty of descriptions that make clear that their hulls were sewn, rather than nailed. The Arabs may have had good reasons for this practice, among them superstition, but sewn hulls made for generally leaky ships. If just one of the fibers broke at sea, the crew could be faced with disaster, and there were plenty of those.

The Arabs seem to have accepted this as part of the business of sea trade. But European writers were universally unimpressed. "These ships are mighty frail," wrote John of Montecorvino. "The men always, or nearly always, must stand in a pool to bail out the water," added Jordanus, another European observer. And Marco Polo, the dean of Europe's medieval travelers, was downright condescending: "These ships are wretched affairs," he wrote, "and many of them get lost."

As unimpressed as they were, these Europeans were writing several hundred years after the Arabs had begun undertaking the long sea voyage to Cathay. By that time the Arabs had controlled the trade between East and West for nearly half a millennium, a feat that required outstanding nautical skills. Marco Polo and his contemporaries failed to give credit, simply from a lack of information. They would not be the last to do so. Even today, the Arab contribution to sea power is seldom fully recognized.

To be fair, today's Asian ports have little to remind one of that Arab presence of a thousand years ago. Where once hundreds of dhows jostled for a place along the harbor, there is now hardly a Middle Eastern flag to be seen. Instead, most of the East-West trade is carried by European, American, and, increasingly, Asian ships. In fact, the Asian contingent—Taiwanese, Korean, Japanese, and Chinese—now accounts for the bulk of it.

Kaohsiung, Taiwan—first stop on the *Envoy*'s eastbound voyage.

In Kaohsiung another 680 containers holding
the riches of the East are taken aboard.

So too in Kaohsiung, Taiwan's southern port and the first stop on the *Envoy*'s east-bound voyage. Most of OOCL's transpacific vessels call at this bustling port, reflecting Taiwan's importance in the world of trade. And OOCL's ships are certainly not the only ones to do so. As the *Envoy* glides to her berth at the terminal, she passes a veritable *Who's Who* in the world of international shipping: ships of Taiwan-based container giant Evergreen and its compatriot Yang Ming, and of Maersk from Denmark, Nedlloyd from the Netherlands, Hanjin from Korea, Mitsui and K-Line from Japan, CGM from France, and APL and Sea-Land from America—all of them here to load Taiwan's "riches" and carry them onward to "the West."

Kaohsiung provides about an eight-hour layover, and thus a chance to explore the city, but it is still raining heavily. When it finally clears somewhat, the radio officer tries to call a taxi, but he reports back that the drivers change shifts at 2:00 P.M. and are "too busy" right now. Better to try again in a couple of hours, he suggests. I obediently wait and ask "Sparks" to call again around four or five, but all the cabs are still "too busy." Actually, they are just conveying that the terminal is too far out of the way, and that business is more lucrative downtown. So my visit to fascinating Kaohsiung remains limited to a brief walk around the container yard. Not what I had in mind, but at least it's some exercise.

Meanwhile, the loading continues, some 630 boxes this time, most of them filled with textiles, sneakers, stuffed animals, and who knows what else. A good many of them seem to be deposited right in front of my cabin, which involves a good bit of clanging and banging, so it is a bit difficult to write. Fortunately, Martin drags me away to show me his newest toy, an experimental on-board guidance system (or OGS) that goes by the name Ocean Routes. Located in the ship's office, the system consists of a personal computer, two monitors, and a modem that links up to Ocean Routes' headquarters near San Francisco via satellite.

It takes me about thirty seconds to become a lifelong convert. First Martin downloads the system, which takes a few minutes. Then the fun begins. On the graphics monitor appears a map of the Pacific, showing surface wind speed and direction. Martin zooms in somewhat, to the area he is most interested in: the seas between Kaohsiung and Nagoya. In addition to average wind speeds, he also pulls up maps showing barometric pressure, currents—in this case the track and surface strength of the Kuroshio (the Japan Current)—and an outline of the ship herself, with arrows showing where the wind and the ocean swells are coming from.

It doesn't take an expert to figure out that these factors affect the vessel's progress, so Martin plots a course between Kaohsiung and Yokohama and then moves it around a bit to take advantage of the northward-flowing Kuroshio current, for instance, or to stay away from strong headwinds. Occasionally glancing at the weather fax map he brought down from the bridge, he decides to stay close to the coast of Taiwan to get a better lift from the Kuroshio. Winds are projected to be fine along the way, quite strong but coming from abeam the entire way, so there are not many adjustments that can be made there.

As it turns out, Ocean Routes was not entirely on the mark. It got the wind's strength right (about 25 knots), but not its direction. Once we pass the northern tip of Taiwan, the wind is dead ahead rather than abeam, and it continues like that for most of the remainder of the trip. Fortunately, for much of that time we are smack in the middle of the Kuroshio—the water temperature will tell you that—which gives us a boost of 2 to 3 knots, so the adverse winds don't cost us too much time.

We are sailing past Miyako-Jima, Okinawa, and the rest of the Ryukyu Islands—places that used to have a subtropical ring to me, but not this time. It is always either raining or cloudy, and with a relative wind speed of 50 knots—the 20 knots the ship is making plus the 30 knots of wind she is fighting—my sunglasses and suntan lotion stay safely out of sight. It is not until we approach Nagoya Bay on Tuesday morning that the weather finally clears out and there is a chance to spend some time on the bridge wings without running the risk of getting blown off.

Martin told me that it gets awfully busy in Nagoya Bay, so I head forward to the fo'c'sle to spend the three-hour trip from Kamishima at the entrance of the bay to the port. It is wonderfully quiet here; the engines eight hundred feet further aft cannot be heard, and there is none of the constant vibration brought about by a 40,000-horse-power engine turning a propeller shaft at 115 revolutions per minute.

The bay is quite pretty, though some of the nicest stretches have been spoiled by attempts to imitate Waikiki and thereby attract gullible tourists and honeymooners. But just watching the traffic pass by, from high on the bow of a giant ocean carrier, is glorious. Martin is true to his word: it is very busy. Aside from the ferries and fishing boats, an awful lot of car carriers make their way out of the bay. In just one hour we pass at least twenty of them—some large, others small, but all equally hideous. Martin later tells me that Toyota has one of its main factories here, so that explains it. That evening I read in the port of Nagoya's fancy brochure that more than half a million cars leave from here to all corners of the globe.

No such volume for us in Nagoya. Only fifty-nine containers need to be discharged and fifty-one taken aboard, so we are in and out in less than three hours. By 22:00 we are under way, back through the bay and its resident population of car carriers, then along the coast of Honshu toward Tokyo Bay and Yokohama, our last port before the crossing.

Arriving in Nagoya. Captain Martin Weir and the pilot direct the action from the bridge wing.

Previous page: Leaving Yokohama, the *Envoy* begins her nine-day Pacific crossing.

Early the next morning we pass Ō-shima Island and merge into the traffic heading for the ports of Tokyo and Yokohama. This is one of the busiest stretches of water in the world, but the bay pilot guides us expertly through the congestion and the myriad fishing boats, which seem to live by their own Rules of the Road. Martin keeps a watchful eye throughout, however. Although the pilot is directing the helmsman, the master remains in command at all times. If something were to go wrong, it's his neck that's on the line. Only in the Panama Canal does the pilot actually take over command of the ship.

We dock around 12:30 on Wednesday and are off by 17:30. The moment we clear Tokyo Bay, Martin asks me whether I want another Ocean Routes demonstration—the "real thing," as he puts it. So we head back into the ship's office and wait for the system to download. Martin keys in the latest vessel specifics: things to do with the ship's draft, stability factors, drag, and the "area of lateral wind resistance." Next, the North Pacific map appears on the screen, but this time with a yellow line between Yokohama and Seattle. For some reason the system already seems to know that the *Envoy* will be heading from one to the other, and the yellow track shows the route it recommends. At this scale the route looks like a great circle, but when Martin zooms in it becomes clear that the track actually diverges here and there.

It is now that I begin to understand what Ocean Routes can really do. The system is not simply trying to come up with the shortest route between the two cities; anyone can do that. Instead, it presents the most economical route, using the latest weather information to dodge strong headwinds or adverse currents and other factors that affect progress, and hence operating costs. And that's the bottom line. In addition to providing information on expected weather conditions, the system predicts how much fuel will be consumed along the way, or how much more money you, or rather the company, will have to shell out if you opt for another route.

Martin wouldn't be a Scot if he simply settled for what a machine, even a smart machine, tells him to do, so he plays around a bit with alternatives. Eventually he decides on a slightly different route, passing into the Bering Sea at Adak Island and heading from there to Unimak Pass and the Gulf of Alaska for a straight shot to Puget Sound. One touch of a key, and the system tells him what the diversion will do to the ETA (estimated time of arrival) in Seattle and the fuel bill. Martin's route would actually cost $160 more. The system always wins, theoretically at least.

Once we are out of the bay, the new course is marked on the chart, and we get ready for the long Pacific crossing. Aboard are 1,422 containers, nearly all of them the forty-foot kind, the others small twenty-foot boxes or the larger forty-five-foot variety. Yokohama gave us an even trade: 175 boxes loaded and 180 boxes discharged, including the last remnants of the Seattle cargo. Three of them contained, of all things, bales of hay—pure American hay, probably from the Midwest, which moves on to feed finicky Japanese thoroughbreds.

Martin knew about this one, because hay can cause spontaneous combustion and is therefore classified as a Class 4 Dangerous Good. He generally knows only the dangerous goods the ship is carrying—anything from asbestos to chemicals and hay—and the contents of the refrigerated containers, known as reefers. As far as the rest is concerned, "Your guess is as good as mine," he shrugs. The usual stuff: videocassette recorders, stereo equipment, computers, beer, *sashimi*, auto parts, tires, chopsticks, you name it.

 It used to be that Japan, or Cipangu as it was called at the time, was known for other treasures: silver and gold, for instance, and especially silk. Before the country sealed itself off from the outside world in the seventeenth century, there was a flourishing trade in these goods. But it was not the Japanese who dominated it, or even the Chinese or Arabs. It was the Europeans, first the Portuguese and later the Dutch and English, who grabbed it the moment they arrived in the East and managed to control it for several hundred years.

The West's domination of this most lucrative of all sea trades dates back nearly five hundred years, when Vasco da Gama rounded the Cape of Good Hope and reached the Indian Ocean. Interestingly, even while slowly making his way up the East African coast, da Gama had no idea where exactly he was, much less how to get to India. But in the Kenyan port of Malindi he found a pilot who showed him the way. Ironically, it was an Arab who guided him, possibly Ahmad Ibn-Majid, one of the most skillful navigators of that time. Without realizing it, Ibn-Majid gave Portugal the key to India, sealing the Arabs' fate as middlemen in the commerce between East and West.

Guiding the Portuguese to India was no more than the final act in an inexorable progression of events, however. In many ways the Arabs had been sowing the seeds of their own demise for much longer. While much of Europe lay steeped in ignorance, Arab scholars were translating the wisdom of the ancients and accumulating a body of knowledge unsurpassed in the world. To this they added their own observations: sophisticated mathematical treatises, for instance, and detailed geographical accounts. They also developed advanced astronomical techniques and instruments—things like astrolabes and astronomical tables, which enabled them get an accurate latitude reading. And to top it off, they perfected a different type of rigging for their ships: the lateen sail. A simple innovation, or so it appears at first, but one of great importance, for it allowed ships to make headway into the wind.

Taken together, these advances provided the basis for venturing beyond the confines of the known world. And Europe accepted them readily. Through the Moorish kingdoms in Spain and Portugal the writings of the ancient Greeks were reintroduced in the West, revolutionizing people's view of their world. Nautical technology too was transferred, for the first time allowing Western mariners to consider sailing in unknown waters. Along with precise geographical and astronomical information, these were the tools needed to gain access to the East by sea, and the Arabs handed them over, one by one. When they realized their mistake, it was too late. Within a matter of years the Europeans had forced the Arabs out of the trade altogether.

But Europe's oceanic breakout took more than Arab technology and information. There were also factors like greed and envy—less tangible, perhaps, but no less important. The West had never lost its appetite for the riches of the East, not even during the Dark Ages, but it had never seen any of the profits. Instead, the money always flowed back to the Arabs and their middlemen—into "infidel" hands, a fact that created even greater resentment. Gaining access to the East could thus achieve a dual objective: making money and wiping out the Muslims. It proved to be an irresistible temptation.

Much of the credit for the first attempts to seek a sea route to the East belongs to one nation, and in fact to one person in particular: Dom Henrique of Portugal, third son of King John I. History remembers him as Henry the Navigator, though it is a somewhat misleading name. Henry never navigated anywhere, except once, in 1415, from Lisbon to the Moorish stronghold of Ceuta in North Africa, just across from Gibraltar. He was only twenty-one at the time. The siege of Ceuta was a turning point in Henry's life—not because it won him knighthood and military honors, but because it allowed him to see the Arabs' wealth firsthand. Ceuta was one of the terminals of the North African gold trade, offering access to spices and other luxuries in quantities seldom seen in the West. Gaining access to these riches and, in the process, dealing the Muslims a terrific setback became Henry's obsession.

In 1418 Henry abandoned the Portuguese court so that he could devote his attention fully to the sea voyages that would occupy him for the rest of his life. He moved to the Algarve, in southern Portugal. Operating at first out of the city of Lagos, he assembled cartographers and astronomers, to make sure that his mariners would have the best tools and information at their disposal before heading into unknown seas. His shipwrights built vessels suitable for exploration. They decided on a small, sturdy vessel, lateen-rigged, of course, so that it could return against prevailing winds.

Henry then began to send out expeditions, one after the other. The going was slow at first, for no matter how convincing a patron and how great his support, his sailors did not necessarily share his vision. They were far more inclined to agree with the prevailing notion that somewhere south of Portugal there was a Green Sea of Darkness, where the sun passed so low that the sea actually boiled. And the first voyages seemed to confirm these speculations. The mariners returned with frightening tales of a desolate coast, thick fogs, and swift currents—clear warning signs, it seemed, of an impassable region further south.

To Henry's credit, he got his captains to disregard these superstitions and to inch their way down, pushing back the edge of the unknown with each voyage. In 1434, after at least fourteen tries, they reached Cape Bojador, just a thousand miles southwest of Lagos. Thereafter the pace picked up. By 1446 they had rounded Cape Verde, Africa's westernmost point. In 1455 they got to the Gambia River, and by 1460, when Henry died, they had made it as far as Sierra Leone—still only one-third of the way down the continent, but nobody knew that.

After a ten-year interruption the voyages continued, this time directly administered by the Portuguese crown. One after another the expeditions left from Lisbon for the African coast, cautiously making their way further south. Along the way trading stations were established where gold and slaves from the African interior were gathered and sent back to Portugal, generating handsome profits. But the ultimate prize was still far off. In 1473 Lopo Gonçalves crossed the equator. By 1484 Diogo Cão had reached Cape Fria, in what is now Namibia. And just four years later Bartolomeu Dias went the final thousand miles to the southernmost tip of Africa—a point he called the Cape of Storms but his superiors renamed the Cape of Good Hope. Good Hope, for now the way to the Indies was finally open. Ten years later, on 18 May 1498, Vasco da Gama attained that objective, reaching India's Malabar Coast after a voyage of more than ten months. He took four ships, two of them specially designed cargo carriers. They both returned the following year after a voyage of twenty-seven thousand miles. Da Gama and his companions received a tumultuous welcome in Lisbon. They brought back only a handful of spices, but that was irrelevant. What mattered was the information they brought back, information that secured the sea route to the Indies and its riches.

Within a year Portugal had another expedition on its way East, this time a massive fleet of thirteen armed cargo ships under the leadership of Pedro Cabral. Following da Gama's example, Cabral led his fleet wide to the west of Africa to take advantage of the trade winds. But he went a little too far and landed in Brazil, which he claimed for his homeland before pressing on. Despite the detour and atrocious weather near the Cape of Good Hope, he reached Calicut after a six-month voyage. Seven of his ships eventually returned to Lisbon, deeply laden with spices. A new expedition was already prepared to sail, and from then on Portugal sent out annual fleets. Before long the Portuguese had doubled Europe's supply of pepper and spices, much to the dismay of the Venetians, who had controlled the European end of this lucrative business.

Portugal's neighbor Spain was equally interested in this spice trade, but it decided to go west in its search for the Indies, as had been advocated by Christopher Columbus. Genoan by birth, Columbus had calculated that reaching the Far East would entail a voyage of less than four thousand miles. He was off by more than twice that much, but fortunately for him, the vast American landmass stood in the way. The "discovery" gave Spain access to the resources of a totally unexpected continent, resources that, though seemingly meager at first, soon began to supply the Spanish treasury as nothing ever had.

Within thirty years of these major voyages of exploration, no more than an instant in time, Spain and Portugal were regularly sending out additional expeditions, taking measure of virtually the entire world. The expansion culminated in 1521 with the voyage of Portuguese-born Ferdinand Magellan around the world, a passage that made clear that all the world's countries were interconnected by water, and hence accessible by sea.

Even more remarkable, within that same time span both countries succeeded in dominating their newfound possessions. By 1512, less than fifteen years after arriving in the Indian Ocean, the Portuguese had taken control of the entire East African coast, Hormuz in the Persian Gulf, and large parts of western India. Within years they had also gained control over Malacca and the ultimate prize, the Spice Islands of Indonesia. Spain too moved with lightning speed. In 1519 Hernán Cortés, with only a handful of men, crushed the Aztec empire, the most powerful in Central America. Using Mexico as a base, others moved on, eventually subduing the resplendent Inca empire in Peru and all lands in between.

It was, and in retrospect still is, an unbelievable achievement: a few men conquering whole empires and civilizations, often far greater than their own. But it was also a tragic period in human history, for these men achieved their goals with brutal repression. The Indian Ocean, for hundreds of years a region of relative peace, was stunned into submission by the brutality of the Portuguese invaders. Vasco da Gama at one point saw fit to capture a dhow full of Muslim pilgrims, hanging everyone aboard and sending the cut-up remains to a rebellious sultan, with a letter suggesting that it might make for a nice curry.

Spanish chronicles too reflect the miseries that befell the Indians of South and Central America—tales of cold-blooded massacres, torture, and white men taking demonic pleasure in the worst of human suffering. "The Spanish began to commit murders, and strange cruelties: they entred into Townes, Borowes and Villages, sparing neither children nor old men, neither women with childe, neither them that lay in, but that they ripped their bellies and cut them in peeces, as if they had beene opening of Lambes shut up in their fold." So wrote the Dominican friar Bartolome de las Casas. Still tormented by the sight, he went on: "They laid wagers with such as with one thrust of a sword would paunch or bowell an man in the middest, or with one blow of a sword would most readily and most deliverly cut off his head, or that would best pierce his entrals at one stroake. They tooke the little soules by the heeles, ramping them from their mothers dugges, and crushed their heads against the clifts." The list of atrocities went on and on: "I saw there so great cruelties," de las Casas admitted, "that never any man living either have or shall see the like."

Just as the Age of Exploration reflected some of the best in Western man, so the subsequent Age of Exploitation exhibited some of the worst. It was a black page in the history of native peoples the world over, all of it put in motion by the quest for the riches of the East and the desire to make up for lost ground when that goal was finally reached. The benefits to Spain and Portugal were huge. By the end of the sixteenth century Spain was the richest and most powerful nation in the world, ruling an empire that stretched from Europe to the Americas and beyond to the Philippines. Portugal too, before it was absorbed by Spain, controlled an enormous trading empire, gaining wealth and power unparalleled in its history.

Few people in Madrid or Lisbon gave a moment's thought to the people at whose expense this newfound wealth had come. After all, was not all of this part of God's great scheme to bring the true faith to the heathen inhabitants of these lands? And so along with the merchants and the soldiers went the priests. "If there were not merchants who go seek for earthly treasures in the East and West Indies, who would transport thither the preachers who take heavenly treasures?" So wrote Antonio Vieira, a seventeenth-century Jesuit observer, implying that spiritual guidance—or "heavenly treasures," as he called it—seemed a fair trade for the riches stripped from overseas possessions.

However patronizing this may appear in hindsight, at the time it provided both Spain and Portugal a measure of justification for the brutal exploitation of their territories. But mixing religion with commerce often proved to be counterproductive. The Portuguese in particular experienced trouble in trying to impose Christianity in the East—upon Hindus, Buddhists, and Muslims, all of them having well-established religious beliefs of their own. In some places the missionaries managed to win a few converts, but in the long run these efforts only added tension to an already volatile situation. In 1640, for instance, after a hundred years of trade, Japan ordered the Portuguese to pack their bags, largely as a result of a growing distrust of their missionaries (who were executed). Elsewhere too the Church's interference created antipathy, making it increasingly difficult for Portugal to hang on to its far-flung possessions.

Eventually Portugal lost its monopoly of the spice trade. Like Spain, it treated its possessions as places to be exploited rather than as entities that could be developed for the mutual good of colony and parent—an obvious source of resentment among the conquered. But there were other factors. As its possessions grew, the country's resources became too thinly spread. Here was a nation of no more than a million people trying to control a trading empire stretching over more than ten thousand miles. There was simply no way it could be done. And most important, there was increasingly strong competition for this rich prize, not just from local rulers, who eventually figured out that the Portuguese were not supremely powerful, but from another European contender—a nation of sailors and traders who left God out of their business dealings. That nation was Holland.

Holland was superbly placed to go after Portugal's commerce. By the late sixteenth century it had become the principal merchant carrier of Europe and possessed one of its strongest navies. It had just triumphed in its struggle for independence from Spain. That victory, against nothing less than the mightiest nation on earth, gave the Dutch a great deal of confidence. Nothing was going to stop them from going after the trade of the world, and especially the rich East Indies trade.

Of course, to get to the Indies one needed a bit more than a sturdy ship and an experienced crew. Knowing how to get there was just as important. Like most European contenders, the Dutch had a rough idea of the passage, but the Portuguese guarded the details closely. They could not, however, keep all of it secret. In 1596 the Dutchman Jan Huyghen van Linschoten published an account of his travels and observations in Asia. In addition to providing a good bit of information on life in India, where he had spent several years, van Linschoten's account made clear that Portugal's control of the Indies was not what it was built up to be. In fact, the book suggested that the mighty Portuguese navy of earlier in the century was barely hanging on. Van Linschoten also published a book of sailing directions to the Orient, which caused an even greater sensation. To the dismay of the Portuguese, it revealed just about everything they had so desperately tried to keep secret.

Another Dutchman, Cornelis Houtman, took a slightly different approach. In 1592 he went to Lisbon, disguised himself, and managed to get aboard a vessel that sailed for the East Indies. When he came back a few years later he was unmasked, and promptly thrown into a Lisbon jail. Fortunately for Houtman, some Dutch merchants paid his ransom, and the Portuguese let him go. Back in Holland, these benefactors set up a shipping company of their own, provided Houtman with four ships, and asked him to repeat the voyage—this time for their account.

Houtman returned more than two years later, after having reached Bantam, one of the key trading ports in the East Indies. Only 89 of his 249-man crew made it back, and their cargo was not as rich as hoped for. But the sponsors considered it a great success, for Houtman had shown that it was possible to get to the East and beat the Portuguese at their own game. That, and the prospect of rich profits, enticed other merchants to invest. More than twenty ships were fitted out the following year, some of which returned with heavy cargoes of pepper and cloves. They made their investors a great deal of money, causing even more ships to be sent out. Between 1598 and 1602 no fewer than sixty-five of them set sail for the Indies, much to the dismay of the Portuguese, who saw their lucrative monopoly seriously threatened.

If there was any doubt left that the Dutch were going after Portugal's spice trade in a big way, it was dispelled on 20 March 1602. On that day the Dutch States General founded the Vereenigde Oost Indische Companie (United East Indies Company), soon to be known as the VoC. Its establishment turned out to be a smart move. Not only did the company bring the many trading ventures of the previous years under single control, thereby reducing internal competition; it also received whatever powers were needed to bring about a total monopoly of the spice trade. Hence, the VoC was given the authority to maintain an army and a navy, to build and fortify trading centers, to declare war and peace, to implement and enforce its own laws, and even to coin its own money. Clearly, this was no longer a simple company; it was a state within the state.

The newly formed company set about its tasks with a vengeance. In 1603 its ships reached Ceylon. One year later, VoC representatives arrived in China and tried to establish direct trade. That same year another fleet launched an unsuccessful attack on Malacca. In 1605 a fleet of heavily armed merchantmen captured the Portuguese fort at Ambon in the Moluccas and turned it into a trading base, the first of several that would follow. And in 1610 they captured Ternate, one of the main spice-producing islands.

At first, local rulers welcomed the Dutch, assuming that they could not be worse than the arrogant Portuguese. But these hopes were soon crushed. The new traders were just as cruel and intent on enforcing a monopoly as their predecessors had been; perhaps they were even worse. The Dutch offered nothing in return for what they took, not even heavenly salvation. Money was all that mattered, and they used brute force to amass plenty of it.

At the height of its success in the 1660s and 1670s, the VoC controlled a principal base in Batavia (now Indonesia's capital, Jakarta), and trading posts in Malacca, Ceylon, India, Ambon, Sumatra, Java, and Ternate—all places with direct access to the major spices. The company also had a base at the Cape of Good Hope, where its vessels could provision prior to setting out for the East Indies, and its officials were the only Westerners allowed to trade with Japan—another trade that made them a bundle. In addition, it possessed 150 massive armed merchantmen, 40 warships, and an army of 10,000 soldiers. "We cannot carry on trade without war nor war without trade," one VoC official wrote to his superiors in Holland. That might as well have been the company's motto.

For much of the seventeenth century these resources enabled the Dutch to control the spice trade from East to West, successively defeating the Portuguese, the English, and anyone else who might have had an eye on their monopoly. But the massive overhead that came with maintaining an army and a navy, not to mention thousands of officials throughout the East Indies, eventually wore the company down. By the end of the seventeenth century the VoC was actually losing money, though its cumbersome accounting system did not reveal this until many years later. The high cost of guarding against each and every incursion was crippling. The outflow of money eroded the company's control, and things grew worse. Every year the mountain of debt grew. Corruption was rampant. English, French, and other traders began to circumvent the Dutch monopoly. Under those conditions the mighty VoC could not survive. A hundred years later, it folded.

Despite this unglamorous ending, for two hundred years the Dutch East Indies Company poured enormous wealth into Holland, as is still evident in Amsterdam and the other VoC cities, and in just about any Dutch art museum. With this newfound wealth, life changed in fundamental ways. Though luxuries like silk and pearls remained the exclusive domain of the wealthy, spices became relatively affordable, enhancing the drab diet of seventeenth-century Europeans. Cotton from India provided them with inexpensive undergarments. Later introductions such as coffee and tea dramatically changed their drinking habits. Not everyone was affected, of course. The poor remained as poor as ever and probably saw very little of this. But for Holland's growing middle class, the luxuries of the East for the first time were within reach, making life somewhat more pleasant.

Life changed at the other end of the trade route too, with many islands in Indonesia, previously independent in their own right, forced to adopt the ways of the new rulers. The Dutch would actually stay for more than four hundred years, as did the English in India and Malaya. Only Japan and China, by hermetically sealing their borders, were able to keep the foreigners out. But they could not do it forever. In the end they too succumbed to the West's obsession with Cathay.

Three days out of Yokohama, the *Envoy* is midway between the northern tip of Hokkaido and Adak Island in the Aleutians. The weather is calm—"Definitely late spring or early summer type patterns over much of the North Pacific," Ocean Routes advises us. And so it is, with winds of 10 knots or so on the quarter and isolated patches of fog, and the *Envoy* lazily rolling through the gentle swell.

Every morning Martin downloads the OGS system, to check what it has in store for him and to verify how well it predicts actual conditions, information he will later relay to the programmers at Ocean Routes headquarters. There is no doubt that he is impressed with the system's performance, averaging 60 to 70 percent accuracy in the western Pacific and as much as 90 percent on the eastern side, along the Alaskan coast. It strikes me as considerably better than the average of local forecasters, even when they're just theorizing about tomorrow's weather.

The daily download sessions are actually fun, because it is possible to compare forecast with actuality, and Ocean Routes is performing admirably. Glancing at the screen, Martin often mutters, "That's exactly what we have" or "Looking good" or, when checking what the next few days have in store, "This is great." Of course, he's

Third officer Poon Kwok Ming on watch as we approach the Aleutian Islands.

looking at a dream crossing: light winds on the stern, light swells, wonderful every-thing. I'd like to see his reaction when the system informs him, say in mid-February, of gale-force headwinds, subzero temperatures, and an iced-up ship, but then again, I'm glad to be aboard now rather than then. This is definitely the way to go.

Being the only Westerners aboard, Martin and I tend to seek each other's company. Before long, we've established a daily nightcap routine, which gives me a chance to ask him questions about the ship and the business of getting it back and forth across the Pacific. But invariably our chats range far beyond, from the family in Edinburgh and the house that overlooks the Firth of Forth to a discussion of the greatest sea novels.

Martin's twenty-seven-year career at sea provides enough material for a few night-cap sessions as well. "I always wanted to go to sea," he tells me, "so I left school at age sixteen to head out." First he joined the Ben Line, a job that gave him an AB (able-bodied seaman) ticket and a deeply ingrained dislike for "chipping"—the tedious business of hammering paint and rust out of steel decks. "The only time I ever came near the wheelhouse was to scrub it," he reminisces.

Next came two years ashore to obtain a second mate's license. By late 1970, only twenty-one at the time, he was shipping out as second mate, making him the youngest such officer in the company. Two years later Martin left the Ben Line to join CP Ships, then a rapidly expanding Canadian carrier. He spent seventeen years there, shipping out on product tankers, North Sea oil tankers, VLCCs (very large crude car-

Martin doing what he likes best: birdwatching. The North Pacific provides him with plenty of sightings.

riers), and bulk carriers. In 1973 he set foot aboard his first containership. "I didn't like it," he admits, "for we were no longer in control of the cargo the way we were on a conventional break-bulk ship. But I knew immediately that this was what it was going to be like from then on."

By the late 1980s CP Ships was running into financial difficulties. Its fleet shrank from forty-four ships in 1980 to no more than five in 1989, giving Martin severe doubts about his chances of shipping out as captain. So he left for OOCL, finding himself mate of the *OOCL Freedom* and then the *OOCL Charger.* A year later he finally got his first command: the *OOCL Alliance,* a feeder shuttling between Hong Kong, Korea, Taiwan, and Japan. Then, after a three-month leave, he returned to take command of the *Envoy.* He likes the ship and her route, though he admits to having been puzzled at first about his assignment. Why was he assigned to the Pacific, which he didn't know that well, when OOCL also services the North Atlantic, which he had been crossing for five years? Presumably there are Chinese captains on OOCL's transatlantic vessels wondering the same thing.

Having been aboard more than a week, I am also getting to know some of the other officers. Chief officer Liu Cheung Sing startled me the first time I met him on the bridge by volunteering how much he hated the sea. Later I found out that he had not been given much notice about this trip and had been literally dragged out of a well-deserved leave with wife and son in Hong Kong, so I understood his lack of enthusiasm. I soon realize that most of the Hong Kong Chinese aboard feel this way as well. They're not here because they feel any particular attraction to ships or the sea. They're here because it's a job, and it's good money. If there's any other reason, they aren't telling me.

This is Liu's first trip as chief officer, and as the days pass, the lines of care become more deeply etched in his face. True, he does have a lot of work. In addition to being the captain's right-hand man—and understudy, in case something happens—he stands watch from four to eight twice a day; supervises the loading, unloading, and carriage of the cargo (which precludes any time off in port); oversees deck maintenance (keeping things like winches, hatches, ropes, and lines in order); controls all ballasting operations; and keeps track of fresh-water supplies. The latter in particular is giving him (and Martin) a major headache, because consumption is far higher than normal, and water supplies to the cabins have to be rationed. Not that it matters to me all that much. My shower gives me a choice between cold and icy water one day, and hot and scalding the next, so I'm already inclined to be economical.

Second officer Shi Hau Kit—Simon, to us—is on his fifth trip aboard the *Envoy* and has just one more to go before going on leave. Perhaps that puts him in a good mood, but he strikes me as being one of those people who are always pleasant to be around. His plate is quite full as well. Besides the twelve-to-four watch, which is the worst, he is responsible for navigation and any medical emergencies. Martin's affection for Ocean Routes has made some of the navigational demands somewhat lighter, but there are still a good many actual calculations to be done.

A first-timer aboard the *Envoy* is third officer Poon Kwok Ming. Bee, as he is called, is very good-natured, even though his next leave is at least seven trips away. "Early December," he tells me, laughing at the thought. "That gives me Christmas and New Year's and everything else." Now there's someone with a positive attitude, I think, but he's always like that. "Five-minute walk to the gate," he tells me in Kaohsiung, though it turns out to be at least fifteen.

Bee used to be on OOCL's Middle East service, heading for Singapore and ports like Dubai, Abu Dhabi, and Bahrain, and once also Kuwait (the port reopened in late 1991 for commercial container traffic). He likes this route better. Sure, it's boring, he admits, but it gets him to Hong Kong and his girlfriend once every thirty-five days, rather than once every forty-five. His family—parents, brothers, sisters—no longer live there, however; they have all moved to Toronto. Yes, they're lonely there, and very cold during the winter, he adds. "But it's better than staying in Hong Kong, no? Never know what China will do to it."

Bee has the eight-to-twelve watch, the only one that doesn't interfere with normal sleeping patterns, so he looks a bit better rested than his colleagues. His additional responsibilities are also somewhat less demanding: maintain the life-saving, fire-fighting, and signaling equipment. Then again, he also has a lot yet to learn.

Rounding out the deck complement is Leung Po Cheong, or "Sparks," the radio officer, who prefers that I call him Andy. I always know when Andy is in the mess-room, because he slurps his soup, even when it's stone-cold, with a great deal of noisy enthusiasm. The rest of the meal is put away with audible relish as well, with a smart smacking of the lips punctuating every bite. It sounds sort of like a wet duck walking across a marble floor. Actually, everybody here eats quite noisily, which is probably considered polite in China, making Andy a very polite young man. Here is someone, I reflect, who not only follows audible dining etiquette to the letter, but also pays tribute to shipboard cuisine by stashing away formidable amounts of food despite what can't be much more than a five-foot frame.

All kidding aside, Andy is my link with the outside world, sending out faxes and delivering the occasional reply. The radio officers of old were busier than he is, but satellite communications have done away with much of the fidgeting with dials and radio transmissions. Telex and fax, relayed via one of the maritime satellites, are far more efficient. To ensure that Andy is not left unoccupied, Martin has handed him some of the responsibilities of the erstwhile purser, a position that no longer exists aboard OOCL ships in these budget-conscious times: dealing with provisioning, taking care of some of the accounting, handling shore leave, and the like.

The *Envoy*'s wheelhouse.

Junior engineer Tsang Wing Kit, who goes by Terrance, is more communicative than his colleagues. Though his mastery of English is a bit shaky, he guides me around the engine room, explaining the machinery that keeps the *Envoy* going.

As far as the engine compartment is concerned, they strike me as an uncommunicative bunch. Seven days aboard now, and the most I've gotten out of them is a passive "Good morning" or "Good evening," depending on when I see them, usually in the mess. I later gather that it is not because they are a particularly grumpy group of people, but because most of them were born and raised in mainland China, and they feel less comfortable than the others with their English. Chief engineer Cheng Shi Wai is particularly quiet around me. Always impeccably dressed, his perfectly starched uniform worn over a matching sport shirt, he has yet to crack a smile. The engineers' discussions during dinner can get quite animated, but of course I don't understand a word of it.

Junior engineer Tsang Wing Kit, who goes by the name Terrance, is the exception. Terrance grew up in Canton, and he loves to practice his English, even though it's a bit shaky. At least he makes an effort, all the while apologizing for his pronunciation. "Sorry my English very bad," he smiles, and I graciously accept the apology, not realizing until later that my accent probably baffles him just as much.

It is Terrance who one day guides me around the engine room, where the 40,000-horsepower Sulzer diesel engines tirelessly toil to turn the propeller shaft. Occasionally he stops to yell an explanation into my ear—"GENERATAAH," then "BOILAAH" or "PURIFYAAH"—all of them equally intimidating. Later I ask him where he and his friends got their English names. I'm curious, because I don't know many people named Terrance. "Our English teachers assign them," Terrance replies, thereby answering any questions I might have had about his command of the language.

On the other side of the ship is the crew's mess, and on Saturday evening Martin and I head over there, armed with a few goodies to loosen up their tongues. Martin is in search of crew reactions: complaints, concerns, and whatever else may be on their minds. I tag along, hoping to get to know them a bit better. Unlike the officers, virtually all of the ratings are Filipino; perhaps they'll be a bit more animated.

At first the discussion is quiet and polite, with topics ranging from promotion to contracts and overtime. The Filipinos have brought some of their own treats: fresh mango, which is heavenly, and something called *dilis*—little dried fish, the smell of which clears my stuffed-up nose in a matter of seconds. There's money in this, I observe, though we're going to have to do something about the scent.

I want to get a few reactions about the Philippine elections, which took place just a few days earlier, but I don't get very far. "Aren't you concerned about who wins?" I ask. "Yes, sir," is the reply. "What about Imelda? Unbelievable, no?" "Yes, sir." After a string of polite Yes-sirs in response to my increasingly provocative questions, I begin to assume that the reports of Filipino election passion are grossly overstated, but Martin later tells me that politics is tabu on the ship. "That and religion" he adds, "and on British ships, football. They're the sort of thing that can cause friction. It's just not worth having them affect the team spirit."

No Imelda-bashing, in other words, but they have something far better in store. "Do you believe in ghosts?" Joel Molinos, the young mechanic, asks me at one point. "Ghosts? I'm not sure," I reply vaguely, "but I don't think so." "I didn't believe in ghosts either," Joel goes on, "but I do now. I've seen one on this ship, in the starboard tunnel." Joel is dead serious. I glance around the room to check the others' faces, and they're dead serious too. They may not have seen anything, but if Joel has seen a ghost and sworn by it, then that's good enough for them.

I have read the stories of the *Marie Celeste* and the *Flying Dutchman* and scores of other "strange" ships, but a haunted containership is something new. So I readily accept Joel's invitation to inspect the starboard tunnel tomorrow and visit the place where he saw the ghost. "No mistake about it," he continues, describing the experience in eerie detail. "It was as clear as I see you, only further away." Since the sighting, which took place just three months ago, the others have noticed weird things happening as well: the elevator going up and down repeatedly with no one in it, for instance, or the sound of a voice in deserted spaces. Even Martin has a few stories to add: clear knocks on the door of his office when no one is around, and other unexplained noises. I look at him, and then at the bottle in front of us, but it's well above the level where a man like Martin would begin to imagine things. "But it's a good ghost," he reassures us. I half expect him to tell us that he's training it to take over some of the (erstwhile) steward's duties, but he too is dead serious. Or at least he pretends to be, to let the weight of the issue settle in. Not that there's any need for that, as far as I'm concerned. Already I'm frantically searching for excuses to postpone tomorrow's visit to the starboard tunnel.

Nonetheless, the next day I meet Joel as agreed in the lower engine room. Since the noise is overwhelming, he takes me into the engineers' control room to provide a quick introduction to ghost watching. "You'll know a ghost is around," he says, "when the hair on your arms stands up straight." If that's the case, I want to tell him, they're having a party here, because my arms already look like pincushions. But I'm wearing a sweater, so Joel doesn't notice. We proceed to the starboard tunnel, which has to be the eeriest place on the ship. Running underneath and along the entire length of the main deck, the starboard tunnel provides access to the various cargo holds or, as Joel contends, accommodation to the *Envoy*'s ghost. It makes sense. If I were a ghost, this is the place I'd pick as well: long, dark, narrow, and, yes, a bit scary.

Entrance to the tunnel is gained through a small watertight door, and the moment we get in, the hair on my arms nudges up a bit—a sure sign that someone is watching us. Joel feels it too, but then again, he's the resident medium. Very calmly he describes where he saw the ghost. "I was doing some cleaning right here," he explains, "and all of a sudden felt someone was watching me. I look up, and then I see him, right there." Joel walks over and imitates the ghost. "He was tall," he continues, standing on his toes, "and very slender. He looked at me for one …two … three … seconds and then disappeared into the end of the tunnel. No feet," he adds, "or at least I couldn't see any."

We walk the length of the tunnel. Most of the time the hair on my arms continues to point straight up, but sometimes it relaxes a bit. Perhaps it has something to do with Joel's calm voice. "Here I feel it very strongly," he whispers, and immediately my arms agree. But it isn't a scary presence. "He's a good ghost," Joel confirms. I don't quite know what to make of it. All I know is that if anyone is trying to play a practical joke

on me, he's having a field day. But I'm not the only one. As we leave the control room, I notice the small altar with a few additional incense sticks burning in front to appease the spirits. "Did you do this?" I ask Joel. "No," he replies, "the engineers did it."

 As we glide comfortably across the Pacific, it is difficult to imagine the appalling dangers the East-West trade routes concealed in the old days. Innumerable ships were lost—victims of sudden storms, uncharted reefs, fires, navigational errors, and other misfortunes. Of the twenty-two ships that left Holland in the year following Cornelis Houtman's voyage in 1596, only fourteen returned. That was not an unusual proportion, at least in the early days. The Portuguese too lost many ships, as did the English and others who set out to claim a share of the Cathay trade.

Even the ships that made it back safely paid a heavy price, with most of them losing an appalling number of men. Vasco da Gama brought back only 55 out of 170; a hundred years later Houtman returned with just 89 men, 160 less than the original 249. Such losses were not uncommon. The dangerous work aboard was complemented by miserable living conditions, atrocious food, and diseases, among them the most dreaded ailment of all: scurvy. Brought about by a lack of fresh fruits and vegetables, scurvy turned strong men into living corpses. First their gums rotted, oozing black blood; their joints began to swell, making it difficult to move; and then their legs turned gangrenous. After a few weeks the victims slipped into a coma and died, to be pushed overboard by those still strong enough to do so. It was a fate shared by thousands.

The journals of those who survived speak of a fate hardly more desirable. Consider the account of Christopher Schweitzer, who took passage on a Dutch East India-man during the 1680s. After watching sixty-three persons die during a nine-day period, he reported, "we expected every soul should die out of the ship." Storms terrified sailors and passengers alike, and for good reason. Wooden sailing ships stood little chance against the typhoons that tore through the Indian Ocean. "We had another very sore storme," wrote an English merchant on an early-seventeenth-century voyage, which "strooke a present feare into the hearts of all men." Fortunately, his ship survived the watery onslaught, but untold numbers never had a chance.

Aside from shipwrecks caused by storms, many ships were lost through navigational errors. Seventeenth-century sailors could determine their latitude quite accurately, measuring the angle of the sun above the horizon and using tables of declination to figure out where they were in relation to the equator. But their longitude—their exact position east or west from home—they never knew in open seas. The best they could do was deduce it on the basis of experience, as well as speed, winds, currents, leeway, and whatever else was thought to influence a ship's progress—dead reckoning, as it was known. But dead reckoning was never more than an educated guess, and often a wild one, especially when ships were away from land for days and weeks on end.

No wonder there were errors, sometimes very costly ones. The Dutch, for instance, lost several ships on their way to the East Indies. They preferred a southerly route, sailing beyond the tip of South Africa to the gale-force westerlies of the "roaring forties." The advantage of this route was that it took only half the time of the old passage along the East African coast and across the Indian Ocean. The disadvantage was that it was difficult to know when to turn north for Batavia and the Spice Islands. Leaving the roaring forties too early could lengthen the voyage, which inevitably affected conditions among the many people packed aboard. But waiting too long could be even more disastrous.

One of the first ships to find this out was the *Batavia*, a massive East Indiaman that left on her maiden voyage in the fall of 1628 with three hundred crew, soldiers, and passengers. The ship made it to the roaring forties without major problems and then turned east, running before the strong westerlies. She made good time—much better, in fact, than anyone had anticipated. On 3 June 1629 Captain Franciscus Pelsaert figured that he should take advantage of the steady winds for several more days before turning north, but he was wrong. Early the next morning, under a perfectly clear sky, the *Batavia* ran aground on the Abrolhos Islands, some fifty miles west of the Australian mainland. No one, least of all Pelsaert himself, had thought it possible that they had already come so far east.

Almost everyone survived the grounding, but the *Batavia* was a total loss. Pelsaert accordingly divided the sailors, passengers, and soldiers among the various islands and set out with a skeleton crew in one of the ship's boats to find water and perhaps a more hospitable refuge. But there was nothing to be found on the Australian mainland. Pelsaert therefore continued on to Batavia, hoping to come back with help. He succeeded, but by the time he returned three months later, 125 people had been massacred by a small group of mutineers. Many more had succumbed to disease and malnutrition. After the mutineers were executed, only 74 of the 260 survivors were left to make the voyage to Batavia.

The *Batavia's* maiden voyage and the macabre details of its aftermath made for a popular book in seventeenth-century Holland. So did the adventures of Willem Bontekoe, another East Indiaman captain, who survived several calamities at sea. Once his ship blew up after a fire reached its stores of gunpowder. He and seventy-one survivors spent several weeks at sea in two small boats. Many more died before they finally reached a Dutch settlement in Java. On another voyage six years later, the two East Indiamen that accompanied Bontekoe from Batavia to Holland disappeared. One sank during a typhoon in the Indian Ocean; the other was probably attacked by pirates—another menace East Indies sailors had to face, from North Africa all the way to the South China Sea.

Few, if any, of these dangers still exist. In some regions pirates are still quite active, though most of them prey on victims much smaller than a ship the size of the *Envoy*. The Straits of Malacca, for instance, have a nasty reputation in this regard, as they have had since time immemorial. So do some ports along the West African coast. Along the west coast of Latin America there have been instances of marauders crawling aboard huge ships and holding their crews up at gunpoint. Sometimes the pirates even have copies of the cargo manifest, allowing them to go straight to the containers filled with the most valuable goods. Piracy appears to be a well-organized business in some of these areas.

Here, in the middle of the North Pacific, the menace of pirates is the last thing on Martin's mind. During one of our evening chats I ask him whether he has ever had any trouble of this nature elsewhere. "Not on any of my ships," he replies, "but the company has had incidents." As it turns out, an OOCL-owned ship, the *YS Prosperity*, was attacked by pirates in the Straits of Malacca, as was one of its smaller feeder vessels. In both instances the robbers got away with most of the cash from the ship's safe. First officer Liu also remembers the incidents, though I have a bit of trouble understanding him at first, since he seems to keep referring to parrots. "Parrots big problem in Strait of Malacca," he insists. "They attack many ships. We think they are part of Indonesian navy."

In response to this Hitchcockian threat, company headquarters sent out a circular to all vessels advising them of "Actions to Be Taken in Certain Waters," meaning the approaches to Singapore. Martin sailed there when he was on OOCL's Round the World service. "We used to rig fire hoses on the quarters, lash them in position, and turn on the water pressure," he explains, "making it very difficult for anyone to board." In addition, all lower deck doors were locked, one radar would be specifically monitored for small targets at short range, and the ABs would patrol the deck at night, armed with pickax handles. Martin adds, "I don't doubt for a moment they would have relished bashing them onto a pirate's skull."

Weather also has been almost entirely ruled out as a concern, with only the most vicious storms temporarily halting or rerouting the big containerships. Ships still sink, but container vessels have a remarkable safety record. It is a major news event, at least in the industry, when one of them is lost.

Much more affected by severe weather are smaller cargo vessels, of course, and large bulk ships such as tankers and coal carriers. Dry-bulk carriers, which carry anything from grain to iron ore, appear to be especially at risk, with no fewer than nineteen of them and hundreds of lives lost during 1990 alone. The reasons are many. Most of the casualties were older ships carrying very heavy cargoes, a factor that puts enormous stress on the hull. Moreover, bulk commodities like iron ore and coal can cause corrosion, further weakening the hull. During a severe storm the constant pounding of waves can rupture a hull, and when that happens, disaster strikes quickly. Some ships did not even have time to send out an SOS, and vanished literally without a trace.

Few of these concerns affect ships like the *Envoy*, which are well built and maintained. The worst she has experienced thus far is cargo damage, with containers stacked on deck, especially those along the periphery, taking a beating during a storm. During really bad storms they even get knocked overboard, though the *Envoy* has not had such a loss during Martin's tenure. But OOCL, like its competitors, has had its share of casualties. For the shipping companies this is considered a straight loss, with container and contents supposedly disappearing into the deep and insurance settling the claims. But sometimes these things float around for weeks on end, presenting a serious hazard to smaller vessels.

In general, people feel safe aboard this vessel, even in the worst weather, though that doesn't mean they disregard it. As far as I can tell, every member of the crew has had an interesting brush with the sea at its most intimidating, but like seamen the world over, they consider it part of the business. Having witnessed the unbelievable damage the sea can inflict on a ship, they do not expect to escape its occasional fury unscathed.

The main concern imposed by severe weather these days is that it can cause delays. Shipowners are constantly fretting about "schedule integrity," and like other containerships, the *Envoy* sticks to a strict schedule. The schedule is not as tight as it used to be, because some of the other vessels on the same service are a bit slower, giving Martin more anxiety about whether he can slow down enough to make the ETA. But whether it is a matter of slowing down or speeding up, punctuality is the name of the game. Shippers—the customers of the shipping lines—have come to expect fixed-day arrivals and departures as well as on-time performance.

There is a lot of competition in the East-West trades these days (some say too much), giving shippers plenty of opportunity to switch carriers if they are not pleased with the service they are getting. And that is something most carriers want to avoid at all costs. Customer loyalty is a priority, and they will do whatever is needed to retain it: match price cuts, guarantee on-time delivery, go overboard on quality assurances, offer volume discounts—you name it. Scanning the shipping ads, one sometimes feels as if one were in the middle of a supermarket-chain war.

To get an idea of what this has done to shipowners, listen to what Ole Skaarup, the chairman of an American bulk shipping company, has to say. One of the United States' most outspoken shipowners, he points out time after time that shippers—his customers—have been getting a terrific deal. The examples he provides are startling. When he started his company in 1951 it cost $7.50 to send a ton of coal from the United States to Europe. Today it costs less than that, in constant dollars. The same is true for grain: $10 per ton in 1951, about the same forty years later. During the same

Following page: A view from the bridge. The *Envoy* is carrying 1,107 containers on this trip, most of them the 40-foot kind.

period, however, the cost of staying in business has risen dramatically. A twenty-thousand-ton bulk carrier that cost $2.5 million in the 1950s would cost a minimum of $20 million today. Fuel prices have gone up even more: shipowners today pay about fifty times what they paid forty years ago.

The situation is the same in the break-bulk market, much of which relies on container carriers. Here too the cost of ships keeps rising, from $35 million in 1985 for a ship of three thousand TEU (twenty-foot equivalent units) to around $65 million in 1991 and a projected $100 million by the end of the decade. Everything else goes up as well, from crew wages to bunker fuel to the price of the meals served aboard—everything, that is, except freight rates, which in some cases have fallen even more dramatically than their counterparts in the bulk sector. "Some people ask me if you can still make a small fortune in shipping," jokes Conrad Everhard, a U.S. shipping executive. "And I reply, Sure—as long as you start with a very large fortune." The punch line invariably gets a massive howl from executives at carrier meetings, though they realize all too well that the joke is on them.

To some extent lower rates have been made possible by economies of scale and much greater efficiencies, but that does not account for all of it. Much of the downward pressure is caused by the simple fact that there are too many ships on major trade routes such as the Atlantic and the Pacific. Overcapacity means bargains for shippers, but hard times for shipping companies. In fact, when analyzing the industry and its prospects, one often wonders why shipping companies bother to stay in business. Some of them operate in the red for years at a time, hoping for the change that will finally allow them to earn a decent return on investment. Whether they can hang on long enough is anyone's guess. Like old soldiers, shipping companies never seem to die; they just go bankrupt or get absorbed.

In short, shipowners may no longer have to be concerned about the perils of old, and they do not have to wait months or even years to find out whether their ship made it back. But they have plenty of other concerns. In a very real sense the trade wars of the seventeenth century have been replaced by rate wars. They are less bloody, perhaps, but no less deadly—their victims entire companies, either absorbed by their competitors or gone bankrupt. It is virtually impossible to count how many of them have gone that way in the last thirty years. The United States, for instance, which had some twenty international liner carriers in 1960, has seven left, only two of which command a respectable market share. Gone forever are such names as American Export, Bull, Delta, Grace, Isbrandtsen, Pacific Far East, and States Marine (absorbed) or Seatrain and U.S. Lines (bankrupt). The same is true elsewhere: Britain now has only one major container operator; Germany, Norway, the Netherlands—the same picture. Even Japanese shipping lines have had to consolidate.

Many shipping executives predict that the field will be narrowed down even further. Conrad Everhard anticipates that there will be only eleven global megacarriers by the end of the 1990s, and many of his colleagues agree. Some of them will be joint ventures, with the partners gradually merging their identities; others will remain nationally controlled. The downward pressure on shipping rates, exercised by increasingly powerful shipping groups, will weed out everyone else.

I have little doubt that OOCL will be firmly entrenched in the survivors' club. The company is already one of the world's largest container carriers, operating thirty-three container vessels at latest count. In addition, it owns several container terminals and a vast number of containers and chassis. To achieve economies of scale, OOCL will undoubtedly continue to work with other carriers, but it will not be absorbed by any one of them. A company literally perched on the front step of the largest producer and (potential) consumer market in the world, and having excellent ties to it, will do well in the years ahead. But just a few years ago the picture did not look so rosy, and OOCL had to scramble hard, very hard, to keep its head above water.

An able-bodied seaman ties up the safety net under the gangway.

Founded fifty years ago by legendary shipping tycoon C. Y. Tung, Orient Overseas Line, as it was initially known, grew rapidly during the postwar years. In addition to conventional break-bulk ships, it began to acquire tankers and bulk carriers, and it was here that Mr. Tung excelled. The big supertankers became the company's hallmark, culminating in the *Seawise Giant,* at 564,763 tons the largest ship ever built. At the time, C. Y. Tung controlled a fleet of more than 150 ships totaling over eleven million tons, making him the world's largest independent shipowner.

Orient Overseas Line quickly caught on to the benefits of containerization, becoming the first Asian line to deploy fully containerized ships. In the early 1970s the fleet began to operate under the new name Orient Overseas Container Line, and it expanded rapidly. New ships were ordered regularly, new services were added, and a number of terminals were acquired around the world. Business looked good, but during the mid-1980s the bubble burst. Like so many other shipping companies, Orient was hit hard by the economic slowdown. Strapped for cash, it virtually defaulted on its ambitious expansion plans.

Fortunately, the company got bailed out. As part of the multibillion-dollar deal it was restructured, with the container fleet emerging as a separate entity under the new name OOCL and the bulk sector going its own way. It was a risky loan, but OOCL performed well during the next several years, despite poor business conditions. In fact, financial experts were surprised at the carrier's consistent performance. Here was a company, it seemed, that had managed to weather the storm, even in the leanest of times.

Wong Ka manages to produce several hot meals for the entire crew on less than $100 per day.

Climbing out of the hole took considerable discipline. The first priority was to seek out cost efficiencies and economies of scale. At first this effort gave OOCL the reputation of being something of a no-frills carrier, so an extensive quality-assurance program was implemented, because that's what customers demanded. Economies of scale were achieved by cooperative ventures with other carriers, such as the United States' American President Lines, OOCL's partner on the transpacific routes. And rounding out the company's strategy was an emphasis on financial strength—a strong cash position, according to C. H. Tung, C. Y. Tung's son and successor. OOCL had learned its lesson once, and that was enough. From then on the company took a decisively more conservative approach, refraining from the ambitious expansion announcements its competitors occasionally succumb to. "We buy and upgrade vessels as the need arises," is how Stanley Chen, OOCL's corporate marketing manager, puts it. "Our strategy is to be the most profitable carrier, not necessarily the largest."

To achieve that goal OOCL must run a tight ship, or rather thirty-three of them. The company buys bunker futures, for instance, so that it doesn't get hit too hard by fuel price fluctuations. Crewing costs too have been gradually brought down. Martin fondly remembers the days of the thirty-plus crew, which included a couple of stewards, two cooks, a purser, and a cabin boy. On the *Envoy* there is no steward, no purser, no cabin boy, and only one cook. Everything is strictly self-service, from serving the food down to doing the dishes.

Catering was not the only department to suffer from the shipping lines' budget cuts. Most ships now sail with one less engineer, leaving only four: the chief engineer and the second, third, and junior engineers. The ratings complement was also cut: two ordinary seamen (OSs) became one; four able-bodied seamen and four deck hands became four ABs. The carpenter—gone. The deck boy—gone. The *Envoy's* crew totals eighteen (nineteen, if you believe in ghosts): nine officers (four deck, including the captain, four engineers, and the radio officer) and nine ratings (three ABs, one senior AB, one bosun, one fitter, one mechanic, one OS, and one cook). "Is it sufficient?" I ask Martin one evening. "It depends," he replies. "To cope with day-to-day maintenance or even with an emergency, say a fire aboard, yes. But not to cope with all the company's expectations, or to get back what's already been lost."

If past experience is any indication, there will be further cuts. Some European lines are already sailing their big container carriers with crews of thirteen or fourteen, a savings achieved by computerizing the engine room in its entirety and monitoring it by closed-circuit television. That leaves a need for only two engineers, who do duty in a control room not unlike that of any power plant. The number of deck officers is difficult to cut, because you need someone on the bridge, but the number of ratings can be lowered. Take the example of the German company that installed a glass-walled lavatory on the bridge so that the officer on watch could fulfill his duty even when nature called. That enabled the company to cut one of the AB lookouts. "Not everyone is happy about it, but you get used to almost anything," one of the ship's officers remarked.

Pressed for further savings, shipowners will undoubtedly come up with more experiments, down to removing everyone from the ship altogether and having it "manned" by robots, so that even the glass-walled toilet can be used elsewhere, perhaps in company headquarters. But there is one approach that Martin absolutely abhors. "The French," he confides, shuddering at the thought, "have experimented with what they call a ship manager. And to get this ship manager, they put the chief engineer through his master's ticket. That way they have a combination of captain and chief engineer. Horrific," he mutters, still shaking his head. "For a while they abandoned the experiment, but I recently heard that someone else is considering it."

There is another item where shipping lines can cut: "victualing," as Martin puts it, a.k.a. provisioning. On the *Envoy* the route from the provision locker to the table passes through the galley, where stern-faced Mr. Wong Ka rules with ruthless efficiency, providing the occasional bit of comic relief.

I once sailed across the Atlantic on a Belgian containership that provided a more conventional culinary setting. Breakfast, lunch, and dinner were served with real silverware, on real plates, with wine in real glasses and menus describing what was available, and with a steward constantly hovering about to make sure that the steak was *à point*. If it wasn't, it went back until the galley got it right. Not that I ever had the nerve to send anything back, but it almost got to the point that the chief cook came out at dinner to explain what he "would like to propose" that evening.

As it turns out, Martin at one point sailed on the same line, though not the same ship, and the fond remembrance of those passages becomes a bit of a standard joke. "I'll have the cheese omelet," I tell him before heading down to the mess in the morning. "Champignons, the trimmings?" he asks before heading down himself and cracking up, his hearty laughter filling the stairwell. Reality is slightly different, with breakfast generally consisting of *congee* (Chinese porridge), noodles, or the inevitable soup with seaweed and "the trimmings," including things I am not accustomed to seeing that early in the morning.

To be perfectly fair, Mr. Wong, after something of a slow start, is doing admirably well. One has to remember that the provisioning budget for this ship is not luxurious. For the price of one nice dinner for two in Washington, wine and tip included—call it $100—he feeds nineteen men three hot meals a day. And lunch and dinner always include a soup, a vegetable, rice, and two entrees. Once I even discovered a veritable feast: a massive plate of shiitake mushrooms, which I proceeded to heap onto my plate under the approving eye of Mr. Wong. They were somewhat chewy, I recall, but then again I presumed that they had probably been on board for a while or hadn't been soaked long enough. Later Martin asked me whether I enjoyed the tripes. Mercifully, it was much later.

I assumed that Mr. Wong doesn't speak English, but that proves to be incorrect. "FOOUUH," he barks when I try to scoop a fifth prawn onto my plate, "TOOO" when I eye the spring rolls. The man does have a soft heart, however, because occasionally he whips up a treat just for the Western contingent: "COOUUH MEEE" (cold meat), for instance, and once a fried chicken leg with peas and fries that could have held its own in any English guesthouse. The cook, it is said, is the most important person aboard, because good food keeps the crew happy. If that's the case, the *Envoy* is a happy ship, at least as far as her Chinese majority is concerned.

On the bridge, Simon takes over the twelve-to-four watch from Bee and begins to prepare his noon report. First, he marks up the ship's position on the plotting chart and then compares it with yesterday's. This information is then keyed into a small pocket computer, and out comes the distance sailed: 461 miles over the past twenty-three hours (twenty-three because we lose an hour every day)—just a tad over 20 knots. Only a thousand miles left till Seattle. Martin is fretting because we're still going too fast, even though he has ordered a slowdown. But bringing down engine revs even further isn't very good for the engine.

At this rate we will hop across the North Pacific in just nine days, a trip that took the sailing ships of old weeks and sometimes months. On the Far-East-to-Europe service the performance is equally impressive. From Hong Kong to Le Havre, for instance, takes a bit over twenty days on OOCL's ships. It took the East Indiamen sometimes as long as a year to make the same trip.

Presumably there was not so much demand in those days to rush things to the market; simply getting back was enough of an achievement. But during the 1650s a commodity arrived in Europe that would eventually change these rules: tea. The English quickly took a liking to the new beverage, almost to the point of revolutionizing

Simon prepares his noon report.

their drinking habits. It also revolutionized the ships that brought it to the West, though that admittedly took much longer. Here too the trade was at first monopolized, and monopolies did not do much for innovation.

For much of the seventeenth and eighteenth centuries this monopoly was held by the English East Indies Company, founded, like the Dutch East Indies Company, in the early 1600s. The two companies were quite similar in purpose: to obtain a major share, preferably an exclusive one, of the rich Cathay trade. But the English East Indies Company was not quite as successful as its Dutch counterpart; the mighty VoC saw to that. To prevent it from gaining a foothold in the East Indies, the Dutch made life impossible for the English company—sometimes literally. In 1623, for instance, they executed the entire English contingent of traders at Ambon in the Moluccas, causing a massive outcry in England. But English indignation did not change the situation; the Dutch were far too firmly entrenched. The English East Indies Company, or John Company, as it was known by then, decided to focus on the rich Indian subcontinent instead.

After many years of struggle against the Dutch, French, and Portuguese, as well as against local Indian rulers, John Company emerged in control of the rich Indian trade with Europe. By the early eighteenth century it was raking in enormous profits, much of it from Indian tea. The company next set its sights on China, the other major Asian tea producer. In 1699 the ruling Manchu dynasty permitted company agents to set up a factory at Canton, albeit under extremely strict supervision. English merchants purchased many commodities: silks, porcelain, lacquer ware, camphor, and especially tea. From a mere handful in the mid-1600s, tea imports increased rapidly, to 90,000 pounds in 1715, 238,000 pounds in 1720, and more than 5 million pounds in 1750. The Chinese allowed other Europeans to trade in Canton as well, but none of them took to the tea trade with such fervor; they simply did not have the demand for it back home.

John Company continued to dominate the trade for most of the eighteenth century, shipping the annual tea harvest to England in its stately East Indiamen. It was a well-organized trade, but a slow one. In fact, it still took the ships six months to a year to cover the distance between East and West, much the same time it had taken a hundred years earlier. But the company was not interested in speed; it was satisfied with its slow, bulky ships because they could carry a lot of cargo. Besides, there was no one to compete with them.

Across the Atlantic, in America, the situation was different. For one thing, there were no East Indies Companies or deeply rooted traditions there to stifle ingenuity and innovation. Instead, there was a vibrant and competitive shipping industry, operating out of busy ports like Charleston, Baltimore, Boston, Philadelphia, and New York. Their ships were among the finest and swiftest in the world. Of course, there was a good reason for this. During the Revolutionary War the rebelling colonies had had to build fast ships to circumvent London's harsh laws. A generation later, during the War of 1812, fast ships again proved useful as privateers and blockade runners.

What made the American ships so fast was a knifelike bow, a high length-to-beam ratio, and a V-shaped hull. Some, such as the rakish two-masted Chesapeake Bay privateers, became known as Baltimore clippers—clippers because they "clipped" the time taken by traditional vessels. After the war some of these vessels prospered in the "blackbirding" trade, carrying slaves from Africa to America and the West Indies, and in other questionable activities for which speed was essential. But many clippers also operated in legitimate trades, ferrying cargoes along the coast from one port to another.

Tea would bring these innovations to large ships. By the early nineteenth century Americans had cultivated a strong demand for tea, and so their ships joined the English in Canton to load the first pickings. When more Chinese ports were opened up after the Opium War, they sailed there as well. Unlike their English counterparts, the

American ships always loaded quickly and left. Since tea leaves could turn moldy in sea air, American customers felt that the first tea to arrive from China was the best, and they were willing to pay for it. So traders began to offer premiums for early arrivals, giving shipowners, in turn, a strong incentive to hurry home.

Speed came at the expense of cargo capacity, but the premiums were sufficiently high for shipowners to consider new vessel designs. Some went as far as incorporating clipper characteristics such as the sharp bow and V-shaped hull into full-rigged three-masted vessels, along with lofty masts to carry more sail. The first such ships were greeted with considerable skepticism by old-timers, who were convinced that they would plow themselves straight to the bottom in a heavy swell. But the results quickly silenced the critics. The first two clippers to enter the China tea trade shaved weeks off the traditional passage. In 1844 the New York–based *Houqua* sailed the fifteen thousand miles from Canton to New York via the Cape of Good Hope in an astonishing ninety-five days—sixteen days less than the best previous time. The return leg she managed in ninety days—twenty-three days less than the previous record. The *Rainbow,* launched nine months later, did not do quite as well on her first voyage, but on her second she shattered the return record: eighty-four days from Hong Kong to New York.

The *Cutty Sark,* permanently docked in Greenwich, England. She is the last remaining clipper, and her Far East career was preempted by the opening of the Suez Canal.

More important—for the owners, at least—was the fact that both ships, as the first tea-laden ships to reach New York, earned more than their construction costs in single voyages. So much for those claiming that it did not make sense to sacrifice cargo space for speed. Before long, American shipyards were swamped with orders for clippers, all of them vying for the distinction of being fastest from the East. In 1847 the *Sea Witch,* on her first voyage, returned from Hong Kong in eighty-one days. Her second return trip took seventy-seven days; the third, in 1849, no more than seventy-four days—a record that has never been broken.

That same year, the British government repealed the laws that for centuries had reserved British trade to (mostly) British ships. American clippers immediately entered the profitable China-to-London tea trade and for several years clipped the time taken by British vessels by days, and sometimes weeks, cashing in handsomely on the rich premiums offered by London merchants. But their success was not destined to last. It did not take long for British shipowners to catch on and begin ordering clippers of their own. Built somewhat smaller than their American counterparts, they quickly proved themselves outstanding competitors. Ships like the *Taeping,* the *Ariel,* and the *Serica* became famous throughout the shipping world for their heroics on the long passage home. Some were even able to cash in on that fame. Cargo that had been carried on a well-known clipper often commanded higher prices—a glamour premium.

Despite the increased competition, there was plenty of work for all. The discovery of gold in California in 1849 tied up many American clippers, which made immense profits carrying men and supplies from New York around Cape Horn to San Francisco. In fact, the first clipper to make the West Coast run, the *Memnon,* clipped eighty days off the traditional six-month travel time for the fifteen-thousand-mile passage around Cape Horn. Two years later the *Flying Cloud* did it in eighty-nine days, another record that has never been surpassed. Ships like the *Flying Cloud* became the stuff of legend, in no small part because they had to deal with the worst weather anywhere on earth. But many of them perished in the fierce storms around the cape, driven to the limit by captains who refused to shorten sail in their quest for a record-breaking passage.

The discovery of gold in Australia kept the growing contingent of British clippers busy, and here too traditional passages were shattered. In 1854 the *James Baines* reached Melbourne with seven hundred passengers, fourteen hundred tons of cargo, and over three hundred mailbags after just sixty-three days. And even that was not a record. Twelve years later the *Thermopylae* took barely fifty-nine days on the London-to-Melbourne run—another passage that stands firmly in the record books.

By that time the clipper era was coming to a close. America's clipper fleet suffered from the severe economic slump of the late 1850s and received a final blow during the Civil War, when trade was carried by ships sailing under neutral flags. The fleet actually appeared and vanished in less than twenty years. British clippers managed to hold on slightly longer, but for them too it was just a matter of time. For the famous tea clippers, the end came in 1869. The opening of the Suez Canal brought the Far East within the range of steamships, virtually halving the passage time around South Africa. With time still of the essence, there was no way clippers could compete. A few of them continued to make their way to China, but not for long. By the late 1860s sailing vessels, which had connected East and West for well over two thousand years, had been all but forced out of the trade.

Since their introduction on the major trade routes, steamships have continued to improve on passage times, to the point that it now takes an average of ten days to get across the North Pacific or just five to cross the Atlantic. Some of the containerships deployed by the American shipping company Sea-Land did even better, racing across the Atlantic at speeds of 30 knots or better, but the fuel bills for their turbine engines proved uneconomical. Today, most containerships, like the *Envoy*, move on at about 20 to 24 knots—about twice as fast as the early steamers.

But it is not just speed that distinguishes containerships from their predecessors, or even size. A far more important difference is the way they handle cargo. The first steamships were like sailing ships: the cargo was stowed piece by piece in the holds, the ships went off, and at their destination the cargo was unloaded piece by piece. Aside from their paddle wheels, they even looked like sailing ships. Many of them retained masts and sails, just in case the engine broke down, and had the flush decks of their sailing predecessors, with the exception of a central superstructure built across the top of the paddle boxes.

Toward the end of the nineteenth century steamships began to change, taking on their typical "three island" profile, with forecastle, bridge house, and poop deck as the islands and the cargo holds in between. But this change in appearance did not affect the way cargo was handled. Ships still loaded, stowed, and unloaded their freight in much the same way they had for hundreds of years. In subsequent years they grew larger and more efficient, installing such equipment as heavy-lift derricks that allowed the cargo to be lifted aboard, but again cargo handling hardly changed.

Even World War II, which claimed a staggering 14.5 million tons of merchant shipping, brought about few apparent changes. Of course, some things changed. The massive shipbuilding programs of Britain and especially the United States led to a number of standardized ships—"Liberty," "Empire," and "Victory" carriers, all built in a matter of weeks and turned out by the dozens during the war years. These programs revolutionized ship construction, but they hardly touched the ships themselves. Loading or unloading them remained a piece-by-piece affair that could take several days, sometimes weeks, at either end of the trip.

Nonetheless, the war was at the root of important changes in this way of doing business. Throughout the hostilities U.S. military planners were faced with improbable transportation challenges. Hundreds of thousands of men, their supplies, and war materials had to be moved, especially across the Atlantic to the European front. To get

The need to move massive quantities of men and materials during World War II led to cargo-handling innovations such as the LST (landing ship tank) seen here approaching the Normandy coast. LSTs were the precursors of the roll-on/roll-off ships introduced by commercial shipping companies a few years later.

everything there as quickly as possible, transportation experts began to experiment with new cargo-handling techniques. Their work led to a number of new ship designs: landing ship tanks (LSTs), for instance, onto which tanks and armored vehicles could be driven, and landing ship docks (LSDs), which could carry a number of barges. The military also took to prepacking certain materials in containers that could then be unloaded directly from trains or trucks onto ships sailing for the front.

These concepts facilitated the mass movement of men and materials to Europe, but it took a while for shipowners to recognize their commercial potential. When the war was over, they simply reverted to the old way of doing things. Virtually all of the ships ordered in the postwar years were of the traditional break-bulk type, designed to handle freight piecemeal. Sometimes it was possible to make up sling loads or pallets of freight, which sped up the process somewhat, but loading and unloading still consumed a lot of time.

During the 1950s people began looking for a more efficient way. The process of loading and unloading not only took too long; it also cost too much. Ships often spent twice as long in port as at sea, and the handling costs of the cargo usually far exceeded the cost of the voyage itself. To reduce these costs, some of the military's earlier war designs began to be integrated into commercial shipping. In 1953, for instance, the *Comet* was launched, the first commercial vessel designed to move cargo on wheels. It resulted in considerable time savings: roll the cargo on to load, roll it off to unload—a process that led to their becoming known as roll-on/roll-off ships, or RoRos. Of course, there was nothing spectacularly new about the *Comet* and her many successors; they were directly derived from the U.S. military's landing ship tanks.

The most important change came three years later, when the American trucking company owner Malcolm McLean began thinking about simpler ways of getting freight from his trucks to ships. What he came up with was deceptively simple. Don't run the whole truck onto the ship, as in the case of RoRos, he argued. Instead, take the freight container and leave the truck and its chassis at the port to haul other freight. If another truck and chassis are waiting at the other end to take the container to its destination, the ship won't have to spend so much time in port waiting for her cargo to be unloaded.

McLean's concept was not entirely new. Army planners had made use of containers as well, but McLean went beyond the idea of simply prepacking some freight. He felt that most break-bulk cargo could and should be moved in containers, and he proposed that the containers be standardized so that they would fit on any truck or train anywhere in the world. To prove his point he bought the Pan Atlantic Steamship Corporation, a shipping company with some thirty-seven vessels, and converted six of them to carry containers on deck. On 26 April 1956 the first of these, the *Ideal X,* sailed on a trial run from Port Newark near New York to Houston with sixty containers lashed to her decks. Few people noticed her departure that Thursday morning, but the *Ideal X* and McLean's "experiment in integrated truckship freight distribution," as he called it, changed the shipping industry as nothing had done before.

American shippers liked the idea, and containerization took off quickly in the United States. McLean renamed his company Sea-Land and began to refit most of his vessels to carry containers, not just on deck but also below, in the holds. Other companies followed suit, and before long there were fully containerized ships sailing in all of the United States' coastal trades. Since few ports had the equipment needed to load and unload the containers, the ships at first carried their own gantry cranes. But soon Sea-Land began to install specialized dockside cranes at its main ports of call, pioneering a remodeling trend along the waterfront as well.

In the spring of 1966, ten years after the *Ideal X's* trip, Sea-Land and its main competitor, U.S. Lines, added European ports to their containerized services. It took a little longer to convince shippers there of the value of this new way of doing things, but once they were, there was no turning back. Within five years all major shipping

The *Ideal X,* Malcolm McLean's "experiment in integrated truck-ship freight distribution." A converted World War II tanker, this ship was the first to carry containers on deck.

Following page: Into the Strait of Juan de Fuca. Only a few hours left before the *Envoy* reaches Seattle.

lines had either converted or bought containerships, and most of the world's major trades switched to containerization. Never had the world's merchant fleet gone through such a radical change in such a short time.

It was not just the ships that changed. Ports too were obliged to restructure and modernize so that they could accommodate this new concept in cargo handling. It required massive investments from everyone involved, but they appeared justified. McLean's way of doing things was simply much more efficient. Ships make money only when they are moving cargo between ports, not when they are waiting for it to be loaded or unloaded, so from the shipowner's perspective the system made sense. Shippers realized major savings as well. Not only did their freight take much less time to reach its destination; the cost of sending it around the globe also came down.

Throughout the 1970s and 1980s containerization made further inroads, affecting not only the maritime industry but just about every transportation sector. For one thing, to make the concept work properly the equipment had to be standardized all over the world, requiring not just shipping lines but also trucking firms and railroads to adapt. Some rail companies began specializing in carrying the containers from ports to their inland destinations. So did a number of trucking companies, gradually extending the shipping industry's reach not just from port to port but from door to door. The container was no longer merely packing in which to stow freight. It had become the centerpiece of the international transport chain, a unit that fit onto virtually every containership, truck, or train in the world.

Waterfront labor was also affected. The days of the old break-bulk carriers, when ships stayed in port for weeks to be loaded and unloaded, were labor's glory days. Thousands of longshoremen were employed in every major port to handle the vast flow of commerce. But containers changed all that. Where once dozens of longshoremen were needed for several days when a ship reached port, now only a few were required for a much shorter period. Waterfront unions tried to stem the inevitable job losses by dictating a variety of work rules. They imposed a specified number of longshoremen to handle containers, for instance, usually more than strictly necessary. Their members were guaranteed a certain wage, even if their jobs were gone and they did not actually get to work. One port even ruled that its longshoremen would not

work when it rained, though they would get paid. These were desperate attempts to keep people employed, but the unions were fighting a losing battle. With every contract negotiation, the work rules were relaxed a bit. Competition among ports for cargoes and revenues saw to that.

Not only the shipping industry was affected; so were producers and consumers worldwide. Containerization has made the world much more of a global market. Take the Far East, for instance. Just twenty-five years ago Hong Kong's exports were still loaded piece by piece from junks onto break-bulk ships. This time-consuming way of doing things added a substantial cost to the price of Eastern products and physically limited their flow to the West. The same was true for just about every other port in the Far East.

Today, containerization has increased the flow of Asian consumer goods severalfold and has reduced transportation costs, thereby enabling Asian nations to project their economic might into Western markets with unparalleled ease and efficiency. There is little doubt that the process has aided the Far East's meteoric rise in the world of finance and trade and the parallel decline of the West. The humble box has thus had a great deal of influence on the redrawing of the world's economic map. Trade wars between East and West, recessions, unemployment in traditionally strong industries—all of these issues become much clearer if we correlate them with the number of boxes flowing from East to West.

And so the trade between East and West continues to affect the shape of the world. Perhaps it is easier to understand how this happened in the past. After all, those nations that expanded their horizons and boldly ventured out to sea often dominated the world. But today is no different. The trading tables have turned, perhaps, with Asian nations now taking the lead, but those that take the initiative at sea are still likely to have an edge. The only difference is in the sea itself. Sure, it is still large and at times intimidating, but it is no longer the obstacle it once was. Today one no longer needs a fleet to succeed in the world of international trade. There are plenty of those around, running back and forth across the oceans with clockwork efficiency. In fact, it sometimes feels as if the seas have been virtually paved over.

We're just a day out of Seattle now, with the weather becoming warmer by the day, so I decide to go for a walk and hang out on the fo'c'sle. When I get there, I'm not the only one. Martin is there too, scanning the waves through his binoculars. He told me that he's a birdwatcher, a bona fide member of the Royal Navy Birdwatching Society, but this is the first time I've caught him at it. Not being a birdwatcher myself, I didn't exactly seek out the experience, but here on the fo'c'sle in the early-afternoon sunshine, with the Gulf of Alaska on its Sunday-best behavior, it's easy to understand the appeal of watching sooty shearwaters, tufted puffins, ancient murrelets, and long-tailed jaegers gracefully skim the waves.

The next morning Martin is all business, pacing up and down the bridge. He stays there all day as we sail past the coast of Vancouver Island and into the Strait of Juan de Fuca, where we briefly halt to pick up a pilot. The final leg of the voyage is glorious, with the snow-capped mountains of Olympic National Park on one side and Mount Rainier giving a credible imitation of Mount Fuji in the distance. Never having been here before, I hadn't realized that this region was so stunning.

Just before sunset we reach Seattle, one of the major gateways for Asian goods. We have arrived ahead of schedule, so the gantry cranes don't swing into action yet. But early the next morning they do so with a vengeance, managing to replace virtually all the containers aboard the *Envoy* in less than twenty-four hours. By the end of the day most of the arrivals are on their way to their destinations. Some left on trucks,

Seattle is the *Envoy*'s only U.S. port of call.

others on a double-stack train that left at 18:00 for Chicago and the East Coast. Here too time is obviously of the essence. OOCL promised its customers one of the fastest transit times from East to West, and it lives up to that commitment. It has no choice.

As always, this means that the *Envoy* and her crew don't get much of a rest. Early tomorrow morning she'll be on her way to Vancouver, then back across the Pacific to Kobe, Kaohsiung, and Hong Kong. Thirty-five days from now she'll be here again, having completed another 12,425-mile voyage. And she'll keep doing that with the precision of a clock until her owners decide to deploy her elsewhere, or until it is time for her to be replaced.

Passage to Paradise

"**P**ort of Miami" the sign says, but this place doesn't much look like a port. At least not the first part of it. Stretched alongside a long pier lie what I know to be ships, though they don't look like it. Instead, they resemble big, glitzy hotels ten or fifteen stories high with lots of white surface and glass. I realize that these things strike some people as being the pinnacle of nautical elegance, but to me they look like something decidedly different. Impressive in a way, yes, but not in the way of a ship.

To be perfectly frank, I have come here this Sunday morning with a bit of apprehension. What I like about being at sea, what I probably like best about it, is the sense of peace and solitude. Travel at sea creates a rhythm, punctuated by simple things—the sea's swell, for instance, or meals, or even the vibration of the engine. Once at sea, life becomes straightforward and, in a certain way, less complicated.

Another appeal of life at sea is its quietness. There are exceptions, of course, but most of the big commercial vessels are manned by crews of twenty or thirty—large enough to supply a bit of company at some times, small enough to be avoided at others. Yet here I am not only boarding something I'm not even sure what to call, but about to do so along with more than three thousand others. I am not altogether convinced that this is my idea of a good time. In fact, as I prepare to enter a gleaming white mass of steel and glass called the *Majesty of the Seas,* I begin to wonder what this has to do with sea power.

The *Majesty of the Seas,* the proud flagship of Royal Caribbean Cruises Ltd., is one of the largest cruise ships in the world. She measures some seventy-four thousand gross register tons, which is big by any standard. Among passenger ships only the *Queen Elizabeth,*

Above: The *Majesty of the Seas,* one of the world's largest cruise ships, docked at her first port of call, Mexico's Cozumel.

Left: The *Majesty's* pool deck makes clear that we're not really here to travel, but to get away from it all.

89

Streamers and rum punches in hand, the *Majesty*'s passengers watch the ship glide out of Miami harbor.

Queen Mary, and *Normandie*—ships from the legendary liner era of the 1930s—were bigger. And like the ships of that time, the *Majesty*'s owners resort to quoting trivia to put these dimensions in perspective. The ship's 880-foot length equals nearly three football fields; her 170-foot height matches that of the Statue of Liberty. Interested in the engines? The four main engines generate 29,700 horsepower, as much power as 432 Honda Civics. The 1,500-horsepower bow thrusters, in contrast, generate the equivalent of 272 lawn mowers (a string of them a quarter of a mile long—a figure that suburbanites no doubt find much each easier to grasp). And the list goes on: 40 miles of piping, 800 miles of electrical cable, 14,000 tons of steel (two Eiffel towers), 150,000 square feet of open decks (fifty tennis courts), 700 tons of desalinized water a day (11,255 showers), 4 miles of corridors (the distance between my house and the post office). I could go on, but you get the idea.

Boarding this assortment of nautical superlatives is an interesting experience. In fact, if it weren't for the "To the ship" sign, I would hardly realize that I just got on one. Quickly sidestepping the inevitable photographer, I feel like I am walking into the lobby of a stunning hotel—one of those places that feature an atrium with glass-walled elevators, sweeping stairways, lush carpets, fountains, and tasteful art on the walls. Having been told that the ship is fully booked, I am expecting a mob scene, but like a luxury hotel, the setting is subdued, even quiet. A few decks up, I run into more people: my fellow passengers, many of them scratching their heads while trying to figure out how to fit their belongings into something that looked a lot larger in Royal Caribbean's brochures. But the cabins are attractive and functional, and everyone goes good-naturedly about the business of trying to fit what will prove to be far too much luggage into a single closet.

I run into hundreds more people during the first official activity aboard: the general mustering, called to let people know what to do in the "very unlikely event of an emergency." It is not a pretty sight. Unlike the cabins, most of the passengers are considerably larger than their counterparts in the brochures, and the sight of them, with their life vests sticking out in front, gives me terrifying visions of maritime disaster. We are herded around for a while in the vicinity of our respective lifeboats, with Norwegian Captain Eigil Eriksen explaining why this exercise is needed, but the drill is mercifully short. The point clearly is to go through the motions of a regulation routine, not to get people needlessly concerned.

With life vests securely stowed and tales of "unlikely emergencies" put out of their minds, most of the passengers next troop to the upper decks for the bon-voyage activities, an exercise designed to remind them that they are here to have fun. I obligingly follow everyone to the pool deck, where a Caribbean band cranks out appropriate tunes and waiters in brightly colored shirts pass out servings of rum and other concoctions by the hundreds. Slowly the ship (and the party) works up steam. With her passengers lining the decks, streamers in one hand and a rum punch in the other, the *Majesty* slowly glides out of the channel, leaving Miami and the setting sun behind.

There's supposed to be something majestic about a big ship's departure, about gradually seeing the shore fall away, but the *Majesty* belies her name. Perhaps it has something to do with the steel drums and the Caribbean beat, which don't quite convey a sense of dignity. Or perhaps it has something to do with the fact that we're not really going anywhere. All the *Majesty* will be doing for the next several days is making a big loop through the western Caribbean, and in less than a week we'll be back here in Miami. Sure, there are ports of call in between: Mexico's Cozumel, the Cayman Islands, Jamaica, and the Bahamas, but they're sort of incidental to the experience. For most of the people aboard, the *Majesty* herself is the destination. After all, we're here to relax and be pampered, not necessarily to travel.

Yet before long the sea begins to cast its spell on those aboard. I notice it in some of the passengers who remain on deck after the Miami shoreline has fallen behind.

Before long, the sea begins to cast its magic spell.

Previous page: Every Sunday afternoon, fifty-two weeks a year, the *Majesty* can be seen leaving Miami harbor.

They are standing there, hands on the railing, taking deep breaths, as if that will help them gain their sea legs. And they're looking forward, toward open seas, not back toward the land. Herman Melville had a nice way of describing this—that "mystical vibration, when first told that you and your ship are out of sight of land," he called it. As I watch some hardy souls take in this "mystical vibration," perhaps for the first time ever, I begin to sense that, despite the reggae beat and the streamers fluttering in the wind, this trip may have something to do with sea power after all. But I'm not sure yet just what.

 As the *Majesty* heads toward Cozumel with me and my twenty-four hundred fellow passengers, most of them Americans, I am reminded that it was not so very long ago that these people's ancestors arrived here. And for most of them too it was their first time aboard a ship, though that is where any similarities end. The difference between their departure, not to mention the trip itself, and that of their affluent offspring is nearly unimaginable.

To begin with, the emigrants did not go to sea for leisure. They went because they had do. Poverty and social chaos, rampant in Europe during the first half of the nineteenth century, drove them to leave their homes and seek a new and better life across the Atlantic. For many, the mere trip to a port from their homes in Ireland or Central Europe was a long and difficult journey that severely depleted their meager resources. Then, upon arrival, they faced a veritable army of petty criminals out to get whatever was left. Most of the emigrants were naive; they wanted to believe the people who offered to help. But they were fleeced. Brokers sold them tickets for nonexistent ships, innkeepers overcharged them, provisioners sold them the bare necessities at appalling prices. Many people never made it to a ship, left penniless by the systematic system of plunder that awaited them in Liverpool, Hamburg, Le Havre, and the other gateways to the New World.

Those who went on had little way of knowing that the worst was yet to come. Before steamships imparted a bit of reliability to shipping schedules, the trip across the Atlantic could take anywhere from four to ten weeks, sometimes even longer.

But even a relatively quick crossing often turned into an ordeal. To shipowners of the early nineteenth century, emigrants were another cargo—and a profitable one, provided they could be crowded together. On many ships the emigrants were accordingly crammed into rough bunks on a temporary deck laid over other cargo along the entire length of the ship. That was their home for the next several weeks, with everyone berthed together, regardless of age or sex. Privacy and comfort were nonexistent.

To make matters worse, many emigrants had to endure brutal crews. Stories of extortion by captains and officers were common, as were reports of assaults on female passengers. Laws were passed in response, by European as well as American authorities, but it appears that few offenders were ever prosecuted. Of course, there also were responsible captains, who treated their passengers with dignity and decency. But when reading eyewitness accounts of those trips, one gets the impression that such captains were the exception rather than the rule.

Charges of a few pounds or dollars per head left little room for acceptable provisions. As a result, the food was horrible. Even people who had not seen much of it in the places they came from described it as revolting. "The bread is mostly condemned bread," the British consul at New Orleans observed, after inspecting a Liverpool ship early in the nineteenth century. "It would kill a horse." Even something as basic as water was often atrocious. "When it was drawn out of the casks it was no cleaner than that of a dirty kennel after a shower of rain," one Quebec-bound passenger wrote of the water aboard. "But its dirty appearance was not its worst quality. It had such a rancid smell that to be in the same neighbourhood was enough to turn one's stomach."

These were strong words coming from someone who had shipped aboard an early-nineteenth-century emigrant ship, and should thus have become inured to the conditions. Ventilation hardly existed on most of the ships, for air had to move through the hatches, which had to be closed in bad weather. With hundreds of people crammed together, the atmosphere rapidly grew foul. There were some lavatories, but hardly enough. On rough crossings people were seasick. Add to that the filthy habits of some of the passengers themselves, and it was no surprise that port officials on the other side of the Atlantic often "recognized" a crowded emigrant ship long before she docked.

Overcrowding, poor food and water, and a lack of ventilation invariably made for unhealthy conditions. As a result, many emigrants ships were ravaged by epidemics such as typhus, also known as ship's fever. Carried by lice, typhus often spread like wildfire through steerage. The disease could be treated, but not on an overcrowded and filthy ship, and the mortality rates were sometimes frightening. In 1847, for instance, more than seven thousand people died during the Atlantic crossing, and another ten thousand after their arrival in North America—more than 17 percent of the people who had left British ports. Most of them were Irish who had fled their homeland during the worst of the potato famine, only to meet a ghastly end at sea.

William Smith from Manchester described one of these crossings in *An Emigrant's Narrative; or, A Voice from the Steerage*. Traveling aboard the *India* during the ill-fated winter of 1847, he watched his shipmates succumb to typhus. "The scenes I witnessed daily were awful," he wrote. "To hear the heart-rending cries of wives at the loss of their husbands, the agonies of husbands at the sight of the corpses of their wives, and the lamentations of fatherless and motherless children; brothers and sisters dying, leaving their aged parents without means of support in their declining years." It was by no means an isolated account. The bark *Ranger* from Liverpool—ninety-six passengers infected. The *Phoebe* from Liverpool—eighty-nine passengers infected. The *Sir Henry Pottinger* from Cork—ninety-eight dead during passage and one hundred sick upon arrival. And worst of all, the *Virginius* from Liverpool—158 dead during passage and 106 sick upon arrival (out of 476). The few who managed to make it on deck when the ship reached her destination were described by a doctor as "ghastly, yellow-looking spectres, unshaven and hollow-cheeked. . . . the worst-looking passengers I have ever seen."

Other ships were hit by outbreaks of Asiatic cholera, which caused death after a few hours of violent cramps and vomiting. The disease was transmitted by contaminated water, but no one knew that at the time. Instead, it was blamed on the ships, which were disinfected. But the passengers were not screened, even though one infected person could threaten an entire ship. Major cholera outbreaks occurred on emigrant ships in 1832, in 1848, and in 1853, when more emigrants died at sea than in any other year except for 1847. The Liverpool–New York route was the worst affected, with no fewer than forty-six ships being hit that autumn, out of seventy-one sailings.

Typhus and cholera outbreaks did not go unnoticed, not least because they often led to epidemics in North American ports, where thousands of people died as well. There were calls for action, for stricter laws that would do away with the unseaworthy ships on which the outbreaks were blamed. By the 1850s regulations had been implemented on both sides of the Atlantic. They were a far cry from what had to be done to make conditions aboard acceptable, but at least they made the passage more bearable.

Of course, government regulations could do little to control the sea itself. Storms also claimed their share of victims. In 1834 seventeen timber ships sank in the Gulf of St. Lawrence, taking 731 emigrants down with them. The timber ships, which took wood one way and emigrants the other, had a terrible reputation, but even the best-built ships occasionally fell victim to the fury of a North Atlantic winter storm. People also perished in fires, a constant risk on wooden ships. In August 1848 the *Ocean Monarch* caught fire, still within sight of Liverpool, and 176 passengers were lost. A year later 101 emigrants burned to death on the *Caleb Grimshaw,* north of the Azores. Fifty-one people perished in the burning of the *St. George* in mid-Atlantic, and four hundred in 1865 on the *William Nelson*—the worst sailing-ship fire of the emigrant era.

Despite the fires, the storms, the epidemics, and the miserable conditions aboard, people kept flocking to the ports to book passage to America. Seven and a half million people left the British Isles between 1800 and 1875, with more than half of them coming from Ireland—a country that lost nearly 4 percent of its population to emigration in one single year, 1851. Many millions more left from continental ports, all of them believing that life across the Atlantic would be far better than what they left behind. And so it proved for some of them, as the Bogduslawskis, the Colangelos, the Garcias, the Goldsteins, the Mullers, and so many other names on the *Majesty's* passenger list make clear.

The *Majesty* is in no hurry to reach Cozumel. Cruising at a leisurely 13 knots, it takes the ship nearly forty hours to cross the Gulf of Mexico, giving everyone aboard the chance to spend a first full day at sea. Though that may be saying a bit much. If it weren't for the fact that we are surrounded by water, you would hardly know we were at sea. As might be expected of a ship carrying nearly twenty-four hundred landlubbers, the *Majesty* has been designed to minimize such disturbing things as rolling and pitching. There's nothing wrong with the sea, as long as it can't be felt. And with seas as calm as can be, there is no danger of that on this trip, even though a good many passengers are walking around with seasickness patches stuck behind their ears. Better safe than sorry, I guess.

If the sea has been relegated to no more than a scenic role, so too the *Majesty* is more of a resort hotel than a ship. Sure, there is a bow and there is a stern, and the

Passengers watch the ship glide out of Miami harbor.

computerized elevator voices inform us that we're arriving on the eighth *deck* (not *floor*), but in between there is very little that looks, feels, or smells nautical. Instead, there are facilities we tend to associate with a shore-based existence: a shopping mall, for instance, several restaurants, an exercise facility and health spa, a casino, a disco, two swimming pools, a cinema and a thousand-seat theater, several bars and lounges. One of them, the Schooner Bar, smells somewhat nautical, with a bit of tar strategically applied to some fake rigging, but that's it as far as the sea is concerned. Elsewhere you would think you were in New York, Las Vegas, or a fancy midwestern shopping mall—anywhere, in short, but on a ship.

Moving endlessly through this nautical wonderland are my twenty-four hundred fellow passengers, holding video recorders and cameras ready to record every bit of it for posterity. Like most of the *Majesty's* weekly passengers, it is a pretty heterogenous group: young and old, fat and thin, sophisticated and not so sophisticated, couples and singles, and a few families with children, all happily soaking up the wonders of life at sea.

The American contingent, which makes up about 90 percent of the passengers, appears to come from all over the country, as the cheering during the evening entertainment makes clear. "Do we have anyone from Boston here tonight?" cruise director Jeffrey Arpin typically asks, and a small section of the audience goes wild. Iowa and New Jersey draw particularly loud cheers, either because these people don't hold their liquor very well or because there are more of them (both, I think). There are also a good many company groups, and a large number of repeat passengers: seven hundred have been on a Royal Caribbean ship before. Taken as a whole, I imagine, the group represents a cross-section of middle-class America, perhaps not unlike the emigrants who preceded them a century or two ago.

But the emigrants' affluent offspring have no reason to complain about the conditions aboard this ship. The food is quite good, though most people seem to be interested in quantity rather than quality. Not that this poses any problem, for there are eight meals offered every day, from the sparsely attended "early-bird coffee" to the midnight buffet, a show of culinary excess that has become something of a holy rite of cruising. There are occasional glitches, but these must be unavoidable when there are eleven thousand meals to be served every day.

Eating, just like everything else aboard, is part of the entertainment, with dinners turning into "international" events. One night we eat French, the next Oriental, then Caribbean or Italian and so on, each time with a bit of amusement thrown in by our waiters. At first I dreaded the thought of five-course dinners that would turn into hours of small talk, but they pass quickly and pleasantly. To my amazement, I am beginning to enjoy myself.

I imagine this change of heart has something to do with the fact that the *Majesty's* staff has everything down to a science, from the ideal length of a meal to the evening entertainment to any of the countless activities that are scheduled every day. Their objective is to make the cruise experience as perfect and comfortable as possible, and to do so for people with a wide variety of interests. And they succeed. Sometimes the whole experience strikes me as being a bit like summer camp for grown-ups, albeit camp with much better food: we're fed, we're kept busy, and we have nothing to worry about.

Making sure that Camp *Majesty* is filled with 2,384 happy souls is a staff of 827, only 96 of whom are involved with the business of actually running the ship. The remainder are "hotel" employees: room stewards, cooks, waiters, pursers, sales clerks, hairdressers, cleaning personnel, casino dealers, and everyone else needed to keep a resort hotel afloat. They are headed by "hotel manager" Barry Jones, a friendly Liver-

The cabins are small but attractive and functional . *(Photo courtesy of Royal Caribbean Cruises Ltd.)*

pudlian who has spent most of his life at sea, first aboard passenger vessels and now aboard cruise ships. "Do you consider yourself a seaman or a hotel manager?" I ask Barry at one point. "A seaman," he replies without so much as a moment's hesitation. "My position used to be called chief purser, which has more of a nautical ring to it, but they changed it to hotel manager. I guess that's a little easier for the passengers to understand."

Whatever the position is called, Barry and his staff are doing a wonderful job. In fact, as far as the hotel side is concerned, this floating one is better run than most hotels I have visited ashore. The entertainment is superb, the service smooth and expeditious, and the people never without a smile. They hail from Jamaica, Portugal, Great Britain, the United States, the Philippines, and some forty-five other countries, but never do I see a single one roll his or her eyes in exasperation at yet another silly question or request. Instead, everyone bends over backwards to make certain that the cruise develops, as billed, into the seven most perfect days anyone could imagine.

And thus we float around in a dream world of sorts, with every whim just a snap of the fingers away and the realities of daily life left back on shore. Though television and a daily news bulletin keep us informed of what is happening in the real world, we're mostly oblivious to it. This is not the place to bemoan the plight of Somalia or Sarajevo. The purpose of cruising is "to get away from it all," and the *Majesty* provides a splendid setting to do so. During the course of our trip we will circumnavigate Cuba, sometimes coming as close as a few miles from its shore. "The mountains you see on your left are part of Cuba," Captain Eriksen will say over the public-address system, and everyone looks over, but I doubt anyone gives a moment's thought to the fact that at this very moment people there are trying to escape, on anything that floats, to the dream world that America is for them. We'll sail within a few miles of Haiti, where people are planning similar escapes, but all we ever regret is that the ship won't stop at Royal Caribbean's private resort on the island's north shore, because of the economic embargo against the Haitian regime.

Although our floating island of excess and indulgence allows us to keep past and present problems securely out of mind, we don't have to look very far to see them. Every port we visit hangs out welcome banners for the tourists whose fat wallets provide a steady source of income, and yet just beyond the periphery, in the areas we don't get to visit, is poverty on a scale we can hardly imagine. And we see those problems in the resigned eyes of our Jamaican stewards, whose work of tidying up cabins and catering to our fancies is the closest they'll ever get to the American dream. But we're not looking. That's not what we are here for.

With about fifty nationalities included among her crew, the *Majesty* represents more than the society brought together by the European emigration. Most of the steward's department—the cabin stewards and cleaning people who quietly and constantly wipe away every fingerprint we leave on the brass railings—consists of people from Caribbean Basin countries: Jamaica, Barbados, Grenada, and so on. Their ancestors also arrived there by ship. But they didn't move of their free will. They were forced to do so. They were slaves.

Between the sixteenth and nineteenth centuries nearly ten million Africans were forcibly shipped across the Atlantic. At first most were sent to Latin America and the Caribbean, to replace an indigenous population that was literally being worked to death. It has been estimated that after the first century of colonization, the Western Hemisphere had no more than ten million inhabitants left out of an original population perhaps eight times as large. Mexico, for instance, had an estimated twenty million people in 1519. Less than a hundred years later no more than one million were left.

Above left: A look behind the scenes: the *Majesty*'s galleys handle more than eleven thousand meals a day.

Below left: The midnight buffet, cruising's holy rite.

To replace these workers, the European colonists began to import African slaves en masse. The introduction of tropical crops such as sugarcane increased the demand for cheap labor, and thousands arrived every year to be deployed on plantations. Brazil took no fewer than 3.5 million of them, and millions more were sent to the French, British, and Spanish Caribbean. Slaves did not escape the harsh work in mines either and were sent to work gold deposits in Brazil, Peru, Venezuela, and Chile. There, as elsewhere, they succumbed within a few years of arriving. The appalling conditions limited their working life span to no more than ten years.

North America began to import slaves somewhat later, in part because it took longer to find profitable export crops. But the introduction of tobacco, rice, and especially cotton led to a growing demand for slaves, especially in the southern states. From the late seventeenth century onward, tens of thousands were brought to North American ports every year. By the time the slave trade was abolished some one hundred years later, about six hundred thousand had been ferried into the country.

The carriage of millions of slaves to the Americas sustained an industry dominated by Dutch, French, and British slavers. Especially during the eighteenth century, when more than 5.5 million slaves were imported, this dubious industry thrived, with ships sailing constantly from the slave ports in West Africa to their American and Caribbean destinations. Depending on the distance, which ranged from three thousand to six thousand miles, the trip would take anywhere from forty to seventy days.

Regardless of where they were headed, these vessels were ill kept, their crews among the most brutal ever to ship out. Slaves were cargo, and were treated as such. On Portuguese slave ships they were baptized cargo, because only Christians could be imported into Brazil, but that did not change their fate aboard in the slightest. Like the others, they were shaved, stripped naked, chained in pairs, and crammed aboard. Men and women were put in separate compartments, which averaged no more than four or five feet in height. There was no bedding. Everyone slept on the deck boards or, at best, on rough mats.

Since it was in the interest of traders to arrive with a relatively healthy-looking cargo, the slaves were regularly fed or even force-fed. Weather permitting, they also were given the opportunity to wash themselves on deck—not out of a sense of compassion, but so that they would look better. In the afternoons they were required to sing and dance. Even people chained in leg irons were ordered to stand and join in the motion, because dancing was seen as being part of much-needed exercise.

Despite these precautions, slave cargoes were ravaged by fevers, dysentery, and smallpox. Seasickness and the oppressive heat in the holds compounded the miserable conditions aboard. Virtually every ship had a surgeon aboard to treat disorders, but against epidemics there was little he could do. On longer voyages from Angola to Barbados or Jamaica, mortality rates reached as high as 25 percent. Elsewhere they ranged between 10 and 15 percent. The dead slaves were simply tossed overboard, often attracting sharks, which followed the ships across the entire Atlantic. Sometimes, when bad weather prolonged the passage and created food and water shortages, the weakest slaves—still alive—were jettisoned as well.

Early in the nineteenth century an official end was finally put to this appalling trade. Although smugglers continued to ferry slaves across the Atlantic, plantation owners in the Caribbean and southern United States now had to rely on natural propagation to meet their needs for slave labor. But in some regions slavery was outlawed entirely, so new sources of labor had to be tapped. One soon became the obvious choice, a place that underwent a frightening population explosion during the early nineteenth century: China.

In 1800 about 150 million people lived in China; fifty years later there were well over 400 million. Little was done to feed the additional millions, leading to famine and social chaos. Rather than staying, many Chinese chose to leave, even though emigration was punishable by death. At first they were lured overseas by contracts and acceptable wages, but soon planters and brokers were resorting to fraud. Many Chinese laborers were enticed by promises that were not met upon arrival. Others were simply abducted or sold, to be packed into the first ship that sailed from China to the West Indies.

In the end, tens of thousands of workers—or coolies, as they became known—were sent to the Caribbean and Latin America. Cuba imported nearly seventy-five thousand, virtually all of them to work on the island's sugarcane plantations. Between 1849 and 1874 nearly one hundred thousand were sent to Peru, to work the local haciendas or, worst of all, the foul-smelling guano pits off the coast. Though they were not slaves, their fate hardly differed. Of the four thousand Chinese consigned to Peru's guano islands, not a single one survived his seven-year contract. Of the 150,000 who were taken to South American colonies, fewer than 500 lived long enough to return to China.

The Chinese workers' trip across the Pacific was quite possibly the most atrocious seaborne migration of all. Like the African slaves who preceded them to these areas, the coolies were stripped naked upon departure, and each one had a letter painted on his chest: C for Cuba, P for Peru, or S for the Sandwich Islands, now better known as Hawaii. Hundreds were then crammed into a single ship. Officially each was given eight square feet, an area six feet long and just over a foot wide. But sometimes even that tiny space did not materialize, so that people had to lie virtually on top of one another. Sanitary facilities were nonexistent. The food was poor. In fact, the shipping company often did not provide for it, and the Chinese had to bring their own provisions.

Pacific crossings are among the longest voyages on earth, and the number of deaths grew accordingly. Between Canton and Callao in Peru, ships sometimes came in with barely half of their original complement. On other runs, mortality rates averaged about 25 percent. Sometimes the voyages were far longer than the Chinese workers' provisions extended, so many died of starvation or dehydration. Disease also exacted a brutal toll. And so did inhumane treatment by the crews. In 1855, on a voyage aboard the American ship *Waverly* (now in New York's South Street Seaport), the crew locked rebelling Chinese in the hold. When the hatches were opened twelve hours later, nearly three hundred had suffocated. When the *Don Juan* caught fire at sea in 1871, the crew closed the hatches before abandoning ship, leaving hundreds of Chinese to burn to death. No wonder many Chinese chose suicide over this treatment and what awaited them at their destination.

Eventually a halt was called to this disgraceful practice. First and foremost, during the 1850s China legalized emigration, doing away with the corrupt system that had led thousands of Chinese to death at sea or in faraway lands. The government began to regulate the brokers and demanded that employers provide free return passage after the workers had fulfilled their contractual obligations. It also insisted that indentures be limited to five, rather than seven, years.

Under these conditions the Chinese could begin to leave freely, something they proceeded to do with a vengeance. When word spread that gold had been found in California, thousands left for San Francisco, or Gum San as they called it—the Golden Mountain. Hoping to make a fortune, they worked the surrounding hills, some by themselves, others for Chinese or American contractors. Many opened small stores, worked on the railroad, or did just about anything the white settlers no longer cared to do. They were hardworking and industrious, and never complained. In fact, they had only one wish: to make it back home at some point, preferably after striking it rich. A good number of the three hundred thousand who eventually arrived in California did return, though many did so as no more than a set of bones, sent back to the Middle Kingdom to be interred in ancestral soil.

This Chinese diaspora continues to this day, sometimes under conditions no different from the trips the coolies took more than a hundred years ago. Just before leaving on the *Majesty,* for instance, I was reading about yet another "misery ship" interdicted by the U.S. Coast Guard—a freighter carrying 180 Chinese refugees packed together in a filthy hold, with little drinking water left after a five-week crossing. Some had pooled their life savings to book passage on the freighter, hoping that this would be their ticket to the riches of America. Others had even agreed to indentured servitude in Chinese-owned businesses to pay for the passage. It is difficult to believe that such practices exist in this day and age, but it shows what people the world over will go through to seek a better way of life.

The *Majesty* also includes a group of these newest emigrants—twenty or so mainland Chinese who toil in the ship's laundry to make sure that we never lack for a clean towel or napkin. "How much laundry do you have to go through every day?" I ask the supervisor, but he doesn't have a ready answer. "Very much," he smiles, but I can see that, with piles of sheets, tablecloths, napkins, and towels constantly being transferred from the huge washers to the dryers. He and his compatriots work long days, from three in the morning till late afternoon, day in and day out, for sixteen months at a stretch, but they're not complaining. The pay is far better than anything they would get in China, they have their own cook with them, and they have managed to set up their own little bit of home deep in the ship's belly. As far as they're

Below: The engine control room. I am allowed to take pictures, "but no closeups."

Above right: The *Majesty*'s community of Chinese launderers work long hours for long stretches of time, but none of them are complaining.

Below right: The *Majesty*'s 29,700 HP engines demand constant maintenance.

Safety is a great concern aboard cruise ships, which tend to pack in hundreds—sometimes thousands—of passengers who know little about coping with emergencies at sea. I already conveyed the thoughts I entertained upon first seeing my fellow passengers dressed in emergency gear. It wasn't a comforting sight. Sometimes, while watching a splendid show in the comfort of the theater lounge, I wonder what would happen if all of a sudden another ship plowed into us, causing the *Majesty* to take on massive amounts of water and sink. What would happen? Well, most of us would be dead meat! With my imagination now in full swing, I see the passengers scrambling through the narrow corridors, bumping into one another, losing their life vests, all this while the ship begins to take on a sharp list before disappearing forever. It would be another *Poseidon Adventure,* no question about it.

It isn't until later that I find out that my imagination got carried away. New ships like the *Majesty* are built to very strict safety standards, designed to prevent a sharp list so that the lifeboats can be lowered at all times. And it would take quite a collision to create the destruction I was imagining. Even so, statistics tell us that a disaster like this will happen one day. We don't know when, or where, or how, but it will happen. In fact, accidents happen all the time, though none of the great cruise ships has had a major calamity recently. But ferries have collisions or other accidents involving serious loss of life all the time. Every once in a while we read about another overcrowded ferry in Bangladesh, India, or Haiti turning over, drowning who knows how many people. The headlines are bigger when the same happens in an industrialized nation. Take the capsizing of the *Herald of Free Enterprise* off Zeebrugge in Belgium in 1987, for instance, in which 188 perished. Since then passenger ferries have also sunk or been burned in the Baltic and Mediterranean, each time with great loss of life. One of the most tragic of these took place in 1991, when a car ferry collided with a tanker off Livorno in Italy and burned, with the loss of all save one of the 141 passengers aboard.

The worst calamity of all, a disaster of unimaginable proportions, took place in late 1987 in the Philippines. On 20 December of that year the *Doña Paz,* an interisland ferry, collided with a small tanker in the heavily trafficked Tablas Strait between the islands of Mindoro and Marinduque. The ferry burst into flames and sank, taking all but a few passengers down with her. No one knows exactly how many people were aboard the 2,215-ton *Doña Paz,* but with people heading to Manila for the holidays, there were certainly far more than the twenty-two hundred she was licensed to carry. The few survivors reported that all the decks were crammed with people, as were the passageways and the corridors and just about every available space. In all, more than three thousand people are believed to have perished that night.

The *Doña Paz,* in retrospect, was a disaster waiting to happen. Philippine interisland ferries are a joke as far as safety regulations are concerned, with ships often crowded far beyond capacity and life-saving equipment seldom in working order. I was once on board a ship like that, the *Don Juan,* sailing from Iloilo on the island of Panay to Manila, and was amazed at the conditions. Many of the passengers had brought along chickens and goats, and were spreading their belongings out on deck while I cursed myself for having insisted on taking a ship rather than a comfortable airplane ride. If something goes wrong aboard a ship like that, it does so in a big way, as has been demonstrated time after time by the *Doña Paz* and the Indonesian, Indian, and other ferry disasters we occasionally read about.

By following existing safety regulations, all of which were developed in response to disasters at sea, the death count can be held down considerably, as a survey of passenger-ship incidents in the West shows. Since the advent of cruising for the masses, say a good twenty-five years ago, there have been numerous wrecks and incidents. At least fifty major passenger ships, not counting interisland ferries such as the *Doña Paz,* have been lost since 1968, though almost all without a single casualty. When Holland America's *Prinsendam* burned off Alaska in 1980, for instance, everyone was safely evacuated. Forty or so of the other wrecks also occurred without loss of life, even though the ship in question was a total loss.

Yet sometimes there is no time to save everyone aboard, as happened aboard the Russian passenger ship *Admiral Nakhimov* in late August 1986. She lost nearly four hundred people after a collision in the Black Sea. Reading the authorities' investigative report on this or just about any other recent collision, one is struck by the eerie appearance of fate at work. After all, some of these incidents occur in broad daylight, with the crews of both ships sighting one another and taking evasive action, yet they still manage to plow into one another. Most collisions admittedly occur in poor visibility, but with radar now required on every ship, they are simply not supposed to happen. And yet they do, with a succession of errors in judgment by one crew or the other inexorably drawing the two ships together.

It may be a morbid thought, but one day this will happen to one of these floating resorts. Her crew may be the best in the world—professional, dedicated, and extremely competent—but that may not be the case aboard the ship that may have wandered into her path. So one day there will be a headline reporting a major cruise-ship disaster. A good captain can steer his ship away from uncomfortable weather to give his passengers a smoother ride, but he cannot steer away from fate.

No matter how many people have perished at sea in recent years in cruise and passenger liners, there is only one maritime disaster everyone remembers. It involved the White Star liner *Titanic*, which went down on her maiden voyage in April 1912 after colliding with an iceberg. More than fifteen hundred people died in the icy waters of the North Atlantic that April night, shocking the Western world as had nothing else in memory. Even today, more than eighty years later, the *Titanic* continues to fascinate. Who remembers the *Doña Paz* and her three thousand victims, even though she went down little more than five years ago? Who remembers the *Admiral Nakhimov* and the *Herald of Free Enterprise,* except for those who regularly follow these things? The *Titanic,* in contrast, is known by everyone, even though few of us had even been born when she perished.

Part of this fascination, no doubt, has to do with the circumstances of the disaster: the many celebrities aboard, the mysterious ship that appears to have ignored the calls for help, and the fact that the *Titanic* was on a dangerous northerly course to shave time off her passage. And, as with all such disasters, part of the fascination has to do with the fact that it was not supposed to happen. The *Titanic* was not only the newest but also the most magnificent passenger liner afloat. With her watertight compartments, she was thought to be unsinkable. And yet three days after her triumphant departure for New York, she lay on the bottom of the North Atlantic, with hundreds of passengers trapped inside.

Like the *Doña Paz,* the *Titanic* was a disaster waiting to happen. By the end of the nineteenth century, passenger steamships had developed into the largest and most complex objects ever created by man. Attracted by the profitability of the transatlantic passenger trade, shipowners added new services, and before long almost every Western nation with maritime ambitions had one, and often several, steamship lines linking Europe and America. Competition became keen, and ships gradually became not only larger and more efficient but also more opulent. Comfort and luxury, it seemed, were essential to successful transatlantic operations. But some of this thinking came at the expense of common sense.

Late-nineteenth-century passenger liners reached sizes of fifteen thousand tons and raced across the Atlantic at speeds in excess of 20 knots. Triple expansion engines gave way to quadruple expansion engines, single screws were replaced by twin screws, and additional decks were added to provide passengers with larger lounges

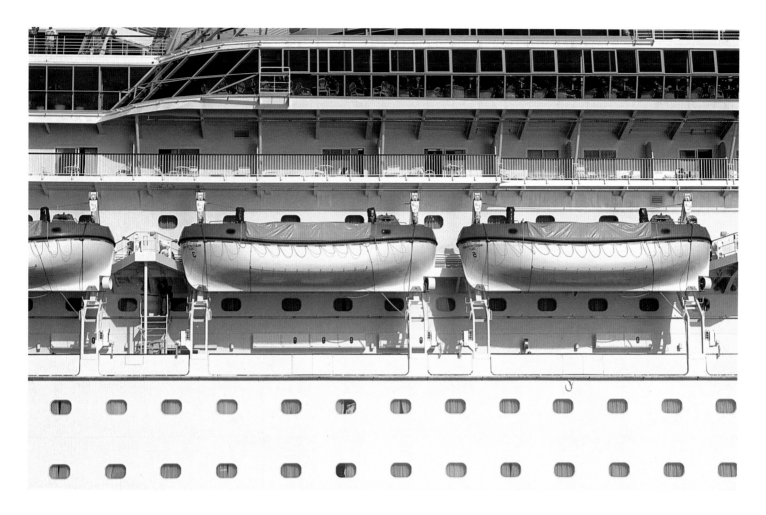

Fourteen stories (or decks) of gleaming white steel and glass.

and more comfortable staterooms. Just after the turn of the century, steam turbines were introduced into passenger liners. Invented by Charles Parsons a few years earlier, they represented yet further savings in space and weight, required far less maintenance, and ran more efficiently. Perhaps most important, they produced little vibration and allowed for even greater speeds. The first transatlantic liner to be equipped with steam turbines, Cunard's *Mauretania,* crossed the Atlantic on her maiden voyage in 1906 at a record speed of 27.4 knots. A year later her sister ship, the ill-fated *Lusitania,* did better, but in 1908 the *Mauretania* reclaimed the Blue Riband for the speediest crossing and held on to it for twenty-two years.

While speed was important, no expense was spared for comfort, opulence, and luxury. Three-quarters of the space on the great ocean liners was reserved for the upper classes. For them, ocean crossings were week-long feasts set in palatial surroundings. Each new ship, it was thought, had to be bigger, longer, and more splendidly luxurious to merit the attention of the high-paying first-class passengers. In the midst of such luxuries, passengers now had the privilege, as one brochure put it, "of seeing nothing at all that has to do with a ship, not even the sea."

Such attitudes gave passengers a false sense of security. These ships were designed to conquer the seas—designed to ignore the seas, even. Then the *Titanic* reminded the shipping lines that one ignored the sea at one's peril, and a proper sense of priorities was restored.

The *Titanic* disaster did not stop people from traveling. In fact, following World War I the liner companies built even larger passenger ships. Growing restrictions on the number of immigrants allowed into the United States did away with the steerage compartments, creating ships that provided cabin accommodations for all passengers.

If anything, the industry was encouraged to focus even more on luxury ships. Increasingly these vessels were seen as ambassadors of national greatness.

France put the contest on an entirely new level when the *Normandie* was launched in 1932. The first ship longer than one thousand feet, she displaced nearly 86,500 tons. Her 160,000-horsepower engines gave her a speed of 31.3 knots eastbound, which entitled her to the Blue Riband, albeit for only a short time. But the *Normandie's* true distinction was her unsurpassed luxury and elegance. Inside this floating palace was a winter garden, several enormous lounges, and a dining room claimed to be larger than the Hall of Mirrors at Versailles. Her 1,972 passengers had a staff of 1,320 to look after them.

Britain's response appeared two years later, in 1934, when Cunard's *Queen Mary* was launched. Slightly smaller than the *Normandie* but with the same size engines, she was somewhat faster and quickly recaptured the Blue Riband for Britain. Four years later the *Queen Mary* was joined by a sister ship of sorts, the slightly longer *Queen Elizabeth*. But the second queen's fitting out was overtaken by the outbreak of World War II. It was not until eight years later that the *Queen Elizabeth* got to make her first regular passenger run across the Atlantic.

Other nations joined in the race to build the best passenger liner. Italy had the *Rex* and the *Conte di Savoia*, Germany the *Bremen* and the *Amerika*, the Netherlands the *Statendam*, and America the *United States*, which in 1952 became the fastest ship yet with a record average speed of more than 35 knots. Only one could be the fastest, of course, but the others focused on other perks—service, cuisine, or accommodations—to ensure a loyal following.

By the time the *United States* made her record crossing, the great liner era was drawing to a close, however. The jet engine had become a reality in civil aviation, giving would-be passengers the option of crossing the Atlantic or any other ocean in a matter of hours, and at a far lower cost than a passage by ship. It turned out to be an easy choice, and gradually the big ships lost their monopoly over the great passenger routes of the world. One after the other they were retired, some to be sold for scrap, others to be redeployed elsewhere. For more than a hundred years they had ruled the Atlantic, Pacific, and Indian oceans. They had weathered storms and disaster; they had withstood the ravages of war; they had even managed to retain sufficient passengers when the gates of immigration to the United States began closing. But in a world that had come to value speed above all else, there was little they could do against jet aircraft. By the mid-1960s their era had ended, and the passenger piers in ports like New York, Liverpool, Southampton, and Le Havre would remain empty for a long time to come.

Many of the ships that had come to symbolize technological progress and national greatness came to an inglorious end. France's *Normandie*, once the largest, fastest, and most sophisticated vessel afloat, was gutted by fire in New York while being fitted out as a troop transport, and she capsized under the weight of the water pumped into her. She lay there for four years before being sold for scrap. The other major French vessel, the *Ile de France*, had to be taken out of service in 1958, the first year a commercial jet aircraft crossed the Atlantic. Germany's *Bremen*, once the flagship of the Norddeutcher-Lloyd Line, did not escape the ravages of war; she was hit by bombs during an air raid. So too the Italian Line's flagship, the *Rex*, was sunk by British bombers as her German occupiers were moving her to block the harbor of Trieste.

Cunard's *Queen Elizabeth* and *Queen Mary* survived the war, performing admirably as troop transports, and continued successful passenger operations on the Atlantic for several years to come. But they could not compete against jet aircraft either, and gradually their losses mounted. On one voyage the *Queen Elizabeth*, designed for more than 2,000 passengers, carried no more than 70 one way, 130 the other. In 1967, with annual losses reaching more than $20 million, Cunard decided to take the two queens out of service. The *Queen Elizabeth* was transferred from one owner to another for sev-

The *Mauretania* was the first liner equipped with steam turbines. On her first transatlantic run she shattered the record for the fastest crossing.

eral years, before being sold to C. Y. Tung, the founder of the Orient Overseas Container Line. Tung planned to turn the ship into a floating university, but it never came to that. In early 1972 the old liner caught fire and burned out. A few days later she turned over in the harbor and had to broken up on the spot. The *Queen Mary's* final voyage was to Long Beach, California, where she was turned into a civic center, and later into a tourist attraction. This one remaining witness to the prewar liner era is not making money in her new role, however, and her future remains in doubt.

The *United States,* the flagship of the United States Lines—which in 1952 captured the Blue Riband for America with an astounding crossing of three days, ten hours, and forty minutes—never managed to operate at anything close to a profit. In fact, her owners could not even pay the interest on her construction cost of $78 million, and if it had not been for a major government subsidy, the financiers would have foreclosed on the vessel within years of her historic crossing. But the subsidy only postponed the inevitable end. In 1969 the *United States* was laid up in Newport News, Virginia, where she languished for thirteen years. She had become a sad symbol of the times. Once a mighty ship, able to race back and forth across the Atlantic in little more than a week, visited and toasted by the rich and famous, the *United States* was now a decaying, neglected mass of steel and aluminum.

Thursday evening the *Majesty* leaves Ocho Rios in Jamaica. On the bridge wing Captain Eriksen is personally backing the ship out of the port. "See that prop wash?" he motions to me, pointing at the churning waters that almost reach the bridge. "Now there is a lot of power for you," he adds. A veteran of the Norwegian navy, he has been with Royal Caribbean from its inception. He obviously loves this ship and the

Leaving Ocho Rios, Jamaica. Captain Eigil Eriksen maneuvers the *Majesty* out of the port.

job that comes with her, even though it entails far more socializing than most seamen would care to handle.

We head north again. On the schedule is another day "at sea," then a one-day stop at Royal Caribbean's private resort island in the Bahamas, and finally the return to Miami, where we will arrive on Sunday morning. But no one is thinking that far ahead yet.

As I walk around the following day, I notice that everyone has grown accustomed to this floating resort. Many of the passengers are relaxing around the pool, a drink in one hand, a book in the other; others are shopping or gambling or playing shuffleboard on the game deck, where one can also drive golf balls into the ocean or try one's hand at skeet shooting. Whatever they are doing, this seems to be a group of happy campers, just as Royal Caribbean told them they would be.

Having looked earlier at pictures and movie reels of passengers aboard the great liners, I notice a certain resemblance between the activities then and now. The streamers handed out during our departure were a fixture whenever one of the great liners set sail. So too the inevitable horse race, the first-night soiree (here called the captain's cocktail party: "This is your chance to *really* dress up"), the last-night captain's dinner,

Following page: Basketball on the high seas.

the shuffleboard, the morning hangover—they're all here, just as they were on the great liners of thirty and forty years ago.

Maritime purists would be offended by the mere suggestion of any similarity between the great liners and these floating resorts, and on one level they're right. Compared with the sleek elegance of the *Normandie* or the *Queen Mary*, the *Majesty*, when seen from a distance, has the elegance of a condominium stuck atop a hull. And something else is missing. One might call it "class," though that sounds a little snobbish. The *Majesty* tries her best to recapture the elegance and savoir-vivre of a past age, with some of the world's top decorators having been brought together to design the various amenities, but she doesn't quite make it. But perhaps that's due more to the passengers than to the ship herself. The *Majesty* caters to a mass market, not to the selected few who crossed the prewar Atlantic in palatial surroundings.

So perhaps it is understandable that some people shudder at the thought of a comparison with the great liners. On the other hand, the development of mass cruising gave some of the old liners a new lease on life. The French Line's sixty-six-thousand-ton *France*, for instance, built to replace the *Ile de France*, proved uneconomical

on the Atlantic. She is now called the *Norway* and spends most of her time on the Caribbean circuit. So too the *United States* may be given a second chance; having been bought by a Turkish entrepreneur, she may make a new appearance in the Mediterranean market.

Yet no matter how we look at it, the *Norway* isn't the *France*, and the new *United States* will never recapture the glamour of the old one, because cruise ships cater to a decidedly different market—a market no longer interested so much in traveling as in vacationing and relaxing. Much of the credit for making this transition must go to Ted Arison, the son of an Israeli shipping magnate. During the early 1970s Arison founded Carnival Cruise Lines, and he subsequently tried to scratch a living (and profit) out of

Back to Miami. In just a few hours the *Majesty* will turn 180 degrees to do its weekly cruise all over again.

cruises to the West Indies aboard the massive *Mardi Gras,* a ship built in Canada in 1961. But the *Mardi Gras* sailed only half-filled most of the time, and Carnival seemed doomed to a quick exit, until Arison realized that his salvation would have to come from beyond the traditions of the shipping business. He hired Bob Dickinson, a marketing expert from Ford and other companies, none of them with ties to shipping. Dickinson took a long, skeptical look at the industry and then proceeded to turn it around.

Rather than advertising the ports of call of the *Mardi Gras,* Dickinson began by promoting the ship herself. He had a full gaming casino installed, expanded the entertainment aboard, and generally improved the facilities, thereby turning the *Mardi Gras* into the destination and the ports of call into a nice extra. Next he convinced the American middle class, which until then had thought of cruising as an elitist experience, that a floating vacation could be fun and affordable. The *Mardi Gras* became the industry's first party boat—the first "fun ship," as Carnival called her. The rest of the story is history. Carnival is now the largest cruise operator in the world.

Poised to take over that position is Royal Caribbean Cruises Ltd., which in addition to the *Majesty* owns and operates eight other vessels in cruise markets all over the world. Founded in 1969 by three Norwegian shipping companies, Royal Caribbean quickly turned itself into an industry leader. In 1970 it launched the eighteen-thousand-ton *Song of Norway,* one of the first passenger vessels built specifically for cruising rather than transportation. Over the next couple of years two similar ships followed. In 1978 the *Song of Norway* became the first passenger ship to be lengthened, with the addition of an eighty-five-foot midsection—an operation that increased her passenger capacity by 30 percent.

With the number of cruise passengers steadily growing, plans to lengthen the other ships were abandoned. Royal Caribbean instead committed to the construction of what was then considered to be a huge vessel: the 37,500-ton *Song of America,* launched in 1982. Six years later that ship was dwarfed in turn by the 73,200-ton *Sovereign of the Seas,* the first of Royal Caribbean's three megaships. Her introduction in 1988 confirmed how much the industry had been transformed, from an odd collection of converted ferries and out-of-work liners into a flashy growth industry. Three years later came the *Monarch of the Seas,* and in 1992 the *Majesty of the Seas.* With them Royal Caribbean not only tripled in size but also became the first passenger shipping company ever to operate three ships of over seventy thousand tons. And the end is not in sight. In early 1993 the company announced its intent to construct up to three new sixty-five-thousand-ton vessels. When these are completed in the mid-1990s, Royal Caribbean will be the largest cruise-ship company in the world.

Other companies are also doing well, as statistics make clear. In 1970 five hundred thousand people booked passage on a cruise. In 1992 that number topped four million, and by the end of the century it is expected to double, to eight million. With an average annual growth of 10 percent, cruising is considered to be the fastest-growing sector of the American travel industry. Elsewhere too more and more people are being enticed to try a floating vacation. And the market is far from saturated. Even though they operate all over the world and target different markets and interests, cruise operators know that they have hardly begun to scratch the surface.

What makes this industry so successful, I imagine, is that it has fulfilled its promise. Cruising is fun, the companies claimed, and I agree, even though I boarded with considerable misgivings. Cruising is affordable, they added, and they stuck to that promise too. True, not everyone can afford to be pampered for seven days aboard the *Majesty,* but there are plenty of alternatives. Even on the three- or four-day mini-cruises out of Miami, people can experience a bit of adventure, some relaxing, culture and entertainment, and some shopping—all this without having to drive or cook, pack or unpack, or do any of the mundane activities that make up life ashore. *Cruising,* in other words, has become synonymous with *escape,* and in a world that is filled with people who want to escape but don't have a lot of time to do so, it has found a loyal following.

Unfortunately, by Saturday night our own escape is about to end. We're having our final dinner aboard the *Majesty.* The theme is American this time: turkey with the works and things like that, with, as an added attraction, our waiters joining in a supposedly rousing chorus of "America the Beautiful." With few of them having ever set eyes on those amber waves of grain, they butcher it, but in truth, these are about the only false notes I have heard during the past week.

Prior to the final show, cruise director Jeffrey Arpin tells us a bit about what we've managed to put away in less than a week: 13,000 pounds of beef, 9,000 pounds of poultry, 1,000 pounds of lobster, 1,800 pounds of shrimp, 22,000 eggs, 4,000 gallons of milk, 7,500 pounds of vegetables, and—as befits a ship with a large American contingent—600 gallons of ice cream. Nothing to be particularly proud of, I remember thinking, having witnessed how much of it has to be trashed, but the figures are heartily applauded. Then again, so is everything else. People are in a giddy mood, greeting each silly joke with roars of laughter. Realizing that their floating dream world will soon end, they want to make sure they get in one last laugh. Tomorrow it will be over. We'll arrive and head back home, leaving the *Majesty* and her crew just six hours or so to replenish and turn 180 degrees to start the whole circuit over.

Following the show, I roam around a final time. Just a few days ago I wondered what this experience had to do with sea power. It soon became clear. I first noticed it at dinner, where a sense of camaraderie developed among people who otherwise would never meet or talk to one another. I guess our headwaiter expressed it best. "Are you part of a group?" he asked our table of eight the first evening. After we told him we weren't, he said, "Well, you are now. You're all in the same boat." I thought that was right on the mark, not only because it was cute, but because it was true. Once we left terra firma, we crossed a boundary of sorts. We joined the brotherhood of the sea, a place where different rules and conventions apply. A place that changes people forever, whether they realize it or not.

Cruising has a strong link to sea power, though it is difficult to discern at first. There is a connection because there is simply no better way to learn to appreciate the sea than by experiencing it. Just one week at sea teaches a lot about the ocean; almost subconsciously it creates a "sea-mindedness" of sorts, a new respect and appreciation for something most of us have simply come to take for granted. And that too is part of sea power. Nations do not become sea powers merely by virtue of a long coastline or maritime resources. They do so by virtue of the sea-mindedness of their people, including those who don't go to sea to make a living. Not my words, but Alfred Thayer Mahan's. He was right.

Ruling the Waves

~~~

There is something that makes young men behave a bit cockier than usual in the vicinity of carrier-based aircraft. Even here, around the lonely C-12 parked on the steaming tarmac at Al Fujairah on the Persian Gulf, they walk with a lanky self-confidence, inspecting the propellers and the fuselage, chewing gum, and talking just a bit louder than necessary. Their nicknames are stitched on to their flight suits, names like Booger, Squirt, or Blues. Generally considered to be the carrier's equivalent of a delivery truck, the C-12 that Booger and Squirt fly isn't really a sexy plane, but that doesn't seem to matter, at least not here on the tarmac at Al Fujairah.

Perhaps they are entitled to their cocky ways, I reflect as I watch them go about their business. The carrier world is a man's world, which seems to invite this sort of behavior. Perhaps it helps them deal with life aboard a ship for six months with five thousand others. Meanwhile, the C-12 is getting ready to take off. An airman gives me a cranial with ear protectors, along with a life vest, and asks me to board. There are about eight rows of seats in the plane, all of them facing back, with just one window on each side. Since I'm out of luck as far as the view is concerned, I settle down in the back and look around. Overhead is a tangle of wires and hydraulic lines. The seats look and feel as if they have survived a couple of crashes. Comfort obviously was not high on the list, but then again the C-12 is a delivery craft, not a passenger plane. Besides, doing away with the paneling makes it easier to get out in case the plane goes down. Just get onto the seat and push out the escape

Above: The USS *Ranger,* heading full speed toward Mogadishu. There are more than five thousand people aboard this floating airbase.

Left: Members of the *Ranger*'s flight deck crew take a brief break. Because the overwhelming noise on the flight deck makes speech and hearing all but impossible, communications take place by gesture and color. Crew members wear different color shirts, depending on their tasks: yellow for directing the aircraft; brown for readying them for flight; white for safety; red for ordnance (weapons); green for aircraft maintenance; and purple for refueling.

125

hatch, the accompanying airman tells us. As he continues his safety briefing, my seatmate leans over and cautions me to remember that. "You'll need those instructions in the unlikely event of a landing on the flight deck," he grins.

After a bumpy two-hour flight, I feel the plane beginning to descend. Not being near a window, I have no idea how far we are from touching down, but the pilots have figured out their own way of letting us know when to brace. Just before landing, they go into a stomach-tightening turn, and moments later we slam onto the flight deck. While the C-12 is quickly directed out of the way, the cargo-bay door is opened, so we can look outside. For a moment it looks as if we have landed on another planet. It is not the noise or the planes; I was expecting that. No, it is the people. Night has begun to fall, and as we maneuver to a safe spot, I see shapes scurrying all over the place, but not a single face. They all wear helmets with ear protectors and goggles, and some have scarves over their mouths. The orange lighting near the control tower casts long and eerie shadows, making everything look slightly unreal. I'll never forget this first look at the USS *Ranger.*

During the next several days this initial impression lingers. There is very little that seems "normal" about this ship. Even the people aboard have many opinions. Some compare her, somewhat unimaginatively, with a floating airport. Others think of her as a city at sea, and a few, presumably those nearing the end of a six-month tour of duty, call her a floating madhouse, albeit somewhat in jest.

It doesn't take me long to figure out that life aboard a carrier has elements of all that, and everything in between. With more than seventy aircraft aboard, there is no doubt that the *Ranger* is first and foremost a floating air base. On this deployment the ship has been assigned Carrier Air Wing Two, which is composed of two F-14A Tomcat squadrons, one A-6E Intruder squadron, one EA-6B Prowler squadron, a group of E-2C Hawkeyes, an S-3 Viking squadron, and finally a number of SH-3H Sea King helicopters. Each type has different tasks and capabilities. The Tomcat fighters, for instance, provide air defense for the carrier. If necessary they can also go on the offensive, as the 1991 Gulf War demonstrated. The Intruders are attack aircraft, especially well versed in all-weather bombing runs. The Prowlers support the fighters and the bombers by providing electronic countermeasures—that is, by jamming enemy radar and communication transmissions. The Hawkeyes soar high above the others to give tactical airborne warning and control. Finally, the Vikings and Sea Kings concentrate on submarines, the first at long range, the second nearer to the battle group. The helos also have search and rescue capabilities, which means that they are always the first to leave the carrier when flight operations begin and the last to return.

Supporting this floating air base is a crew fifty-one hundred men (and a few women) strong, all of them crammed into a ship not much longer than the *Crown* or the *Envoy.* Perhaps that accounts for the occasional reference to a floating madhouse: there always is noise, and life aboard seems frantically busy. The atmosphere certainly explains the floating-city analogy. On the schedule prepared for me by public affairs officer Rod Hill are visits to massive galleys and dining halls, laundry facilities, immense food-storage rooms, machinery shops, hospitals, chapels, power generators, a radio and television studio—just about everything a small city would have.

As I tour some of these facilities in subsequent days it strikes me that of all the things she has been called, the *Ranger* appears least of all like a ship. I sense that when I get lost for the umpteenth time in one of the vessel's endless corridors, with no clue whether I am heading fore or aft. I sense it when I meet people in various places who hardly ever get to see the sea. Most of the time they don't get to feel the sea either, for the *Ranger* hardly rolls or pitches, except in the heaviest weather. And I sense it when Rod tells me, contrary to the procedure on just about any other ship, to stay put during a fire alarm. "Don't forget, this place is like a city," he explains. "In a city, people don't assemble in one place when there's a fire somewhere." In a strange way life here seems further removed from the sea than aboard any other type of ship.

Sunday morning finds the *Ranger* and two of her escorts, the *Valley Forge* and *Kinkaid,* speeding at 25 knots along the south coast of the Arabian Peninsula. Two days ago the ships didn't even know they would be here. They had been assigned to the northern Persian Gulf, to provide support for Operation Southern Watch: the monitoring of the Iraqi no-fly zone below the 32d parallel. But during these past few days the American government has begun to implement plans to help starving Somalia. Though no one expects any military opposition of consequence off the Somali coast, it was thought a good idea to have a carrier on hand, and the *Ranger,* at that time the nearest to the Somali capital, Mogadishu, was the obvious choice.

More than 560 years ago another fleet was sailing these waters to impress upon others the identity of the strongest power on earth. That fleet wasn't European. In fact, at that time European sailors barely left sight of land. It wasn't Arab either. Arab sailors regularly crossed the Indian Ocean and sailed all the way to China in their dhows, but they seldom set off in fleets. No, the fleet that showed up off the Arabian Peninsula in the spring of 1431 was Chinese. It was the last of a number of massive naval expeditions sent out by the Ming emperors in the early part of the fifteenth century.

Only fragments of this spectacular exhibition of maritime power survive, but what we know is truly astounding. During a thirty-year period no fewer than seven expeditions ventured from China to places as far apart as the east coast of Africa, the Red Sea, the Persian Gulf, India, and Southeast Asia. Each expedition involved thousands of men and hundreds of vessels, among them the largest and most advanced merchant ships in the world. But interestingly, this show of maritime command and prowess ended almost as quickly as it had begun.

The expeditions were the brainchild of Yung Lo, the third Ming emperor. Unlike his father, Hung Wu, who founded the dynasty and forbade all contact with foreigners, Yung Lo was keen on finding out about other nations. China needed a large navy, he felt, to convince other states of the country's supremacy and to help curtail the growing threat of piracy along its southern coast. Accordingly, Yung Lo called for a mammoth expansion in China's sea power. In 1403 construction began on a large number of seagoing junks.

In command of China's maritime expansion plans was Cheng Ho, the emperor's superintendent of the office of eunuchs. Appointed admiral of the Ming fleet in 1404, Cheng Ho oversaw the preparations for the first expedition, which left from Nanking one year later with a force of more than twenty-seven thousand men aboard 317 ships. Among these were sixty-two treasure ships (*baochuan*), so called because they carried "unnamed treasures of untold quantities." These were the largest ships ever constructed by the Chinese, or by anyone else, for that matter. Ming records mention nine masts and a length of 44 *chang* (approximately 440 feet). Most experts feel that the vessels would actually have measured a maximum of three hundred feet and three thousand tons, which was still considerably larger than anything that existed elsewhere.

According to the records of the first voyage, Cheng Ho visited several Indonesian islands and Ceylon before heading on to Quilon and Calicut in India, where tributes, acknowledging the Chinese emperor as the "ruler of all mankind," were received from various local rulers. On the return voyage the fleet defeated the forces of Chen Zuyi, a Chinese pirate chief who operated out of Palembang in Sumatra. Delayed by this action, the fleet did not return to China until the fall of 1407.

Cheng Ho did not accompany the second expedition, though he was its official commander. This time a fleet of 249 ships and an unknown number of men headed back toward Calicut, stopping in Thailand, Java, and Cochin. The third expedition was also directed to visit the "seas of the west." That fleet, consisting of forty-eight ships carrying thirty thousand men, left in the fall of 1409, just a few months after the second expedition had returned. It called at Champa (Vietnam), Java, Malacca, Semudera, and Ceylon before sailing onward to the Indian west coast.

In the fall of 1413 the fourth expedition was sent off. It followed the usual route to the Indian subcontinent, but after calling at Calicut the fleet sailed on, crossing the western Indian Ocean to Hormuz. The fifth expedition left in the fall of 1417. There is no information on the number of ships and men involved, but we know that the principal objective of the voyage was to escort the ambassadors from nineteen countries back to their homes, and to bring gifts to their rulers in return for their tribute. The ambassadors came from places as far away as Malindi (Kenya) and Mogadishu, and accordingly Cheng Ho's fleet sailed for the first time to the East African coast. It returned to China in the summer of 1419.

Two years later a fleet of forty-one ships and an unknown number of men followed a similar course to return another group of ambassadors. But in 1424, shortly after the return of this sixth expedition, Yung Lo died and it appeared that an end had come to China's age of maritime questing. Yung Lo's successor, Jen Tsung, was not interested in exploration, and he immediately suspended all overseas expeditions. But his successor, Hsuan Te, ordered one more voyage to the "Western Sea." In 1430 the seventh and last expedition set out, consisting of 27,750 men in one hundred ships. It returned to Nanking on 7 July 1433, after having visited some nineteen countries.

During the thirty years between the first and last of these voyages, China possessed the most powerful navy in the world. At its height it numbered 400 major warships based in Nanking, 2,700 warships of the coastal guard stations, 400 armed grain transports, and 250 treasure ships, each capable of carrying at least five hundred men. Yet after the return of the seventh voyage, the entire fleet was dismantled. China's new emperors were no longer interested in maritime exploration, and the country turned its back on the sea. Two years later Cheng Ho died, and within a generation few Chinese even knew of his achievements and adventures.

To understand why China so abruptly renounced its maritime supremacy, we have to understand why it had sent out the expeditions in the first place. Clearly, Yung Lo was interested in enhancing China's prestige by an impressive display of maritime might. Then as now, big ships did that better than anything else. The voyages also helped reestablish China's complicated tribute system. And finally, it was hoped that the voyages would stimulate the flow of goods to and from the West.

The seven expeditions appear to have achieved these objectives, but they were very expensive. Perhaps if they had been properly planned, the gains could have offset the costs, but China never undertook these voyages with the intent of merely making money or monopolizing trade. "Your minister hopes that your majesty…would not indulge in military pursuits nor glorify the sending of expeditions to distant countries"—so wrote a high-placed Ming official in 1426, voicing the opinion of many in the court. "Abandon the barren lands abroad and give the people of China a respite so that they can devote themselves to husbandry and to the schools." We have no business overseas, he meant. There is nothing to gain; we should focus on our own concerns.

Other factors also played a role. The reopening of the Grand Canal in 1411, for instance, enabled grain shipments to travel the inland route. As a result, the coastal route lost its importance, and this diversion was soon felt in the shipping community. And during the early fifteenth century China experienced trouble along its continental borders, particularly in the north. Not surprisingly, this had to be attended to first, diverting resources and attention from maritime endeavors.

So it was for pragmatic as well as political reasons that China declined to pursue its marine ambitions. In a matter of years virtually all of China's maritime know-how was forgotten. The official records of the voyages were destroyed, lest others should try to repeat them. By the end of the fifteenth century no shipbuilder knew how to build the great treasure ships that had sailed the "Western Seas." In fact, by the early sixteenth century it had become a capital offense to build a seagoing junk with more than two masts. Coastal officials were required to destroy all such vessels and arrest their crews.

In retrospect, China's maritime decline could not have come at a worse time. While Cheng Ho was showing the flag off one side of the African continent, tiny European vessels were inching their way south along the other, hoping to find a sea route to the East. By the end of the century they had reached India, and the rest of the East came soon thereafter. Their vessels could not compare with the ships that had sailed under Cheng Ho's command a hundred years earlier, but that no longer mattered. By that time China had nothing left to put in their way.

China's brief show of naval might and splendor has always fascinated me. In fact, as the *Ranger* continues on her course toward Mogadishu, I am struck by some of the similarities between Cheng Ho's expeditions and this American contingent. There is little doubt that the Chinese fleet at that time was the most powerful in the world. So too the U.S. Navy today is the dominant naval force in the world. In fact, this very contingent of the *Ranger* and her escorts probably represents the strongest naval presence in this entire region. With the present composition of Tomcats, Intruders, Prowlers, and Hawkeyes, the *Ranger* can make her influence felt as far as four hundred miles away, and can cause a terrifying amount of destruction in the process. And this task force is only a small part of America's naval power. Like the Chinese fleet of the early fifteenth century, the U.S. Navy is second to none.

Furthermore, like Cheng Ho's fleet, this is a navy facing uncertainty. Emerging from World War II as the most powerful fleet in the world, the modern U.S. Navy was molded to respond to a global Soviet threat. For much of the postwar period it was a serious threat. Having witnessed how Western navies served as vital instruments in containing Communist expansion, the Soviet Union began expanding its own navy in the early 1950s. Under the leadership of Admiral Sergei Gorshkov, its fleet grew rapidly from a coastal defense force into a full-fledged blue-water navy.

Gorshkov had obviously done his homework. The supply routes across the Atlantic are one of the West's weak links, he rightly concluded. Accordingly, the Soviet navy did not try to match its American counterpart's emphasis on aircraft carriers. Instead, it focused on submarines that could interrupt those sea lines, and surface vessels that could defend the Soviet Union, provide submarine protection, and assist the country in acquiring or protecting zones of influence.

Yet today the threat posed by that Soviet fleet has been reduced. In view of the uncertainties that still surround the disintegration of the country, the threat cannot be said to have vanished, but it certainly is not up to cold-war levels. Many of the Soviet navy's vessels are rusting away in places like Murmansk and Vladivostok, victims of the financially ruinous naval race with the United States—a race that basically bankrupted the Soviet system. But gone too is the money that allowed for the U.S. fleet's remarkable naval expansion of the early 1980s. So what happens now? How large a U.S. Navy is needed? And what should it be doing next?

I gain some insight into these issues when Rod takes me to meet Dennis McGinn, the *Ranger*'s commanding officer. We find him after a long climb to the bridge, seated in the captain's chair. Like just about everyone else I have met on the ship, Captain McGinn is extremely welcoming and open. He even invites me try out his chair. "Here, sit down," he says, getting up himself. "Get a feel for what the view is like from this place."

I decline the honor, but his kindness breaks the ice, and before long we are discussing U.S. Navy missions in a changing world. "As you know, the U.S. Navy has traditionally had three missions," Captain McGinn starts: "projection of force, protecting the sea lines of communication, and presence." I nod. These are the standard missions as summarized in any navy briefing.

The USS *Ranger*'s flight deck.

When projected against the backdrop of cold-war anonymity, these missions were quite straightforward. Projection of force meant being prepared to bring military force to bear on the Soviets through amphibious landings, fire support, or whatever else was called for. Protecting the sea lines of communication involved having the ability to neutralize the strong Soviet submarine fleet in case of a conflict, so that it could not wreak havoc on the many merchant ships that would have had to ferry across the Atlantic with supplies. And presence basically involved outdoing the Soviets in using naval units as instruments of foreign policy, something both sides did very well.

"I don't think anyone in his right mind believes that the threat has simply vanished," Captain McGinn continues. "But clearly there has been a need for some refocusing. And perhaps you can consider what we are currently doing as being part of that effort. A shift in attention from the global threat posed by the erstwhile Soviets to regional needs—navies happen to be particularly well adapted to making that sort of adjustment."

Rod next takes me for a brief visit with Rear Admiral William Hancock, commander of the entire battle group, whose flag quarters are also on the *Ranger*. Again I am welcomed cordially. In fact, I am put so at ease by the admiral's friendly disposition that within a few minutes I am proffering my insights on changing naval roles and missions, even though I don't remember having been asked to do so. But I soon realize that I am not there to listen to myself. "Could you call your battle group's role in this Somali campaign a new mission?" I ask Admiral Hancock. "And is this operation part of a search for a new naval role in a changing world?"

It doesn't take the admiral long to formulate a reply. "There are plenty of precedents for a naval role in humanitarian missions," he says. "Take last year's assistance to Bangladesh after that terrifying storm, for instance, or the support we gave to the Kurds following Desert Storm in 1991. What may be different here is that there was no government to ask for assistance; the United Nations asked. In that sense I don't see anything radically different."

When pressed about whether we will see the navy do more of these things, the admiral pauses for a moment. "I think all this is very much in line with the navy's latest White Paper," he finally says. "The *From the Sea* document. You've probably read it. The paper basically states that naval priorities have changed with the end of the cold war, and that there will be a shift of attention from a global threat to regional challenges. And this Somali question strikes me as being a perfect example of a regional challenge. Don't forget that navies don't have to do destructive things in order to be effective. In fact, it has often been said that the ultimate role of a navy is not to wage war, but to preserve the peace."

An F-14 Tomcat comes in for a landing. Once the plane has landed, it is quickly directed out of the way. The next one may be less than a minute behind.

By the time I leave it has turned dark outside, and with the day's schedule of activities over, I head to Vulture's Row near the bridge to watch the planes come in. Below, the

flight deck crews as always are frantically busy. Once on deck, a plane is quickly directed out of the way to make room for the next one, which is no more than a minute away. The noise is overwhelming, for the pilots have to go full throttle when they slam on deck, just in case they failed to hook up with the arresting wire and have to take off again. But the recovery operations go very smoothly tonight. ROARRR…BANG (the flight deck shakes for a moment)…ROARRR…and engines down, the plane is moved out of the way, then one minute later the same thing again: ROARRR…BANG…ROARRR…and so on, until every plane is back and the helos head back in as well.

They really have this business down to a science, I reflect as I head back down to my cabin. But how much will these carriers be needed in a world from which their traditional enemy has vanished? I pull out my copy of the …*From the Sea* document to see what it has to say about that, but it doesn't quite address the question. The paper makes sense: shift attention from a global threat to regional challenges. But does one need aircraft carriers in order to do so? And suppose the experts say yes; can one afford them? Obtaining the funds to keep these ships at work is easier when the enemy is real and threatening than when it has been replaced by a host of "regional challenges." Already voices are calling for a peace dividend. It may be a little too early for that, but never mind. Do not indulge in additional military pursuits or in the sending of expeditions to distant lands, they seem to say, just as the Chinese minister of half a millennium ago advised his emperor.

What will happen to these megaships and their five-thousand-man crews? Will they be around in twenty years, or are they, like Cheng Ho's treasure ships, doomed to be replaced, victims of a changing world?

Perhaps there is nothing new about these questions. In their long history navies have always been faced with uncertainties—uncertainties about their adversaries, the rules of war at sea, technologies, and the tools at their disposal to implement their missions.

If anything has remained fairly constant throughout time, it has had to do with the missions of and reasons for navies. Navies, it is generally accepted, came into being to protect peaceful merchant ships against piracy. This certainly happened in the ancient Mediterranean and in the Far East, and probably wherever richly loaded merchant vessels provoked less than honest instincts in others. Interestingly, virtually every navy in the world still has this same role enshrined in its mission statement. Perhaps not so much protection against piracy, although that certainly remains a problem in some regions, but against anything that threatens maritime commerce, in peace or in war—protecting the sea lines of communication, as it is put in naval vernacular.

Above: The "foreign object damage," or FOD, search involves a meticulous search of the flight deck to remove any small objects. If sucked into one of a plane's engines, they could cause considerable damage.

Left: Flight deck crew.

Fighting at sea is an unnatural activity, yet little time transpired between the appearance of ships designed to protect commerce and the emergence of more aggressive roles for them. Not much is known about the earliest sea battles, but they seem to have been caused by attempts on the part of one adversary to invade the other. That was the intent of the mysterious Sea Peoples, for instance, who fought the Egyptians at sea during the reign of Ramses II—an incident commemorated in the oldest surviving artistic representation of a naval battle. And it certainly was the case when Persia and its allies attempted to invade Greece in 480 B.C., an attempt that led to the first great documented sea battle in history—the Battle of Salamis.

Like all major sea battles, Salamis was the culmination of a long series of events. In 492 B.C. the Persians, under King Darius, attempted to invade Greece a first time, but a storm damaged the fleet of ships that accompanied the Persian army as it marched along the northern shore of the Aegean Sea. Without supplies and equipment, the advancing army came to a grinding halt and had to turn back. Two years later Darius sent a new expedition, this time across the Aegean directly into the heart of Greece, but it too failed. The first contingent of Persians, some ten thousand strong, was defeated by eight thousand Athenians at the Battle of Marathon, forcing the Persians to abandon their invasion plans a second time.

For several years there were no attacks, and when Darius died in 486 B.C., the Greeks grew confident that the Persian threat had been averted. But Darius's son Xerxes was making elaborate preparations to ensure that a third attempt would be successful. In 480 B.C. he amassed 180,000 troops in Asia Minor and sent them north along the Aegean coast. Thousands of cargo vessels plied between bases in Asia and the front to supply the troops. Another thirteen hundred fighting ships, manned by 175,000 men, protected the cargo ships and covered the flank of the army.

In Greece the mood became desperate. For once the Greek city-states had agreed to establish a common defense, but the resources they could muster seemed pitiful in comparison with Persia's might. Athens had the strongest naval fleet, but even when combined with galleys from all the other city-states, the Greek fleet numbered no more than four hundred vessels, a mere third the size of its Persian counterpart. In terms of troops, the Persians held an overwhelming advantage as well. At Thermopylae the Spartan king Leonidas attempted to halt the Persian onslaught, but his force of forty-seven hundred was slaughtered to the last man. The Persian army pushed on, plundering its way into Attica. When the hordes came within sight of Athens, the city was evacuated and the Greeks retreated toward the isthmus of Corinth. Helpless, the Athenians watched their city go up in flames.

The Greeks now had only their fleet left. Even though the odds appeared overwhelming, the Athenian regent Themistocles sent his galleys from Piraeus to the island of Salamis a bit farther west, where they teamed up with the remainder of the Greek fleet. It was here that Themistocles wanted to draw the Persians into battle. He knew that on the open sea his fleet would be overwhelmed, but in narrow waters it stood a chance. And Salamis provided a splendid setting. To enter the waters between the mainland and the island, the Persians had to pass through the narrows, where their maneuverability was constrained. Once beyond the strait, they could bring their numerical superiority to bear, but within it they were vulnerable.

At dawn the next day, or so Aeschylus tells us, the Persian fleet entered the strait. The Greeks faked a retreat, and more lines of Persian ships entered the narrows in pursuit, but then the Greek ships reversed course and attacked. Their rowers, straining at the oars, brought the triremes to top speed and crashed into the first line of Persian vessels, sinking or crippling them. Meanwhile, more Persian galleys entered the narrows. In a matter of minutes the Persians were trapped between the Greeks at one end and their own reinforcements at the other.

By late afternoon the battle was over. The Persian fleet had been annihilated. The Greeks had sunk or disabled two hundred enemy galleys and captured many more, having lost a mere forty ships of their own. Deprived of a fleet to protect and support his army, Xerxes was forced to return. He left an army of fifty thousand to winter in Greece, but the next summer this force was annihilated by the Greeks at Plataea, forty miles northwest of Athens. Later in the year the Greek fleet hunted down the remainder of the Persian fleet and destroyed it off Mycale in Asia Minor. The Persians never came back.

Important lessons were learned from the Battle of Salamis. Navies, it was shown, could be used either to project power (as the Persians had attempted) or to defend against it (as the Greeks had demonstrated). The battle also showed that navies are essential to protect supplies. Xerxes' army was no stronger than its line of supplies, and when that line was severed, defeat became inevitable. And it showed that navies are essential because nations never know what the sea may bring them. The story goes that Themistocles, following the advice of the oracle at Delphi, persuaded his fellow Athenians to renew their fleet of ageing triremes, even though it demanded a financial sacrifice. It turns out that he made the right decision. Without that fleet, history would have taken a different course.

After the Greeks, the Carthaginians gained control of the Mediterranean. Then came the Romans, followed by the Arabs and the Italian city-states. Whenever one power left a void, it was quickly filled. For two thousand years naval warfare in the Mediterranean proceeded largely along the lines of classical battles such as Salamis. There were innovations, to be sure, such as catapults that could throw large stones, or much later a highly flammable mixture of naphtha, sulphur, and pitch that could be blown onto enemy vessels through long copper tubes. But despite these and other inventions, Mediterranean sea confrontations remained mostly battles fought across decks. Victory depended on killing people. Ships could be replaced more easily than men, especially if thousands perished, as was often the case.

In northern Europe, a different type of naval warfare evolved. Galleys were too vulnerable in rough northern waters, so people there relied on longships, and later on broad-beamed cargo ships with a single square sail. Since Europe's feudal lords could not afford to maintain ships specifically designed for fighting, there were no specialized warships until after the Middle Ages. If a conflict called for a battle at sea, the rulers filled merchant ships with soldiers and sent them out to do the work. The ensuing battle usually consisted of grappling and boarding—a fight across decks. At the end, the soldiers on the captured vessels were unceremoniously tossed overboard.

The emergence of the three-masted sailing ship and the appearance of guns changed this way of fighting at sea, for with these innovations ships no longer had to be in physical contact in order to engage. Many of these changes were pioneered in the Tudor England of Henry VIII, the first English monarch prosperous enough to afford ships designed exclusively for fighting. To counter the permanent threat of invasion from France, Henry developed a naval system consisting not only of ships and men permanently in the service, but also of dockyards, building yards, and a Navy Board. As a result, England forged ahead of all other nations in warship design. To accommodate big muzzle-loading guns, for instance, shipwrights cut ports in the side of the vessels, thereby introducing the first broadsides. Henry also ordered the fortification of the English coast, which did much to end the succession of raids and surprise landings from France.

Henry's successors were less interested in naval matters, and after his death in 1547 his navy declined. But during the reign of Elizabeth I later in the century, it received government attention again. This time the work proceeded under the stewardship of John Hawkins, who had been appointed treasurer and comptroller of the navy in 1577. A prosperous merchant from Plymouth, Hawkins was not unfamiliar with sea fighting. But his many years of freebooting against Spanish shipping had left him with a profound dislike for boarding and hand-to-hand combat. He preferred

Medieval sea battles usually consisted of fights across decks. At the end, the losers were unceremoniously tossed overboard.

guns and mobility, and under his direction English naval vessels became floating platforms for guns. To improve the vessels' speed and maneuverability, the high fore- and aftercastles were lowered, and the vessels' length-to-beam ratio was increased. Hawkins also installed long-range guns that could throw a cannonball well over a mile. Slowly but surely a new type of navy emerged: a fleet of fast, maneuverable vessels that actually avoided the traditional way of fighting man to man across decks. This fleet was designed to engage the enemy at long range.

In 1588 this new approach to warfare met with the naval school of thought developed in the Mediterranean. Relations between England, a bastion of Protestantism, and Spain, a defender of Catholicism, had deteriorated. But there was more to the friction than religious antagonism. For many years English sea raiders had been harassing Spanish shipping in the West Indies. At first the conflict remained limited to skirmishes and diplomatic moves, but by 1580 it was being rumored that Spain intended to invade England. The reports were premature because Philip II, the king of Spain, was preoccupied with the revolt in the Low Countries and the threat of Islam in the East. Merely retaining control of his immense empire required all of his resources.

Nonetheless, during the 1580s the prospect of an invasion of England became more realistic. Spain had concluded a truce with the Ottoman Empire, allowing Philip to focus more resources on western Europe. There, the death of a Catholic heir in France broke down the Anglo-French alliance that had been holding Spain back. Further north, the assassination of William the Silent, the ruler of the newly proclaimed Dutch republic, seemingly paved the way for a victory in the Netherlands. Spain had also recently absorbed Portugal, giving Philip access to additional maritime resources. Finally, and perhaps most important, the steady flow of gold and silver from Mexican and Peruvian mines into the Spanish treasury made the preparation of an invasion fleet financially possible.

Philip remained hesitant, but the execution of Mary Stuart, queen of Scotland, in 1587 firmed his resolve to do away with the English heretics. At first the plan was to send out an enormous fleet carrying an invasion army from Spain, but later it was decided to divert troops from Flanders to team up with the fleet and then proceed across the channel to England. Though it numbered no more than twenty-three thousand men, the Spanish force could have been expected to succeed. England had no army to match the well-trained Spanish troops, and the state of its defenses was deplorable. Only the English fleet, by now increased to some 130 vessels, stood in the way of a Spanish victory.

To both sides, the "Enterprise of England" was a leap in the dark. Spain had experience in defending large formations of ships, gained in convoying its rich treasure fleets from South America, but protecting a fleet of 130 sail was a different matter. Moreover, the Spanish fleet had to progress through unfamiliar waters and was certain to be attacked. The English faced equally baffling questions. Their commanders had some sea-fighting experience, but only in small actions. Now they were confronted with a huge and powerful fleet the likes of which none of them had ever seen. No one had any idea how this formidable opponent could be defeated.

If anything was clear, it was that the two sides represented different naval philosophies. On the one side the Spanish fleet, commanded by Alonso Pérez de Guzmán, the duke of Medina-Sidonia, was built to achieve victory by grappling its opponents and fighting it out man to man. Accordingly, most of the Spanish vessels were large, impregnable floating fortresses, equipped with big short-range naval guns to incapacitate any opponent within range, and manned by a large contingent of soldiers to board the enemy ships. The English fleet, in contrast, consisted of Hawkins's small, maneuverable vessels, equipped with long-range guns and manned by sailors who worked the ship as well as the guns. Spain's strategy was to entice the English ships to come close enough to be grappled and boarded. England's was the opposite: stay out of boarding range and pepper the enemy with long-range shot.

The *Henry Grace à Dieu*, launched in 1514, was the nucleus of Henry VIII's national navy.

An English view of one of the Armada
engagements, by an unidentified English
artist (c. 1590).

Each side was well aware of the other's strengths and weaknesses, but the first
encounter of the fleets, on 29 July 1588, was a mutually discouraging experience. The
Spanish were astonished at the speed and the maneuverability of the English vessels.
Their heavy transports and warships seemed like sitting ducks; there was no way they
could hope to force an engagement on their own terms. To the English the Armada,
sailing in a tight crescent formation with the heaviest fighting ships ahead and on
either quarter, was an equally intimidating sight. It seemed impossible to mount an
attack on the Armada without first breaking up this formation.

As the Armada sailed up the channel toward its destination, the English made
repeated attempts to break the Spanish formation, but without much success. When
it reached Calais one week later, the Spanish fleet was virtually intact. Several attacks
by the entire English fleet had hardly made a dent in the Spanish formation, and for
England the situation was very grave. The Armada was only thirty miles away from its
intended meeting point with the duke of Parma in Dunkirk, and unless the rendezvous could be prevented, the country was doomed.

In a final attempt to break the Armada's tight discipline, the English sent a number of fire ships into the Spanish anchorage at Calais. Anticipating this, the duke of
Medina-Sidonia had made provisions, but some of the floating torches slipped
through and caused panic. Most of the ships, which until then had exhibited such
superb discipline, fled in a disorderly mob toward the north. The following day the
duke of Medina-Sidonia succeeded in regrouping his fleet, but his vessels were running out of ammunition and took a severe beating from the English. More important,
during the skirmish the Armada had drifted by the Flemish coast and the duke of
Parma's army, and a brisk southwesterly wind prevented it from reversing course.

There was nothing to do but to return to Spain by sailing north around Scotland.

None of the Spanish vessels was in any condition for such a long voyage. Many had been badly damaged, and most were short of food and water and manned by severely weakened crews. As a result, the return voyage was a disaster. Only half of the fleet limped back into Spanish ports; the remainder vanished without a trace or were wrecked on the rocky coasts of Scotland and Ireland, where their exhausted crews were massacred. Philip II took a philosophical view of the failure of his "Enterprise of England." He wrote, "I sent my ships to fight the English, not the winds and the waves," and in a sense his analysis was correct. It was the elements that scattered his "invincible" Armada, not the prowess of the English navy.

Even so, the failure of the Armada was a turning point. It was a political turning point in that it signaled the beginning of Spain's decline, even though few people would have known it at the time. And it was also a naval turning point. Fighting at sea had changed. It now depended not on hand-to-hand combat between men, but rather on gunfights between ships. This change called for different naval tactics. Guns and broadsides made the line-abreast formation, which had been used in every major battle since Salamis, ineffective. The position of the fleets in relation to wind direction also became vitally important.

But from a broad strategic perspective there were few, if any, changes. Navies remained good at doing what they had always done: projecting power, protecting or attacking supply lines, and establishing presence. And navies once again proved vital as a first line of defense. Without a fleet to harass and contain the Armada, Britain would have become a very different place.

The confrontation with the Armada was too short to integrate tactical changes into new doctrines, but during the seventeenth century the British had plenty of opportunities to practice their fighting at sea, and to become extremely good at it. Their first adversary was Holland, whose domination of commerce and fishing did not sit very well in Britain. Initially the conflict was limited to diplomatic moves and countermoves, but when England's leaders started rebuilding its navy and merchant fleet, competition on the various trade routes became hostile. Before long, armed conflict had become inevitable.

The three Anglo-Dutch wars that followed were principally fought over trade, and though not marked by religious overtones, they were waged with considerable ferocity. All the engagements took place at sea, and they were led by some of the greatest admirals of all time. Not surprisingly, the battles led to major changes in naval tactics. For one thing, the English commanders were appalled at the general lack of organization during naval engagements, with the two fleets merging and ships generally battling it out individually. Accordingly, they adopted instructions designed to do away with the bunching of ships. They also agreed on a number of flag signals, so that the admiral could convey tactical instructions to his ships.

Although none of the sea battles of the Anglo-Dutch wars ended in a decisive victory for either side, Britain fared better than Holland. But the peace that followed in 1673 was short-lived. Under the fostering care of Louis XIV and Jean Colbert, his minister of finance, the French navy had been strengthened as well, and it soon saw action against the Dutch and English fleets. By the end of the seventeenth century a major war had broken out between France and England. It would occupy both nations for most of the eighteenth century.

The conflict was interesting in that it pitted a maritime nation with a strong navy against a continental nation with an army, causing both countries to adopt strategies in accordance with their strengths. After some resounding naval defeats, the French wisely decided to avoid further major engagements, focusing instead on a policy of privateering to disrupt English trade. The English, in contrast, sought to blockade the French navy and merchant fleet in their ports, and made sure that there was a strong British naval contingent wherever trouble could be expected.

Several naval battles were fought, the most important of which came in 1805, when the English fleet met a combined French-Spanish fleet off the Spanish coast near Trafalgar. Britain's victory was largely the result of the tactical genius of Admiral Horatio Nelson, its most celebrated sea commander. Nelson knew that he had to destroy the enemy fleet rather than merely defeat it, and by trapping it between the wind and his own fleet he was able to turn the confrontation into a closely fought battle, where he could take advantage of his superior gunnery. In the process, the French-Spanish fleet was demolished. Eighteen enemy ships were taken, and one was blown up. Casualties on both sides were enormous. Nearly six thousand French and Spanish sailors were killed or wounded, while twenty thousand were taken prisoner. England, in contrast, lost only seventeen hundred men, though among them was Nelson, mortally wounded by a sniper's bullet.

A few weeks later, a grief-stricken England gave its favorite son a hero's funeral. It was a deserved tribute, for Trafalgar forever denied Napoleon command of the sea. And without command of the sea, there was no way he could command the land either. Ten years later, Waterloo sealed his fate. Instead of France it was Britain that emerged as Europe's most powerful nation.

Above left: Admiral Horatio Nelson's tactical genius gave Britain a much-needed victory at Trafalgar.

Below left: England lost seventeen hundred men in the bloody confrontation at Trafalgar, among them Nelson, here seen mortally wounded on the deck of the *Victory*.

The *Ranger's* name is a reminder of this era of fighting sail, for the first such ship in the U.S. Navy was a small eighteen-gun frigate that harassed the British during the Revolutionary War. She was commanded by John Paul Jones, who would go on to fame and immortality, at least in America. The same *Ranger* made history when she received a formal salute from a French flotilla in 1778, now celebrated as the first official act of recognition of the fledgling American Republic.

Since then there have been six other *Rangers*. The second was a schooner; the third, a brigantine that saw action during the war of 1812; the fourth, a fully rigged iron vessel; and the fifth, a coastal minesweeper deployed during World War I. The sixth *Ranger* was the first U.S. Navy ship designed and constructed as an aircraft carrier. She served from 1934 to 1947, to be succeeded by the current *Ranger*, which was commissioned ten years later and has thus been in operation for over thirty-five years—the longest of any *Ranger* yet. Since they depend for their weaponry on their flexible air wing, carriers can lead long lives, yet after this campaign the curtain will fall for the current *Ranger*. In just a few weeks she will be sailing home to San Diego for the last time, to be decommissioned a few months later.

Her current humanitarian mission is a nice way to go out, I suppose, but as with all ships, it is sort of sad. Ships like this don't get "decommissioned." They die, just as their occupants do. Unless she is very lucky, the *Ranger* will be heading for a scrapyard before too long.

Meanwhile, I have been scheduled to leave the carrier for a while. "Today you are headed for the *Valley Forge*," Rod tells me. "Their helo will pick you up around 16:00. I'm not sure whether they're expecting you, but if not just ask someone for the XO [executive officer], explain to him what you're doing, and try to get back here tomorrow."

The *Valley Forge* is an Aegis cruiser, one of the most modern warships in the world. Crammed with radars and sonars, Aegis cruisers are known as the eyes and the ears of the battle group. I have long been wanting to visit one, although I am a bit concerned about just dropping in. But there isn't much I can do about that now, I reflect, as the *Valley Forge's* LAMPS III helo approaches the ship's landing deck.

I run into the helicopter hangar, hoping to find someone to tell me where I can find the XO, but there is no need for that. He is there already, along with Captain Billy Cornett and several of the ship's officers. "Welcome aboard the *Valley Forge*," Captain Cornett says, before introducing me to the others. For a moment I think this is a case of mistaken identity, but he is using my name, so they obviously were expecting me. More than that, they had prepared for it. On the schedule that Captain Cornett gives me is not only an elaborate twenty-four-hour tour of the ship, but also a cake and ice cream social on the crew deck, a formal meal in the wardroom, and even some free time. Then and there, I decide I like the *Valley Forge* a great deal.

That liking doesn't just have to do with an affinity for cake and ice cream. It also has to do with the fact that I feel I'm back on board a ship. There are fewer than four hundred people here, so chances are you'd run into someone more than once. The *Valley Forge* also looks and feels like a ship; she even rolls a bit in the gentle swell. In short, I feel comfortable. On the *Ranger* I always felt like Hansel leaving mental breadcrumbs so that I'd find my way back to my cabin. The *Valley Forge*, in contrast, is manageable. No confusion here about which way is fore and which way is aft.

After showing me my quarters, Captain Cornett guides me into the combat information center (CIC)—the brain of the ship, coordinated by the sophisticated Aegis system. It feels a bit like walking into a real-life video game. On one side are three large, blue display screens, which depict what is going on at any one time at various scales. Today, off the coast of Somalia, there isn't much to see: a few blips ahead representing other vessels, and behind us the *Ranger*. In front of the screens is a row of con-

Above: Captain Billy Cornett, commanding officer of the USS *Valley Forge*.

Left: Guided-missile cruisers like the USS *Valley Forge* are known as the eyes and ears of the battle group.

soles, where the operations officer and combat systems officer are seated. And behind them are various radar screens, each one earnestly monitored by an operator.

Captain Cornett takes me by all of them and introduces me to the operators, who briefly explain what their task is in this mind-boggling operation. Their explanations are brief and to the point, but to be perfectly frank, within a few seconds I am resigned to muttering an intelligent-sounding "I see" now and then. It is not so much my lack of technical understanding (though that too plays a role), but everyone seems to be very fond of using acronyms I have never heard of, and that makes even the simplest explanation incomprehensible.

Nevertheless, from one sympathetic operator I gather that the AN/SPY-1A radar is at the heart of the Aegis system. It consists of four different array faces, he explains, allowing it to look in all directions at once and thereby provide continuous surveillance. There also are an air search radar, a surface search radar, and a surface surveillance and tracking radar, keeping operators informed of the whereabouts of hundreds of contacts.

Adjacent to the areas for antiaircraft and anti–surface group warfare is the anti-submarine warfare area. The operators here have some of the most sophisticated sonars at their disposal, along with the information relayed to them by the ship's two helicopters. All of these activities are eventually coordinated by the captain or the combat systems officers, unless things get so hot that a human mind can no longer follow the action, in which case computers take over.

During the tour of the CIC, combat systems officer Michael Sweeney walks up to Captain Cornett to inform him that the ship's helicopter has spotted a "wooden ship, probably a dhow," whose deck seems to be packed with people who are waving. "We don't know whether they are trying to attract attention or are just waving," he adds. The captain, who was in the middle of explaining one of the sensors to me, looks at

SEA POWER: *A Global Journey*   145

him for a moment, then orders the helo to make another pass to figure out what, if anything, these people need.

We head for dinner in the wardroom, but Captain Cornett is called back to the CIC before we even get to the salad. Next goes XO Alvin Smith, and then Luke McCollum, the operations officer. Every five minutes or so the phone rings, calling another officer away, so that by the time the steaks are served there are only a few of us left. Just as I'm getting ready to finish the dinner by myself, weapons officer Donald Shirey returns to explain that something is up with the dhow that was spotted earlier. "The captain says you're welcome to join him in the CIC," he adds.

I follow Don into the CIC, where Captain Cornett is sitting in front of the blue display screens, which now show the *Valley Forge* heading the other way. Occasionally glancing at the screen, the captain quickly briefs me on what has happened. Apparently the helo established radio contact with the dhow and was told that she was carrying some five hundred Somali refugees urgently in need of food, water, and medical assistance. This is not the sort of request that is taken lightly at sea, so Captain Cornett contacted Admiral Hancock aboard the *Ranger* to determine how best to render assistance. It was agreed to divert the *Valley Forge*. All this took place in the last half-hour, Captain Cornett adds, so that now we are on a northerly course, closing in on the dhow.

With the *Valley Forge*'s helo still circling the dhow, we are able to listen in on its conversation with the Somalis. Since neither the captain of the dhow nor any of his crew speaks English, one of the passengers is talking. "What kind of assistance do you need?" we hear pilot Jim Gillchrist ask. Though filled with static, the response is clear: "We are Somali refugees," it goes. "There are more than five hundred people on this ship, many of whom are sick. We are also short of food and water." Lieutenant Gillchrist asks other questions, but the reply is always the same: "We are refugees from Somalia, and we need help." Eventually we find out that the dhow is headed for Aden in Yemen, and that at least two-thirds of the people aboard are women and children.

For some time Captain Cornett tries to talk the dhow into turning toward the coast to obtain assistance, but having just fled the country, the Somalis obviously would rather press on. Besides, there probably isn't much assistance to be had along the coast. We also begin to gather that the dhow captain is not very keen on the attention his boat is beginning to attract. This is understandable, because there isn't much that is legal about loading five hundred people onto a dhow that is certified to carry half as many, if that. He probably also doesn't have permission to bring these people into Yemen. Our questions regarding the ship's name and nationality therefore remain unanswered.

By midnight the dhow has come into view, and half an hour later the *Valley Forge* is steaming next to her. We can see her name, *Chamsagar,* but no flag. She is perhaps 120 feet long, and even though it is dark, we can see that the deck is crammed with people. In fact, there are probably far more people on the dhow than there are on the *Valley Forge,* which is nearly five times as long.

After some coordination with the English-speaking Somali on the bridge, a first attempt is made to bring the dhow alongside so that food and medical supplies can be transferred. Unfortunately, the waves prove too high for this to be done safely, and the maneuver has to be abandoned. Instead, it is decided to try again during daylight.

The following morning I look at the people aboard through the ship's binoculars. There are some 250 of them topside. All look relatively well fed and clothed, though we have no idea about the 250 of them below deck, of course. Looking at the dhow bobbing up and down in the waves, I assume it isn't a pleasant place to be. With the waves still too high to risk pulling alongside, Captain Cornett decides to transfer the supplies by helo. From the bridge I watch the pilots transfer water, rice, bread, and fruits and vegetables with pinpoint precision onto the deck, where the Somalis eagerly unpack each load and distribute it among themselves.

Executive officer Alvin Smith joins me as I observe this procedure. He looks tired but happy. "No sleep last night," he confesses. "We had a little strategy session during the night to figure out how we could best help these people. But you know, seeing them get these supplies, and seeing how happy they are with them, makes all of it worthwhile. In fact, it makes the last four months worthwhile. We hardly ever get to see who we help." I look at him, and then at the people on the dhow, who are happily munching away and waving. He is justifiably proud, as is the entire *Valley Forge.* The ship and her crew went well beyond the unwritten code that calls upon seafarers to help one another.

By early afternoon the supplies have been transferred, and there is not much more the *Valley Forge* can do. Meanwhile, the *Ranger* has reached Mogadishu. We are about four hundred miles north of there, and since Admiral Hancock is eager to have his cruiser join up again, the engine room is informed that we'll be putting the pedal to the metal for a while. The four gas turbines are cranked up to full power, and the *Valley Forge* literally surges ahead. For a while I watch the dhow become smaller and smaller, until she is no more than a tiny white dot ploughing on toward Yemen and what is at best an uncertain future.

As the *Valley Forge* presses on toward Mogadishu, I get a chance to pick up my visit where we left off the night before. Lieutenant Commander Dan Lien, the ship's supply officer, introduces me to disbursing officer Mark Thomas and food service officer Mark Pimpo, who in turn show me around the galley and the various food-storage and spare-parts rooms. Then it is time for a visit to the propulsion plant, where engineering officer Robert Kerno does the honors. And as soon as I emerge from the engine room, Don Shirey guides me through the various weapons systems that are his responsibility, a tour that takes me from gun and missile control computer complexes deep inside the ship to the Harpoon quad-canister launchers on the stern.

I am utterly impressed with the professionalism not just of these officers, but of everyone I encounter on the tour. There is no choice, for this is no longer a simple warship; she is a floating computer complex, one of the most completely integrated naval combat systems in the world. In the missile compartment I'm told that the ship is capable not only of tracking hundreds of targets at the same time, but also of aiming and firing weapons to engage them within seconds. Of course, while all this is true in theory, no one knows how effectively this technology would function in wartime, when it takes only one enemy missile to slip through the net.

Uncertainty about the effectiveness of offensive or defensive weaponry is an accepted part of naval life. The introduction of missiles a quarter-century ago altered the nature of war at sea as much as the appearance of guns aboard ships did five hundred years earlier. As it did then, the change in weaponry raised tactical questions. How would precision guided missiles affect naval battles? Was there any protection against them? Did they make major warships such as aircraft carriers too vulnerable, or even obsolete? To seek answers, naval experts the world over go into an analyzing frenzy whenever there is a naval engagement. But these studies, while helpful, never lead to conclusive answers. Technology is moving too fast for that, it seems.

 Times of rapid technological change always entail such uncertainties. And while no period in naval history seems to compare with the current explosion in technology, the nineteenth century comes very close. Politically it was a period of relative peace around the globe, enforced by Britain and the Royal Navy. Yet technologically it was a period of phenomenal change. Ships began to make the transition from sail to steam and from wood to iron. In fact, navies and naval strategy changed more during the nineteenth century than in all of previous history.

Previous page: Turning back toward Mogadishu, the *Valley Forge* literally surges ahead.

At first navies were slow to adapt to the changes brought about by the Industrial Revolution. The Royal Navy, anxious to stay with a way of fighting it had perfected, rejected steam propulsion. Initially there were good reasons for this. The action radius of early steam vessels was very small, and a navy that ruled the seas obviously required vessels that were reliable over long distances. Naval strategists also argued that bulky engines and paddle wheels made warships too vulnerable, since one well-aimed shot could immobilize a vessel. And finally, paddle wheels interfered with the positioning of guns. They masked as much as a third of the side of the vessel, dramatically reducing the firing power of the broadside that had served the British so well at Trafalgar.

As a result, the Royal Navy was very little involved in the development of reliable steam propulsion. That work was left to the commercial sector, but progress there was so fast that it was only a matter of time before navies too made the switch. The reluctance to adopt steam-driven war vessels was overcome in particular by the development of screw propulsion during the 1840s. Screws did not interfere with gun placement and were far less vulnerable than paddle wheels. In fact, because it placed the engine under the waterline, and thus out of reach of shot, steam propulsion became a far more attractive proposition. The Royal Navy even converted some of its Napoleonic war veterans to steam and screw, and from the 1850s onward new war vessels invariably included both.

Another development that changed navies was the invention of explosive shells. Until the early nineteenth century cannons had fired solid shot, but against the big ships of the line, this was no longer effective. At the battle of Trafalgar, for instance, thousands of rounds had been fired, but not a single ship had been sunk. Explosive shells were far more destructive. At first they were not very accurate, but soon guns were developed that did away with that shortcoming. Further improvements came when ordnance experts developed the rifling of cannons as well as elongated rather than spherical projectiles.

Explosive shells led to the disappearance of wooden warships. In 1853, during the Crimean War, a Russian fleet armed with shell-firing cannon annihilated a Turkish squadron in a matter of hours, and naval theorists concluded that future fleet actions would take less than half an hour because of the enormous destruction caused by shells exploding inside a wooden hull. But shipbuilders did not agree. They responded by protecting the hulls of ships with thick iron plates, thereby producing the first ironclads. In 1858 the French built the *Gloire,* the first seagoing ironclad. Displacing some fifty-six hundred tons, she was armored with iron plates about twelve centimeters thick. Her steam-driven screw gave her a speed of 13 knots. The British responded by designing the *Warrior,* a vessel with such heavy armament and armor that she required an iron hull. Her launching in 1860 signaled the end of the era of wooden warships.

There were other important developments. Early in the century Robert Fulton, a young American inventor, peddled what he called a "diving boat," first to the French and then to the English navy. Fulton demonstrated the uses of the diving boat, but this revolutionary type of naval warfare was rejected. Another new development was the mine (or torpedo, as it was called then). During tests on rivers, mines proved to be very effective at destroying ships.

Steam propulsion, explosive shells, and defensive measures such as mines were bound to change naval warfare. The shift from sail to steam did away, it seemed, with the naval tactics of the past. Commanders no longer had to worry about what the winds and tides would do to their formations. Moreover, shell-firing guns made the tactics of Trafalgar obsolete. By 1860 guns could fire at a range of five miles—a totally new tactical concept. Even so, while every naval tactician was aware of the changes, no one was certain how this new arsenal of weapons would affect naval warfare. With the exception of some naval skirmishes during the Crimean War, few of these new weapons had ever been tested in combat. But in 1860 war broke out in America.

Naval theorists suddenly had a splendid opportunity to witness how these technologies would perform in a prolonged conflict.

Though the Civil War was not a naval conflict, sea power played an important role in its outcome. The states of the South required supplies of all sorts, most of which they had to obtain from overseas. The North was more industrial and hence self-supporting, but it could not ignore the sea either. To the Union it was vital that the Confederacy's supply lines from Europe be disrupted.

To achieve that goal, the Union established a naval blockade of Confederate ports and began to intercept vessels carrying goods to the South. Although blockading thirty-five hundred miles of enemy coastline sounded impossible, the strategy proved remarkably successful. To obtain its vital supplies, the South first turned to fast ships to run the blockade. Later it used commerce raiders, to strike at the North's trade and

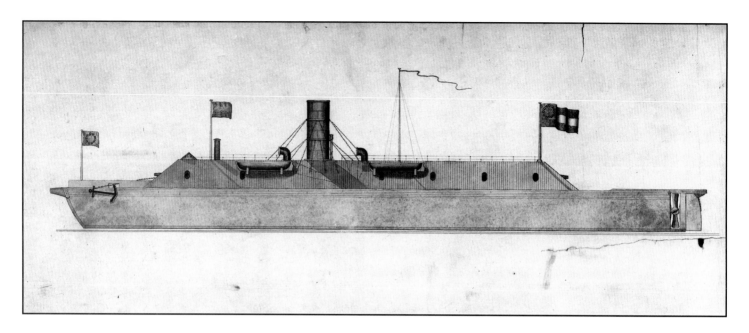

The CSS *Virginia*, also known as the *Merrimack*, introduced a radically different battleship design. Her confrontation with the Union warship *Monitor* on 9 March 1862 proved inconclusive.

to force the blockading vessels to scatter their strength, but still the blockade remained effective.

Desperate to break the stranglehold on its ports, the Confederacy next turned to the new arsenal of naval weapons. Mines were used very effectively, destroying more than thirty Union vessels. The South also built semisubmersible vessels that, armed with a spar torpedo, attempted to ram blockading ships, but this method was only moderately successful. Backed by Southern financiers, Fulton's concept of a diving boat was revived. After several tries, a true submersible was built and christened the *H. L. Hunley*, after her chief backer. Powered by eight men turning a crankshaft to drive the propeller, the vessel had a speed of about 2 knots underwater. But the *Hunley* was not very safe: during trials she had already sunk twice, drowning most of the crew. Even so, a third crew was found, and on 17 February 1864 the vessel rammed the Union sloop *Housatonic* with a spar torpedo, blowing a great hole in her side. The *Housatonic* sank virtually immediately, becoming the first war victim of a submarine. The submarine crew did not get a chance to celebrate the successful attack, however. Sucked into the hull of her victim, the small vessel was dragged along to the bottom, taking all aboard with her.

Aside from applying these new weapons, the South also built innovative vessels, hoping to compete with the Union's larger fleet. This strategy appeared to be successful when, on 8 March 1862, the Confederate ironclad *Virginia* went on a rampage against the wooden Union ships at Hampton Roads, ramming and sinking one vessel, setting another afire, and forcing a third to run aground. The same evening the North's response, the *Monitor,* arrived, just in time to prevent further destruction. The most innovative warship of her time, the *Monitor* had a revolving turret equipped with two 11-inch guns mounted in an armored hull. On 9 March the two vessels fought a battle. Though they fired hundreds of rounds, neither ship seriously damaged the other, and shortly after midday they broke off action.

If anything, the damage caused by the *Virginia* on 8 March showed that the old order of the wooden ships of the line was definitely over. But the battle between the two ironclads the following day was indecisive and provided no insight into how battles between such vessels would proceed. Many nations sent observers to America to witness the impact of the new naval technologies, but their reports remained inconclusive. The Civil War had seen the first encounter between armored vessels, the first submarine sinking, the first torpedo-boat attack, the first use of turret ships, and the first effective use of minefields. It was the first war in which shells were widely used, and the first in which bombardments from ships were successful. It confirmed that these new techniques and technologies were effective, but it provided few clues to the future.

In the years following the Civil War, warships became bigger, faster, and more heavily armed. But there were few opportunities to see how these vessels performed in combat, and naval experts had to rely on theoretical rather than empirical information. Armchair tacticians the world over filled military journals with new ideas. In various countries institutions were established to train naval officers in the art of war and strategy, and to help formulate future naval policy.

Though the growth of navies was accompanied by an increasing interest in naval matters, little time was spent on naval history. In fact, there was a growing feeling that the many advances in technology had made history irrelevant. It was said that Trafalgar, fought just sixty-five years earlier, was a battle much closer to the actions fought in the sixteenth century than anything that could be expected in the years ahead. Moreover, steam propulsion had made useless the elaborate tactical plans of the great admirals of the age of sail, so why study them?

Alfred Thayer Mahan, second president of the recently established Naval War College in Newport, Rhode Island, had a different view. As chief instructor of the college Mahan taught a course on sea power, and during the early 1890s he published the contents of his lectures in two books: *The Influence of Sea Power upon History, 1660–1783* and *The Influence of Sea Power upon the French Revolution and Empire, 1790–1812*. Both works gave a detailed account of the many naval engagements fought between European fleets a century earlier, but they contained something more. From the naval history of the seventeenth and eighteenth centuries Mahan drew a comprehensive theory of sea power that captured the minds of naval officers and governments alike.

In essence, Mahan stated that the sea was a great highway over which men and goods could travel more easily and at a lower cost than on land. Sea power consisted of controlling this highway. This involved not only creating markets and a sufficiently large merchant fleet to carry the trade, but also establishing bases or colonies and, of course, a strong naval fleet to protect commerce and acquire trading stations. The function of this navy in wartime, Mahan continued, was to secure command of the sea in order to maintain effective communications among vessels and bases, and to deny such communication to the enemy. Command of the sea could be achieved only by neutralizing or destroying the enemy fleet, Mahan suggested. This in turn called for a strong fleet—not necessarily a very large one, but one composed of large, powerful, well-manned ships operating on the principle that the best defense is an aggressive offense.

Mahan's work was acclaimed as the most important review of the nature and importance of sea power ever conducted, and it all boiled down to one simple idea: national greatness demanded sea control. Mahan took Britain as his case study, showing how the might and prowess of its navy provided it with such international stature, wealth, and power. If other nations wished to contest that hegemony, they required a powerful navy as well, along with bases and a merchant fleet, so that they could make an effective bid for command of the sea.

Here was a simple recipe for national greatness, and during an age of strident chauvinism, it was not ignored. In England the reception was electrifying. Mahan's work explained to the British how they had won their exceptional worldwide power, and—perhaps more important—it justified the policy through which that power had been maintained: large naval expenditures. The Japanese and Germans also showed a great deal of interest in the studies. The kaiser ordered Mahan's books to be bought for all ship and training-school libraries, and even the German General Staff quoted Mahan's ideas. In Japan the government provided translated copies to its officers, political leaders, and schools.

Alfred Thayer Mahan, the father of modern sea power, believed that national greatness was inextricably linked to sea power.

At first the U.S. Navy was not as impressed with Mahan's work. In 1893 it ordered him to sea again, much against his wishes, as captain of the USS *Chicago*. But in the end the assignment turned out much to his benefit. When his ship arrived in England, Mahan was showered with honors by the British. He was wined and dined by Queen Victoria, the prince of Wales, the prime minister, and the first lord of the Admiralty, all of whom were terribly impressed with his work, and he received honorary doctorates from both Oxford and Cambridge. These accolades did not go unnoticed in the United States. Here also Mahan finally began to receive wide acclaim and, in time, a powerful following.

For someone who only ten years earlier had been in command of small wooden steamers and seemed destined for a thoroughly uneventful navy career, it was quite a change. But it was not undeserved. Mahan's work was extremely well put together. He began by giving a comprehensive overview of the factors that affect sea power, and then gradually developed his thesis—the overriding importance of the sea in world politics—by drawing from the events the past. His lectures, like his books, were extremely well presented, contributing in no small part to their popularity.

But something more than their form accounted for the widespread acceptance and influence of Mahan's ideas. His work appeared at a time when it was bound to have a profound impact. Many nations were spending increasing amounts of money on their navies, and Mahan's thesis seemed to confirm that they were doing the right thing. Moreover, his books coincided with a growing colonialism, and again history, as interpreted by Mahan, seemed to support an expansionist policy. Mahan's work also appeared at a time of great uncertainty about the role of navies, an uncertainty caused by the rapid advances in science and technology. Mahan helped to clear up the confusion by emphasizing in no uncertain terms the importance of big, powerful capital ships. And finally, big ships made big impressions. Increasingly, navies were seen as symbols of national prestige and power. No self-respecting nation, it seemed, could afford to be without a very impressive fleet.

These factors led to an enormous expansion of naval strength at the end of the nineteenth century. Britain, whose fleet had been unchallenged for most of the century, led the way and remained at the forefront of warship design by experimenting with different types of ships and armaments. During the 1890s it launched several enormous steel battleships. They were fourteen-thousand-ton monsters—almost a third of the weight was in steel armor—that carried a combination of large (13.5-inch) and medium-sized (6.0-inch) guns in turrets and attained speeds of up to 15 knots.

Even so, the British lead in naval strength was shrinking by the day. In 1883 the size of the Royal Navy equaled that of the fleets of France, Germany, Italy, Russia, and the United States combined. By 1890 that lead had vanished forever, and the British government adopted a "two-power standard" of naval strength, specifying that the Royal Navy at all times had to match the size of the combined fleets of any two other nations. But by the early twentieth century even that standard had become difficult to maintain.

Britain's chief competition came from Germany, which was emerging as the dominant nation on the Continent. Germany made it no secret that it wished to compete for commercial domination. Believing that such domination had to be backed up by military superiority, it launched a massive naval building program under the direction of Admiral Alfred von Tirpitz. Taking Mahan's lessons to heart, von Tirpitz emphasized the construction of powerful battleships to protect and expand German interests. But the German policy was increasingly seen as a threat in Britain, worsening the already deteriorating relations between the two powers.

Meanwhile, Japan had emerged as a power in the Far East. It too was staking national ambitions on maritime power, and under the stewardship of Admiral Heihachiro Togo the country rapidly expanded its navy. Finally, America was building up its fleet under the direction of Theodore Roosevelt, secretary of the navy. After a period of stagnation several steel battleships were launched, preparing the U.S. Navy to meet its first challenge: the Spanish-American War. With its resounding victory over the Spanish at Manila and Santiago, the United States demonstrated that it was fit to join the ranks of the major naval powers.

By 1904 there were more than one hundred major battleships afloat or under construction. Britain had forty-eight, the United States twenty-four, Germany twenty-two, Russia nineteen, and France seventeen. With its "two-power standard" on the brink of being violated, Britain committed to a revolutionary battleship design. The result was launched in 1906. Christened HMS *Dreadnought,* the vessel displaced nearly eighteen thousand tons, had ten 12-inch guns, and could make 21 knots. Her speed, in combination with her powerful battery of long-range guns, in a single stroke made every other battleship afloat obsolete. But Britain's competitors lost no time in building similar warships, accelerating the naval arms race.

Most of the big battleships had never seen action, but with navies becoming stronger and with their owners becoming more belligerent, it was clear that this situation would not last much longer. True enough, when Japan declared war on Russia in 1904 over the seizure of Port Arthur, Russia decided to send its Baltic Fleet on an eighteen-thousand-mile journey to the Sea of Japan. Seven months later the fleet left French Indochina for Vladivostok, setting a course for the Strait of Korea. At the narrowest part of the strait, near the island of Tsushima, the Japanese fleet under Admiral Togo was waiting. On 27 May 1905 the two fleets met.

On paper the fleets were an equal match, but in the course of the ensuing battle, the Russian fleet was annihilated. Eight Russian battleships, four cruisers, and five

Built in almost complete secrecy, Britain's HMS *Dreadnought* revolutionized battleship design to such an extent that any battleship before her became known as a predreadnought.

destroyers were sunk, some with the loss of their entire crew. Out of a fleet of twenty-eight ships, only three made it to Vladivostok. In a single day Russia's sea power was effectively wiped off the face of the earth. Japan emerged as the dominant power in the Far East.

The Battle of Tsushima was the first major fleet action since Trafalgar and was accordingly studied with a great deal of interest by naval tacticians. In terms of ships and weaponry, there were no longer any similarities. None of the battling ships depended on wind and weather anymore, they fought their gun battles at distances of miles rather than a few hundred feet, and they had to reckon with other weapons, such as torpedoes. Yet even though the tools of naval warfare had changed, victory still depended on crew morale, a well-thought-out tactical plan, and its effective implementation. And perhaps most important, Tsushima appeared to confirm Mahan's thesis: the best way to secure the all-important command of the sea was through big, powerful, and aggressive battleships.

Mahan's thesis did not always hold up, however. On the other side of the world the rivalry between Britain and Germany was taking an increasingly threatening tone. Germany had hoped that by building a very powerful fleet, it could induce Britain to seek an alliance, but things did not work out that way. When Austria, supported by Germany, declared war on Serbia it set the stage for World War I, pitting the Triple Alliance of Germany, Austria-Hungary, and Italy against the Triple Entente of Britain, France, and Russia. On 4 August 1914 the British government declared war on Germany.

World War I was principally a land war, one that reached a devastating stalemate in Flanders and northern France, but navies also played a crucial role, albeit not along the lines Mahan had sketched. Britain entered the war with the most powerful navy in the world, but the fleet rarely ventured out for fear of submarines and mines. Its German counterpart also stayed mostly in port. The two sides instead confined themselves to a number of skirmishes in the North Sea, each one hoping to reduce the strength of the other. The entire fleets of the two countries did not meet until the Battle of Jutland in May 1916. Even then they did not realize, at least at the outset, that they were meeting each other in full strength.

When the two fleets met, a running battle ensued. At first the British fleet had the advantage of being able to position itself between the German ships and their home ports, but during the night the German fleet managed to break through the British line and make a run for its base. The British admiral, John Jellicoe, was unwilling to commit his vessels to a chase for fear of mines, torpedoes, and the risks of fighting at night. By early morning the battle was over.

Germany was quick to call the Battle of Jutland a victory, and in a tactical sense it was. Though the German fleet was weaker than the British main fleet, it had in fact inflicted far more damage than it had sustained. England lost three battle cruisers, three armored cruisers, and eight destroyers with more than six thousand men, while Germany lost one pre-dreadnought, one battle cruiser, four light cruisers, and five destroyers as well as twenty-five hundred men. Given the fleet strength ratios, the German High Seas Fleet had more than held its own against the British Grand Fleet.

In terms of strategic importance, however, the Battle of Jutland was a British victory, because the German fleet remained bottled up in port for the rest of the war, not daring to risk another confrontation. Britain's uncontested command of the North Sea did much to hasten the end of the war, because it enabled the country to impose a distant blockade and deprive Germany of much-needed supplies.

The Battle of Jutland was the culminating action of the era of the great battleship, much as Trafalgar had been for the age of sail. For many years afterward tacticians analyzed it with great interest, but for all its intensity it left few abiding lessons other than Mahan's well-known dictum that sea control was crucial in any conflict, even in confrontations that were fought largely on land. In fact, Mahan had predicted that Britain's command of the sea would grind Germany down, no matter what victories the German armies won on land.

Despite the accuracy of this prediction, it was no longer clear that Mahan's big battleship fleets were the best means of achieving sea control. World War I indeed made clear that other vessels could play decisive roles as well. Submarines, for instance, emerged as excellent commerce raiders. At first Germany was cautious in its submarine operations, for fear of drawing the United States into the conflict. German submarines limited themselves mostly to attacking warships. The first British merchant vessel was not sunk until October 1914, and as was typical of Germany's attitude toward this practice, the vessel was first politely informed that she would be sunk (which the submarine commander proceeded to do by dispatching a boarding party, to save torpedoes). Afterward, the entire crew was towed to safety by the submarine.

The emphasis on undersea warfare intensified in early 1915, when Germany declared the approaches to Britain a war zone and started to attack merchant vessels without warning. A few highly publicized sinkings and the associated outrage from neutral countries, particularly the United States, caused Germany to reverse this policy and to order its submarines to engage while surfaced. But by late 1916 it had become clear to the German leaders that they needed to disrupt Britain's supply lines in order to win the war, and the only way this could be done was through increased submarine activity. Accordingly, an unrestricted submarine campaign was launched, regardless of the risk. It was a desperate move, but it seemed to pay off when the Allies suffered massive losses during the first months of 1917. It was not until an escorted convoy system was implemented later in the year that casualties fell, and that the vital Allied supply lines could once more be secured.

By mid-1918 submarines had ceased to be a menace, and the end of the war had become only a matter of time. Nonetheless, the success of German submarines presented a frightening picture. During the hostilities they sank a total of 5,234 merchant vessels, representing more than twelve million tons, against a mere 187 losses of their own. In addition, they torpedoed nearly fifty warships, including ten major battleships. It was the submarine, rather than the powerful battleship, that nearly decided the war. But few naval leaders were willing to admit it.

This lack of insight caused the Allies major problems during World War II. At the onset of hostilities Germany declared war on shipping, catching Britain unprepared. Perhaps the country had been lulled into a false sense of security by the various naval agreements of the previous years, but there was also a feeling within the Admiralty that the convoy system and the development of underwater sonar had dealt with the submarine threat. Moreover, the Royal Navy still firmly believed in the supremacy of the battleship. Accordingly, few smaller ships suitable for escort duty had been built.

The result was disastrous. Though Germany started the war with only fifty-six submarines, Allied merchant ship losses grew rapidly, particularly after Germany secured submarine bases in Norway and France. Under the leadership of Admiral Karl Donitz the German fleet refined its tactics, increasingly relying on groups of submarines, later called wolf packs, to deal devastating blows to convoys. The vital supply lines between England and America were again seriously threatened.

During the first months of 1943 Allied merchant ship losses reached all-time highs. But better antisubmarine warfare techniques caused increasing numbers of submarines to be sent to the bottom as well, and it became more difficult for Germany to replace its U-boats and crews. The Allies, on the other hand, seemed to be turning out ships faster than they could be sunk. Despite desperate attempts by Donitz and his U-boat crews to turn the tide, by the end of 1943 the Battle of the Atlantic had been decided.

The final tally made clear that it had been another close call. In all, 2,775 merchant ships totaling over 14.5 million tons had been destroyed by German and Italian submarines during the course of the war. They had disrupted Allied supplies to the western front almost single-handedly. It was finally accepted that the submarine was the most dangerous threat to vital sea lanes in time of war, and that it would continue to be so for a long time to come.

Conflict at sea also expanded upward, into the skies. Nothing illustrated this development more vividly than the Japanese surprise attack on the American Pacific Fleet based at Pearl Harbor. Directed by Admiral Isoroko Yamamoto, the attack involved 360 aircraft launched from six carriers, plus twenty-seven submarines. To Yamamoto's disappointment, the Pacific Fleet's aircraft carriers were at sea, but six battleships were either sunk or seriously damaged, along with two cruisers, three destroyers, and many smaller craft. When the British lost two battleships off Southeast Asia a few days later, the Pacific and Indian oceans seemed wide open to Japan's expansionist drive.

Nonetheless, the U.S. fleet recovered rapidly from its setback at Pearl Harbor. By mid-1942 it was ready to oppose its Japanese counterpart. A first strategic victory was

The Japanese surprise attack on Pearl Harbor proved once and for all that sea power now extended to the air as well.

won at the Battle of the Coral Sea, when a U.S. carrier force spoiled a Japanese attempt to invade New Guinea and thereby pose a direct threat to Australia. The next major battle centered around a tiny island in the midst of the Pacific, appropriately called Midway. The Japanese wanted Midway as a forward observation post. They also knew that any Japanese activity there would draw the Pacific Fleet out, because the United States could not afford to lose the island.

The stakes at Midway were enormous. Each side desperately wanted to destroy the opposite fleet, for control of the Pacific could be gained only through naval power. The Japanese fleet approaching Midway in early June 1942 accordingly consisted of four carriers, two battleships, and several cruisers, followed by a heavily escorted occupation force including battleships, cruisers, and destroyers as well as troop transports and auxiliaries. Several hundred miles behind was a powerful battleship force headed by Admiral Yamamoto himself, who had masterminded the operation. Opposing this massive armada was a U.S. contingent of three carriers, eight cruisers, and thirteen destroyers. Though the U.S. fleet faced enormous odds, it had one major advantage: its leaders knew where the enemy was heading, because they had deciphered his messages. The Japanese, in contrast, had no idea were the opposing force was.

Access to this information proved vital, for it permitted the Americans to concentrate their striking power on the vital point. They were also lucky: when the American aircraft sighted and attacked the enemy fleet, they caught its carriers in the midst of changing their airplanes' weaponry from bombs (to attack the island) to torpedoes (to attack the American fleet). The result was a disaster for the Japanese fleet. In just a few minutes American dive bombers destroyed three aircraft carriers. Later in the day the fourth one was hit as well. In one day the Japanese lost four carriers, 322 airplanes, and, most important, thirty-five hundred lives, including many of their most experienced pilots. The Americans, in contrast, lost one carrier, 147 planes, and about three hundred lives. It was by no means a cheaply won victory, but it was sufficient to change the course of the Pacific war.

After Midway the Allies seized the initiative, and over the next three years they recovered one by one, at an enormous cost in lives and materials, the many territories Japan had seized. American submarines, meanwhile, inflicted heavy losses on Japanese merchant shipping, depriving the nation of vital supplies. Like England, Japan was an island nation, totally dependent on overseas supplies to meet its wartime needs. And like England, the country was brought to its knees by submarines.

But it was not the slow strangulation of Japan by submarines or the approaching American forces that ended the war. Instead, it was a long-range bomber that, on 6 August 1945, set out on a mission of unimaginable destruction. The nuclear bombs dropped on Hiroshima and later on Nagasaki finally induced Japan to surrender. They also signaled the beginning of the nuclear era, a shift that would yet again revolutionize the nature of war at sea.

Even at 30 knots it will take the *Valley Forge* until early tomorrow morning to reach Mogadishu and the *Ranger,* so it is clear that I'll be remaining on the cruiser a bit longer than expected. Not that I mind, because there is still plenty to do and see.

As dusk falls I climb up to the bridge. A few minutes later Captain Cornett arrives as well. "Captain on the bridge," the watchman calls, and everyone straightens up or tries to look just a bit busier. It reminds me of the creaking door to the wheelhouse on the *Envoy,* which no one bothered to oil until Captain Martin Weir did it himself one day. Only then did I understand why this creaking door was so valuable to the people on watch. Anyway, no such opportunities exist on board the *Valley Forge,* where Captain Cornett would be hard-pressed to arrive unannounced.

Prior to taking over command of the vessel last year, Captain Cornett was at the Naval War College teaching and discussing, as he tells me, "things to do with naval strategies, Mahan, and all the other things you're interested in." I'm eager to find out what that experience involved, so before long we're chatting about Mahan's theories and their role in a changing naval world. "Is Mahan still relevant?" I ask at some point. "It depends what side of Mahan you're talking about," Captain Cornett replies. "If you're talking about command of the sea, then yes, that, I think, is quite relevant. But don't forget, Mahan wasn't the first one to point out that sea power and sea control were very important; so did many people before him. Perhaps Mahan's strength was in the way he popularized this theory and got others interested in it. In that sense, he made history as much as he interpreted it."

When asked about what a nation needs in order to obtain command of the sea, Captain Cornett seems less precise. "It depends on a great many factors," he finally says, but I get the impression that he is not quite ready to share his thoughts on that topic. Everyone agrees that Mahan's suggestion—big battleships—is no longer applicable. And just about everyone agrees that carriers have taken over that role. But not everyone agrees that they should, or even could, continue to play that role. Perhaps the captain's feelings are along those lines, but if so, he isn't going to tell me.

Early the following morning we arrive off Mogadishu. We missed the actual landing on the beach by a couple of hours, but as I'll find out later, the media were there to immortalize the event. Some landing craft are still ferrying back and forth between the amphibious assault vessels and the shore, and everything seems to be going as planned. I quickly get the impression that this is a textbook operation straight out of *From the Sea*: regional, conducted on short notice, and very effective.

The operation demonstrates some of the traditional advantages of naval forces: flexibility and mobility. Within just a few days the U.S. Navy and Marines managed to have several amphibious assault ships in place off Mogadishu, and now there are also a carrier, a cruiser, and a fleet oiler, as well as three pre-positioning ships, which arrived during the morning with any supplies the task force might need in the next few weeks. And no other nation had to be asked for permission for these ships to get through.

On the other hand, the operation also demonstrates a few traditional weaknesses. Once a ship is at sea, she severs some of the lines of communication we have come to take for granted. The *Valley Forge,* for instance, is positioned in the fire support zone, guns at the ready just in case any Somali rebel feels like taking a shot at her. Here we are, only a mile or two off the coast, but we are limited to what we can see from the bridge or on the display screens in the combat information center; we lack the big picture. In fact, it strikes me that anyone watching these events at home on television knows a lot more about what is going on than we do. I am no expert on these things, but it seems to me that a satellite dish would be a wise investment.

There is another thing that intrigued me while walking around the ship: two chairs placed side by side at the ship's bow. It looks like a great place to catch some sunshine, but that's not what they are there for, of course. They are there so that the lookouts can sit down while watching the sea's surface for mines. This arrangement intrigued me because at one point a radar operator told me that the SPY radar was so precise, it could pick up a bumblebee. This is not done, of course, because along with the bees the radar would pick up every bird and who knows what else, but it shows the remarkable surveillance capacities of the *Valley Forge*. And yet for detecting something as simple as a mine, there really isn't anything like a good pair of eyes. Given the fact that just about anything—from a fishing boat to a submarine—can lay mines, they represent a serious threat.

I stay on the ship another day, but then it is time to get back to the *Ranger.* Early the next morning a helo arrives to take me to the carrier, stationed about twenty miles further out. As we take off I get a good look at the *Valley Forge* and the other ships assembled off Mogadishu. The fact that they are here on a humanitarian mission demonstrates that navies, as Admiral Hancock said, can do many positive things. No doubt they could do a lot of that in other parts of the world as well, but somehow I

suspect they won't get to it. Navies require strong political support, because they cost so much money. Being the world's good Samaritan is fine in theory, but the popularity of such missions may wane when the bills start coming in.

Even so, there's nothing wrong with a bit of positive thinking. Navies have proved very good at certain missions, and there's no doubt they'll keep doing those for many years to come. Mahan was right about sea control. On a planet that is nearly three-quarters covered by water, nations with global or regional ambitions don't have a choice. But there's something else Mahan said that now seems to have been forgotten: sea power also includes the ability to create markets and to carry the trade. And in that the United States and many other industrialized nations have fallen far behind.

I guess that is what distinguishes naval powers from true sea powers. In this day and age sea powers can no longer be measured solely in terms of the number of warships they possess. They are also measured according to how they are able to use the ocean in other ways. And perhaps most of all, they should be measured according to how they treat Mahan's great highway. But that's another part of this story.

Mineral Wealth

"R ocky and sparsely settled" is how *Den Norske Los (The Norwegian Pilot)* describes the Fensfjord in western Norway. And so it is on this early-June afternoon: a rocky and sparsely settled place that looks positively glorious under a deep blue sky. Sometimes a high-pressure
zone settles above this region, producing wonderful weather for days and even weeks on
end, and one feels fortunate to be here during that time. Just looking at the area—the
water, mountains, and islets sparkling in the sunshine—makes you feel healthier.

Not all of Fensfjord remains blissfully undeveloped, however. On its western edge is
the Mongstad Base, a supply base for the rich Oseberg oil field about eighty miles out in the
northern North Sea. Run by Norsk Hydro, one of Norway's largest oil companies, the
sprawling base stocks just about anything needed to keep a massive offshore oil installation
in business, from the omnipresent drilling and casing pipes to cement, chemicals, drilling
muds, food, fuel, and spares for every nut and bolt on the platforms.

Whatever may be needed out at the field is hauled back and forth by supply vessels,
three of which are docked along the quay when I arrive. One of them is the *Far Sky*, a
sturdy 250 feet long, built to handle the most atrocious conditions at sea. With her bright
red hull high at the bow and low at the stern, she is classified as an anchor-handling tug,
meaning that she spends a good bit of her time pulling platforms from one site in the North
Sea to another. But that is not her job at Mongstad. Like the *Far Scout* next to her, the *Far
Sky* is maintaining the daily link between the base and the platforms, and she is scheduled
to go out next.

Above: The *Far Sky* at the Mongstad supply base, ready to depart on another supply mission to the Oseberg
Field Center.

Left: Oseberg Bravo silhouetted against the rising sun. Never far away is the rescue boat, always on the alert
for any mishaps.

While I meet with shipment manager Eirl Marholm to check in on the ship, trucks and forklifts run back and forth between the storage areas and the dock, depositing casing pipes and a variety of small containers. Some are blue, containing spare parts; others are green, filled with food supplies; and a number are clearly marked Hazardous Materials—mostly chemicals used in drilling muds or in cleaning operations. All are lifted onto the *Far Sky*'s loading deck and positioned so that nothing can move. It takes a bit of mental planning to figure out how to do this, but the loading gang at Mongstad is experienced. Every once in a while they have to rearrange something, but other than that the process goes remarkably quickly.

As I board the *Far Sky* I am immediately struck by the size of everything about her. She is not particularly huge as ships go, but she looks oversized, as if someone had taken a regular tug and multiplied the dimensions by two or three. The equipment aboard looks oversized too. Cables about a foot in diameter are wound on massive winches. They hold hooks that weigh at least several tons in their own right. Even the shackles look like they were made for giants.

But it's not just the equipment that's big; so are the amounts of money involved. On her last towing job the *Far Sky* pulled in 175,000 Norwegian kroner a day—more than $25,000. On a job like this she will probably rate about $100,000 a week, which is still a good chunk. I have no idea of the value of her cargo, but considering that all this goes out at least once a day, it is clear that keeping a North Sea platform in operation is an expensive business. And that figure, in turn, pales in comparison with the cost of the platforms themselves. The Oseberg field contains three of them: Alpha and Bravo, which are linked by a bridge, and Charlie, which is located about nine miles further north. Oseberg A and B, along with a pipeline that delivers the oil on shore, required an investment of some 27 billion Norwegian kroner—well over $4 billion. Bringing Oseberg C on line added another $1.6 billion to the bill.

Naturally, all these investments will be recovered quite handsomely. The Oseberg field itself contains enough oil to keep Norway happy for at least twenty years, and it is just one of many along the Norwegian coast. It currently produces about 340,000 barrels a day—depending on daily oil price fluctuations, worth between $7 million and $8 million a day, or well over $2.5 billion a year. Taken as a whole, Norway produces nearly $16 billion worth of oil every year, all of it from its extremely generous continental shelf. And there is plenty left to pad the Norwegian treasury for many years to come.

Below: Supplies for another day on the Ose-berg platforms are loaded aboard the *Far Sky.*

Left: Far Sky wheelhouse.

The magnitude of these figures explains why the development of ocean resources has become such an important component of sea power. In fact, in less than fifty years the offshore industry has grown from a few offshore mining operations into a megabusiness that produces about 20 percent of the world's oil (along with a host of other things). It is no surprise, then, that this relative newcomer has firmly entrenched itself as a legitimate component of sea power, making the field considerably more complicated than it was in Alfred Thayer Mahan's time.

To be fair, Mahan could not have known. He never even referred to ocean resources in his grand sea power theory. Mahan did include access to minerals as one of its key elements, but he was primarily referring to deposits in overseas colonies, which he considered very important. To maintain these colonies, he added, a nation needed the traditional elements of sea power: a navy, for instance, to protect them, and a merchant fleet to transport people and resources back and forth.

Little could Mahan have known that the sea would one day become the source of these resources, rather than just the "highway" on which they were transported. Neither could he have known that once there was no more unclaimed dry land left on earth, nations seeking to expand their territory would begin to look at the sea, and even eye the seafloor itself as a quasi-colony. Nor could he have foreseen the dramatic changes in ocean law that this would trigger.

To appreciate these changes it helps to understand how ocean law developed. Over time two opposing theories developed in regard to ocean ownership: one holding that the sea is free and open to all, and the other suggesting that it can be owned—and thus controlled—by individual nations. The first of these theories is by far the oldest, having originated when nations began to trade with one another at sea. In the ancient Mediterranean, for instance, a body of rules emerged to cover the conduct of this commerce. Addressing such issues as losses at sea or disagreements among merchants from different countries, it proposed that the seas were free to be navigated—or used, for that matter—by all nations.

Similar rules were observed throughout the Middle Ages, although some of the Italian city-states asserted jurisdiction over large ocean areas. Venice, for instance, claimed the entire Adriatic, and there was little anyone could do about it. Further north, Scandinavian countries began to assert rights over their coastal waters as well, particularly in regard to fishing. England, on the other hand, had a different concern. To ascertain whether vessels sailing through its waters were pirates or traders, England demanded that ships in the English Channel lower their sails when passing a government vessel, so that the king's officers could inspect them. Any ship that failed to do so was subject to seizure—provided the king's officers could catch her, of course.

These minor infringements on the concept of a free and open sea were nothing compared with what would happen during the Age of Exploration. In 1494 Spain and Portugal drew a line from pole to pole 350 miles west of the Cape Verde Islands and decided that whatever lay west of it was Spanish, the remainder Portuguese. Naturally, this line did not have to do so much with the water that fell on either side as with the land, though both countries insisted that whatever waters fell under their control were to be navigated by their ships only. A suitable contribution to the Vatican treasury enticed the pope to approve the deal, so other nations took it seriously, at least initially.

Not surprisingly, both Portugal and Spain benefited enormously from this arrangement and the exclusive overseas trade that went along with it. But it could not last forever. Countries such as Holland and Britain were eager to trade with the Indies for themselves, and the moment they realized that neither Spain nor Portugal could enforce its preposterous claims, they made their move. By the late sixteenth century Dutch ships had begun sailing into "Portuguese" waters, despite repeated protests from Lisbon. One thing led to another, and before long the two nations opposed each other in a state of undeclared war.

Hugo Grotius's *Mare Liberum* popularized the theory that the seas are free and open to all nations.

Left: It takes a bit of planning to figure out how best to load the *Far Sky,* but the loading gang at Mongstad is experienced.

Guiding the *Far Sky* out of the Fensfjord toward the North Sea and the Oseberg Field Center is Captain Ollbjørn Austnes.

This tension would have a profound impact on the development of the law of the sea. In 1602 a fleet of Dutch ships captured a richly laden Portuguese carrack in the Straits of Malacca, causing an uproar not only in Lisbon but also in the Amsterdam headquarters of the newly founded Dutch East Indies Company. Several of the company's shareholders felt that this was an act of piracy, and they threatened to pull out. To avert a crisis, the company's board sought legal advice and asked Hugo Grotius, a young lawyer, to provide an opinion.

Grotius, who was only twenty-one at the time, set to work and produced an elaborate defense for the company. It was entitled *De Jure Praedae* (*On the Law of Prize of War*). "No one nation may justly oppose in any way two nations that desire to enter into contract with each other," he wrote, arguing that the Portuguese claim to exclusive trade with the Indies was unfounded. If this right to trade was not reinstated, he added, a nation like Holland had every right to fight for it. In his view, the capture of the Portuguese ship was therefore entirely justified.

By the time Grotius finished his work the crisis had passed, and *De Jure Praedae* was never published. But three years later the company needed Grotius again, this time to counter Spain's claim to exclusive trading rights with the West Indies. Grotius went back to his earlier work and pulled out the twelfth chapter, entitled "Mare Liberum" ("The Free Sea"). It was published this time, but again there was a settlement before it could be used. A few weeks later Holland faced yet another ocean-related crisis when Britain forbade Dutch herring fishermen to fish off its coasts without a license. The herring fishery was vital to the Dutch, so they immediately sent a delegation to London to try to talk the British out of their restrictions.

In *Mare Liberum* Dutch negotiators had a concise set of arguments as to why they considered the British action unjust. Though it had been written to defend the freedom of navigation, its arguments could easily be transposed to defend the freedom of fishing. "The sea, since it is as incapable of being seized as the air, cannot be attached to the possessions of any particular nation," Grotius had said. A bit further on he argued that "the sea is common to all, because it is so limitless." Everyone should be free to fish, in other words, because the sea is inexhaustible.

Unfortunately, Holland did not succeed in working out a settlement this time. Using Grotius's arguments, the Dutch insisted that the sea should be free and open to all. England, on the other hand, asserted that it held sovereign rights over the sea between England and the Continent, and that it could therefore do whatever it wished. It soon became clear that the disagreement could not be resolved by legal means. By the middle of the seventeenth century, war between the two rivals had become inevitable.

The three Anglo-Dutch wars that followed were a disaster for the Dutch. Though none of the ferocious naval battles fought on the North Sea was decisive, Holland lost thousands of its best seamen and never regained its maritime supremacy. The country's only consolation came on the legal front, because it did not take the British long to realize that Grotius's views on the freedom of the seas made sense. In fact, as they became the world's preeminent maritime power themselves, they became one of Grotius's staunchest advocates. Sea power did not necessarily require ownership of the sea, they discovered; it demanded control.

From then on, the freedom-of-the-seas concept became an accepted part of international law. There was one exception to this freedom: most nations agreed that they were entitled to a narrow belt of water along their coast, a zone that became known as the territorial sea. Unfortunately, they could not agree on its width. Some countries argued that the territorial sea should include all water in sight of land, while others suggested that it should extend as far as their command reached.

In the early eighteenth century Dutch jurist Cornelis van Bijnkershoek promoted the command option and proposed that it be defined according to the range of a shore-based cannon. Most nations agreed on the principle, but not on the range of their cannons. Hence, several nations accepted a five-kilometer limit (about three nautical miles), but in Scandinavia the width of the territorial sea was set at four miles. And Mediterranean cannons apparently shot much further than others, because there most countries chose six and some even ten miles.

Despite these varying interpretations, the law of the sea remained blissfully uncomplicated. There was a territorial sea and beyond that the "high seas," free and open to all. That state of affairs lasted until about fifty years ago, when nations began to realize that there was more to the sea than fishing and navigation; there were also valuable mineral resources. To determine to whom these riches belonged, the pendulum would begin to swing back toward more restrictions on the freedom of the seas.

Ten P.M. finds the *Far Sky* plowing at a leisurely 12 knots through an uncharacteristically smooth North Sea. It doesn't quite feel like evening yet, with the sun still high above the horizon and a temperature that stubbornly refuses to drop below the seventies. But I'm not complaining. This is the sort of ship that does a lot of pitching and rolling, especially when unloading cargo near a platform, and my stomach appreciates not having to deal with that.

Up in the large and luxurious wheelhouse, Captain Ollbjørn Austnes is on watch. "Ollbjørn is an old Viking name," he tells me in his singsong English. I have no reason to doubt it. Tall, blond, and bearded, he fits the description. Aside from him there are only seven others on the ship: a chief officer, two engineers, three ABs (able-bodied seamen), and a cook. Except for the cook, they all run two watches a day, from six to twelve, five weeks in a row. Then they get five weeks off to recover.

Like most of his crew, Ollbjørn comes from a seafaring family. "I grew up on a little coaster," he explains, "that went all over Scandinavia." He loved the life, but containers put a lot of the little coasters out of business, including the Austnes family's. So Ollbjørn joined Sverre Farstad and Company, owners of the *Far Sky* and about thirty other supply ships and anchor-handling tugs, and has been with them for the past seventeen years. He enjoys this job too, though he concedes that it can get "a little rough" in the North Sea. "Especially the winter southwesterlies," he adds. "They can really kill you." I nod appreciatively, though it is a little difficult to imagine today, with hardly a wave in sight.

Occasionally Edvin Johansen, the AB on duty, comes up to the wheelhouse. Edvin is a scrappy little guy whose face reflects thirty years of work at sea. "We're the warmest place in Europe right now," he informs me, as has everyone else I've met in Norway. But I feign surprise, not wanting to deny the Norwegians their brief moment in the sun. While we continue to discuss the merits of global warming, Edvin nonchalantly rolls a cigarette with one hand, which is a pretty tricky feat. I guess it comes in handy when it's blowing a gale and you need the other hand to hold on to something.

Aside from the cook and the engineer on duty, everyone else is asleep, so the ship feels quiet and empty. But I'm not about to turn in yet. Far in the distance, a small orange spot has emerged on the horizon. "Oseberg Alpha," Ollbjørn confirms, spreading out a map to show where we are. As we move on, more orange lights begin to appear: Oseberg Charlie, a bit to the right, and Veslefrikk, about two points off the bow.

The Oseberg field, I have been told, was named after a Viking burial ship that was found at the turn of the century and is now displayed in Oslo. With a corporate logo featuring a Viking longboat, Norsk Hydro quite logically chose that name for its prime field. But the name Veslefrikk intrigues me, so I ask Ollbjørn what it means. "Veslefrikk was a character in a fairy tale," he explains. "He was a little man, and this is a small field." Virtually all of the fields in the Norwegian sector have ties to mythology or fairy tales, Ollbjørn points out. "Right now we're sailing over Troll, who was a giant, and this is the largest gas field in the North Sea." So far it all makes sense.

Looking over the map, Ollbjørn continues his introduction to Norwegian mythology. "Here is Odin," he explains, pointing to a gas field southwest of Oseberg. "He was

Right: Finally the size of the platform becomes apparent. My first close look at Oseberg reminds me of science fiction images of future cities on distant planets.

the principal god of the Norsemen, the god of war and wisdom. And right next to it is Frigg, who was his wife. And a bit further south is Balder, who was one of his sons." Far to the south are the Valhall field (named after the hall where Odin entertained the warriors who had been killed in battle) and Gyda (named for Norway's first queen). Odin's eight-footed horse Sleipner is also represented, as are Brage, the god of poetry, and Gullfaks, a ship that could sail as fast on land as at sea. Further north, in the Norwegian Sea, are Heidrun and Draugen—the first a mythological goat that provided the fallen warriors at Valhall with an endless flow of liquor, and the second a mean water spirit. And even further north, well above the Arctic Circle, is Snohvit. "You can probably figure that one out for yourself," Ollbjørn concludes.

In his seventeen years on the North Sea, Ollbjørn has seen virtually all of them, on the Norwegian as well as on the British side, where the *Far Sky* often does duty moving platforms. "But Oseberg is one of the most impressive," he says. It's not just that the platforms are large; the living quarters are reportedly the best in the business. A competition was held to come up with the best design, with the winning entry proposing a plan that included a gymnasium, several recreation rooms, and a lounge with a large fireplace that alone cost several million kroner. "It's probably the most expensive fireplace in the world," Ollbjørn laughs. "Of course, you have to remember that all of this was planned when the barrel price was still close to $40 and the oil companies felt very rich."

Just before eleven the sun sets, and it gradually becomes darker. Ollbjørn has the radio tuned to some jazz station in Bergen, which keeps playing Miles Davis tunes, adding a bit of atmosphere. Meanwhile, the little orange spot of a while ago keeps growing larger and brighter and begins to resemble a platform, though we are still some fifteen miles away. We continue to chat about the North Sea, oil, and what oil has done for Norway, a topic on which just about everyone here has a strong opinion. Like most others, Ollbjørn feels that it has been something of a mixed blessing. Yes, it poured enormous amounts of money into the Norwegian economy, raising the standard of living, but it did so at the expense of high inflation, high unemployment, a somewhat "spoiled" younger generation, and other social ills. "But I don't know what we'd do without the oil," he adds.

At midnight Ollbjørn's watch is over, and first officer Per Gunnar Vasdal takes over. By now we are just a few miles away from the platform, and the size of this thing finally becomes apparent. As we move closer, it reminds me of the cities on distant planets depicted in science fiction novels: towering structures stuck on a narrow base and then widening as they reach skyward. What I'm seeing here is no different. From about a mile away at night, with the hissing gas flare casting an eerie glow, Oseberg Alpha and Bravo look positively futuristic. Jules Verne was on target, I reflect; we did build his cities at sea.

Per carefully maneuvers the *Far Sky* between the two platforms so that the unloading can begin. Then he quickly walks to the other side of the wheelhouse. There is another set of maneuvering controls here, as well as a much better view over the loading deck. He sits down and grabs the joystick, connected to four thrusters, that makes the ship move in any direction. But the point here is not to move; instead, Per uses the joystick to stay right under the huge platform crane, using the thrusters to counteract the effect of winds and waves. On a day like today it may seem relatively easy, but they do this, as Per explains, in waves of up to twenty feet and in winds of 40 knots. When it blows harder than that, they just "wait" away from the platform until it calms down a bit.

I'm not unhappy about witnessing this procedure during a perfectly calm night, though I realize I'm missing out on the real thing. I've seen the pictures of the supply and rescue ships being tossed around during one of these mean southwesterlies, showing what people have to face to extract the riches of the North Sea. The fact that these ships manage to do their job year after year without a single major accident is a terrific tribute to them and their crews.

If building cities at sea and dealing with abominable weather seems like a lot of trouble to obtain oil, consider how it was done in the past. A thousand years ago people began to obtain oil from the sea not by drilling for it, but by hunting whales. Eighteenth-century American whalers turned this hunt into a worldwide industry, involving hundreds of ships and thousands of men. They processed and refined the valuable oil and sent it as far as England to light homes and streets. They discovered scores of new uses for baleen, or whalebone, fashioning everything from buggy whips to skirt hoops out of it. And in the process they discovered, albeit belatedly, that the seas were not inexhaustible, and that some of its stocks could be hunted to near extinction.

This massive industry began innocently enough from shore-based stations along the coast of New England, in pursuit of migrating right whales. But soon there were few whales left close to shore, and New Englanders had to venture out in small boats that could stay out for a few days at a time. In 1712 one of these was driven far off-shore by a storm, smack into a herd of sperm whales. The crew managed to kill one and tow it back to Nantucket, where people expressed surprise at the catch; sperm whales were thought to be extremely rare. If the sighting was true, it was good news, because sperm-whale oil was of far better quality than the oil of right whales.

Before long the people of Nantucket were off to hunt sperm whales, discovering that the whale's lack of baleen was more than offset by the fine spermaceti oil found in its head—up to five hundred gallons of it. When brought into contact with air, the oil solidified into a waxy substance that could be pressed into virtually smokeless and odorless candles, which commanded excellent prices. An additional bonus was found

Previous page: First officer Per Gunnar Vasdal carefully maneuvers the *Far Sky* between the two platforms so that the supplies can be unloaded.

New England's whalers, who turned whaling into a worldwide industry, were among the first to discover that the sea's resources were not inexhaustible.

in the form of ambergris, an accretion of excrement sometimes found in the bowels of whales. When first recovered, it naturally smelled awful, but after a few days the ambergris hardened and actually began to exude a pleasant aroma. As a fixative for perfume, it turned out to be worth more than its weight in gold.

For much of the eighteenth century Nantucket dominated the sperm-whale hunt. In 1740 the island had some fifty whaling sloops, which brought in nearly five thousand barrels of oil valued at $25,000. Within ten years the value of this oil had quadrupled, enticing more people to equip vessels for the hunt. By 1775 there were 150 ships producing more than twenty-two thousand barrels, worth over $500,000. They ventured over the entire Atlantic, locating sperm-whale populations not only close to home in Newfoundland, but also off Bermuda, Guinea, Brazil, the West Indies, and the Azores. Unfortunately, by the late 1780s fewer and fewer whales were to be found on these grounds. Voyages grew longer as captains drove their ships to the far ends of the Atlantic in search of new populations. But none were found, and many a ship returned without a profitable cargo.

There was a vast ocean on the other side of the American continent, however, and to it the Yankee whalers turned next. The news that large sperm-whale herds had been found off the coast of Chile spread like wildfire along the Nantucket waterfront, and within months forty or fifty vessels were headed for the dangerous passage around Cape Horn. What they found on the other side exceeded their wildest expectations. Ships regularly returned with more than a thousand barrels of oil, making unbelievable profits in the course of a single voyage. By the turn of the century a hundred more had joined the hunt. The golden age of American whaling had arrived.

For a while Nantucket retained its position as the principal whaling center, but since its port was too shallow for the larger whalers, these moved on to other ports. Edgartown on nearby Martha's Vineyard soon possessed a sizable fleet of its own, but most of the whalers moved to New Bedford and the neighboring port of Fairhaven. By the 1850s nearly four hundred whalers—more than half of the entire world's fleet—were registered in New Bedford alone.

The returns were phenomenal. In 1858, for instance, the town's whalers brought in $6 million worth of whale oil and baleen, giving its twenty thousand inhabitants one of the highest per-capita incomes in the world. Some shipowners made veritable fortunes from whaling, and many a captain could retire comfortably at an early age. But this wealth came at a terrible price, as the many memorial plaques in New Bedford's Seamen's Bethel show. Hundreds of sailors were lost in confrontations with whales, and hundreds more were never seen again, their ships having vanished on the long and dangerous voyage.

There was yet another price to be paid for this wealth, though few gave it much thought during New Bedford's brief reign as the whaling capital of the world. Even the vast Pacific proved not large enough. In some years more than four thousand sperm whales were taken, and they began to become more difficult to find. The whalers never reflected on the damage they were causing. Instead, they switched to humpback and bowhead whales. Then these too began to be thinned out, requiring ships to stay away even longer before they were filled.

People began to realize that there were too many whalers chasing too few whales, but no one was about to show restraint. Whaling was seen as a god-given right, and few whalers left the business unless poor returns forced them to do so. In the process, New Bedford and its prosperous cousins committed commercial suicide. Longer voyages meant higher costs, which were tacked on to the price of whale oil. In 1845 a gallon of it could still be had for 80 cents; a few years later it had shot up to more than twice as much. At these rates lighting a house or a street became an expensive proposition. More important, at these rates it made sense to look for something cheaper.

It was not long before alternatives were found. One substance in particular proved promising, a substance that until then had been regarded mostly as a nuisance.

Called rock oil or petroleum, it especially annoyed people drilling for salt and fresh water, who often found it contaminating their wells. On the other hand, it was known to be flammable. George Washington, for instance, complained about a spring on his land that was "of so inflammable a nature as to burn freely as spirits." It was no surprise, then, that this substance was first on the list of potential alternatives to whale oil.

During the 1840s people managed to distill petroleum into a variety of burning fluids and lubricating oils. Though none of these products quite matched the quality of whale oil, they demonstrated that distillation could turn petroleum into something useful. This did not escape the attention of Samuel Keir, a Pittsburgh merchant who operated several contaminated brine wells in the wooded hills of northwestern Pennsylvania. Since he had to remove the oil from the wells anyway, Keir set up a small distillation still in 1850 to produce a lighter fraction, which he called carbon oil. The oil proved quite suitable as an illuminating fluid, and its price shot up quickly, from 50 cents a gallon to almost $2.00. At these rates petroleum turned from a nuisance into a valuable commodity.

Skimming oil by hand from wells or natural seepages was not very productive. There had to be a better way, and Keir's salt wells provided the answer. If drilling for brines occasionally struck oil, then presumably one could drill directly for oil and obtain far larger quantities. That, at least, was the opinion of New York lawyer George Bissell and New Haven banker James Townsend. Armed with an analysis from Yale chemist Benjamin Silliman, which stated that the petroleum sample they had obtained from Pennsylvania could "manufacture very valuable products," they decided to form America's first oil company. That way they could raise money to look for oil in a more organized manner.

The Pennsylvania Rock Oil Company, which later became the Seneca Oil Company, hired Edwin Drake, a retired railroad conductor who had convinced Townsend that he would be able to drill for oil. Accordingly, in 1859 Drake was sent to the company's property in Titusville, Pennsylvania, where he built a derrick and engine house and commenced drilling. At thirty feet the drill struck hard rock, and progress slowed to no more than a few feet a day. Drake assumed that the oil lay several hundred feet down, which would take weeks to reach at that rate, and his investors were getting impatient. But on 27 August, at a depth of barely seventy feet, the drill hit a reservoir. Oil began flowing to the surface in quantities larger than anyone had ever seen.

Drake's success marked the beginning of a veritable oil craze. By the end of 1860 there were seventy-four oil wells in and around Titusville. In 1861 the first flowing well was struck. It produced three hundred barrels a day—an unimaginable amount at that time—and people from all walks of life sped to the oil-producing regions, hoping to make a fortune. Oil was later discovered in West Virginia, Colorado, Kentucky, and Tennessee. Geologists and entrepreneurs fanned out across the continent, finding large amounts of oil in Texas, Oklahoma, and California as well.

By the late nineteenth century oil drillers had reached the edge of the continent, discovering that some of the oil fields continued offshore. To get to these deposits they built wooden piers to house their derricks, and they successfully recovered offshore oil as early as the 1890s. But these were no more than hesitant steps, never quite leaving the shore, for drilling at sea required more advanced technology than was available at the turn of the century.

It did not take long for this technology to be developed, however. Throughout the early years of the century the demand for oil continued to rise rapidly, especially as a result of the growing popularity of automobiles. To meet this demand, an intensive search for additional deposits was launched. Geologists were asked to formulate theories on the formation of oil, in the hope that this work would lead to further discoveries. It soon became clear that in addition to massive deposits on land, there was a great deal of oil off the coasts of the United States.

In response, American oil companies continued their explorations at sea. By the 1930s they had proven the viability of recovering oil from platforms that were no longer tied to the land, first in inland waters and later at sea. The first of these appeared in 1937, about a mile off the Louisiana coast. Built by the Superior and Pure Oil Company, it struck oil about a mile deep. Exploiting the Gulf of Mexico, and in fact all of the world's oceans, now became just a matter of time.

～～～

Just over fifty years separate the first Gulf of Mexico platform and the Oseberg installation, but it might as well be five hundred. There simply isn't much of a comparison in terms of size and technology. The small platform that pioneered offshore oil recovery in the Gulf of Mexico weighed less than a thousand tons and operated in fourteen feet of water. Oseberg Alpha, in contrast, weighs more than six hundred thousand tons and is built in 340 feet of water. Ten, twenty years ago this would have been considered out of the question.

Senior safety officer Øivind Berg, who is waiting for me when I arrive on the platform, laces his introductory briefing with more examples of the "impossibles" of yesteryear now firmly proved feasible. There is the pipeline from Oseberg to Norway through the deep Norwegian Trench, for instance, or the system that injects gas from the massive Troll field into the oil deposits. Øivind also mentions predrilled wells and wells that diverge from the platform in all directions. All of these features were considered unthinkable just a few years ago, proving that little is impossible when large amounts of money are involved.

Below: For some time rock oil, or petroleum, was scooped up from salt wells and oil springs, to be sold as a miracle cure.

Left: The rising demand for petroleum set the stage for former railroad conductor and jack of all trades Edwin Drake, seen here in front of his derrick at Titusville, Pennsylvania.

Below left: Only fifty years separates the earliest Gulf of Mexico platform from the Oseberg installation, but the two have little in common.

Following page: The Oseberg Field Center.

After the briefing Øivind offers me a guided tour. We first head for the living quarters, located on the windward side of Oseberg Alpha so that in case of an emergency, prevailing winds would keep the area somewhat protected. As Ollbjørn had implied aboard the *Far Sky*, the setup is positively luxurious. We walk through a movie theater, a gymnasium with a full basketball court, weight rooms, a solarium, a hospital, a library, and then the lofty lounge with its famous fireplace. It is a bit disorienting; one just doesn't expect these things in the middle of the northern North Sea.

Aside from these amenities, there are 284 cabins on the platform. They are small but attractively decorated in light pastel shades. Considering that the three hundred people who work here receive liberal leave (two weeks of work are followed by either three or four weeks off), glorious meals, and wages that are among the highest in Norway, I begin to understand why there is such a long waiting list for offshore jobs.

At first Oseberg was strictly a man's world, but that has clearly changed. During the tour I notice plenty of women in a variety of jobs, even in the drilling tower. "All jobs were opened to women in 1989," Øivind explains. "The moment they arrived, deodorant sales at the store shot up 700 percent." I nod, imagining Oseberg's female contingent lining up to buy toiletries, but Øivind corrects me. "No," he clarifies, "it wasn't the women who began buying these things. It was the men."

Thus Oseberg became a nicer-smelling place as well as a nicer place in general. There is a pleasant, relaxed atmosphere throughout the living area, an impression later confirmed by platform manager Svein Vaksdal. Personality problems are the least of his worries. "There simply isn't enough time for people to get on one another's nerves," he says when I meet him in his office. "People here work twelve hours a day, from seven to seven either at night or during the day, for two weeks in a row. That isn't long enough to create the tensions you might find on a ship. Besides, people are too busy with their jobs."

Svein doesn't have to think long when I ask him what, then, is mostly on his mind. "Safety," he answers. "We have an awful lot of gas going through this platform, so there's always the possibility of a leak." And he doesn't need to be reminded of what a leak can do to a platform. On 6 July 1988 a gas explosion ripped apart the Piper Alpha platform in the British sector of the North Sea. Only sixty-four of the workers aboard survived. Their 167 colleagues never had a chance.

To prevent explosions, people are constantly monitoring for gas leaks, and the safety measures they follow are draconian. Before I head out into the work areas, for instance, I am asked to remove every battery from my camera, down to the tiny lightmeter battery, because the safety managers don't want them around. Regular fire, safety, and evacuation drills ensure that the emergency routines become second nature. "All of them are unannounced," Svein adds, "to keep people on their toes. Sometimes we even throw a dummy overboard, just to make sure that the crew aboard the rescue boat is alert as well."

Even so, it is clear that the possibility of an emergency, however remote, is on Svein's mind. "A crew of three hundred is a big responsibility," he admits, "and combining their safety with the need to keep production stable can make it even harder." These are not mutually exclusive responsibilities, he adds, but they lead to difficult decisions. He just received notice, for instance, that there is a small gas leak from a slightly corroded pipe on Oseberg Bravo. Obviously the pipe needs to be fixed, but to do that some section of the production would have to be shut down, because no one likes to weld near gas. And shutting down production may mean several million kroner down the drain. "I never cease to be amazed at the amounts of money that are involved in day-to-day decisions," Svein concludes.

After ensuring that I am entirely battery-free, Øivind guides me around the various components of Oseberg Alpha. Adjoining the living quarters are the power generators, which produce enough power to keep a city of fifty thousand people in business.

Maintaining a link with the "beach" are
regular helicopter flights.

Next to the generators are a number of complicated-looking modules, which separate the well stream into gas, oil, and water before pumping the oil onward to the mainland. The gas that is recovered is reinjected into the field by means of a compressor module to enhance recovery. Oseberg Alpha also receives enormous amounts of gas via a separate pipeline from the Troll gas field some thirty miles away. After processing, it is injected into the oil deposits as well, thereby allowing as much as 55 percent of the oil in the field to be recovered.

Setting up this gas-injection system required a $600 million investment, Øivind explains, but every additional percent of oil that can be sucked out of Oseberg repays that investment many times over. Besides, most of the gas that is moved from Troll to Oseberg can be recouped when Oseberg switches from oil to gas production in another fifteen years or so. If gas prices have gone up by then, Norsk Hydro and its partners will turn a tidy profit on this operation.

The tour of the platform makes clear that Oseberg is a showcase installation in more than its accommodations. It is the first (and only) installation to deliver its oil directly to Norwegian soil, it is the first to use predrilled wells, and it is the first to make use of an elaborate gas-injection system. The amounts of money that were needed to bring it to this point are mind-boggling, but then again so are the amounts of money that are being (and will continue to be) made. And this is but one field on Norwegian soil. Time and time again the image of a modern-day Heidrun comes to mind, with the brave Norwegian warriors not sucking liquor from the goat's udder but cashing in on a nearly endless flow of oil. If ever there was a winner in the offshore oil sweepstakes, I reflect, it must be Norway.

Actually, Norway did not have to do much to cash in on the jackpot. Much of the preparatory legal work, the difficult task of determining to whom this oil belonged, was handled by the United States, which fifty years ago was just about the only country with the technology to recover oil at sea. By 1941 several offshore wells had been drilled in the Gulf Of Mexico, one of which was about two miles from shore—just one mile short of where the United States' territorial sea, and thus its jurisdiction, ended. So naturally people began to wonder about what to do if they wanted to drill beyond that limit. To whom should they apply for permission? To whom did that oil belong, anyway?

If international law was applied, it could be argued that the oil belonged to no one. After all, if the prevailing freedom-of-the-sea concept applied to all of the ocean beyond territorial waters, the seafloor could be considered *res nullius*—a legal no man's land. The oil, in other words, would be fair game for anyone with the technology to recover it.

The United States made sure that the seafloor would not remain a legal no man's land for long. During the war years some of President Franklin D. Roosevelt's advisers began expressing concern over America's coastal resources. On the one hand, they argued, there were the coastal fisheries, some of which needed protection. But far more important, there was offshore oil as well. And with wartime oil consumption dipping deeply into land-based reserves, the country was going to need those offshore resources.

Harold Ickes, Roosevelt's secretary of the interior, summed up the situation in a letter to the president. "I draw your attention," he wrote, "to the importance of the Continental Shelf not only to the defense of our country, but more particularly as a storehouse of natural resources." What were those resources? In Ickes's view the continental shelf provided "a fine breeding place for fish of all kinds," and "since it is a continuation of our continent, it probably contains oil and other resources similar to those found in our States." Ickes then went on to make a very important recommendation: "I suggest the advisability of laying the ground work now for availing ourselves fully of the riches in this submerged land and in the waters over them."

The secretary of the interior obviously recognized the legal scope of what he was proposing. "The legal and policy problems involved, both international and domestic, are many and complex," he said. "In the international field, it may be necessary to evolve new concepts of maritime territorial limits beyond three miles, and of the right to occupy and exploit the surface and the subsoil of the open sea."

Roosevelt was taken by the idea. He sent Ickes's letter to Cordell Hull, his secretary of state, with a handwritten note. "I think Harold Ickes has the right slant on this," it said. "For many years I have felt that the old three mile limit should be superseded by a rule of common sense." Roosevelt even went on to give a little example of what he meant by common sense: "For instance the Gulf of Mexico is bounded on the South by Mexico and on the North by the United States. It seems to me that the Mexican Government should be entitled to drill for oil in the Southern half of the Gulf and we in the Northern half of the Gulf. That would be far more sensible than allowing some European nation, for example, to come in there and drill."

These informal exchanges led to formal meetings on the topic, and three years later Roosevelt's successor did exactly what was needed to bring a bit of common sense, Roosevelt-style, to the law of the sea. In a proclamation dated 28 September 1945, Harry Truman asserted the United States' right to control and exploit the resources and the subsoil of its continental shelf, basically bringing all of it under American jurisdiction. There was also a proclamation on fisheries, in which the United States asserted rights to exploit and manage "certain high seas fisheries."

Before these proclamations were issued, their text was run by some of America's allies and neighbors to assess the reaction. Not that any reaction would have made much difference. From the records of the various meetings it is clear that Washington was not about to let others interfere. The government simply took the initiative and informed the rest of the world that nothing in international law could prevent a state from claiming the mineral resources off its own coast. It was a rather subjective interpretation of the law—or, rather, of the lack thereof— especially since there was not a single precedent for a claim of this nature. But then again, at the end of the war the United States was by far the most powerful country in the world. That position allowed it to dictate the rules.

Whatever the motivations, the first Truman Proclamation became a landmark document. In retrospect, it was nothing less than the first step toward the enclosure of the oceans, a process that continues to this day. But at the time it seemed to make sense. Though some nations reacted with suspicion to the American move, most thought it a good idea. Geologically speaking, the continental shelf did form part of the continent, so it seemed reasonable to suggest that its resources belonged to the coastal state. Besides, who knew what was out there, anyway?

Nonetheless, it soon became clear that the United States had opened a legal can of worms. For one thing, states like California and Louisiana, which were already producing offshore oil, felt that the continental shelf should be under their control rather than the federal government's. It took several years to resolve the ensuing dispute. And there was not only domestic trouble. A month after the Truman Proclamation, Mexico decided not only to follow the American example but to go a little further. In its declaration, it claimed the Mexican continental shelf as well as its "superjacent" resources, a legal term meant to include the fish above the shelf. This position raised concerns in Washington, because many American fishermen operated in these waters. But with the United States having started this entire process in the first place and having created new "law" to suit its own needs, its complaints sounded hypocritical. Mexico ignored them. American fishing vessels that violated the Mexican claim were detained and forced to pay a hefty fine.

The Mexican example was soon outdone, anyway. Taking the opportunity to adjust supposed injustices, Latin American and Caribbean nations began to extend not just their jurisdiction but their sovereignty over the sea and the seafloor out to a distance of two hundred miles, in effect claiming a territorial sea of that size. Argentina started in 1946, and a year later Chile, Ecuador, and Peru followed suit. Costa Rica made a similar claim in 1948, and El Salvador in 1950. Nations elsewhere began to claim larger chunks of ocean too, leading to a veritable escalation of maritime claims. Before long there was so much confusion over who supposedly owned what that the U.S. State Department geographer Whittemore Boggs was forced to admit in his 1949 Annual Report to Congress, "Never have national claims in adjacent seas been so numerous, so varied, or so inconsistent."

This confusing situation created problems. All nations had for a long time agreed that navigation through territorial waters was subject to "innocent passage." This meant that ships had the right to sail through any nation's territorial sea, provided their passage was not prejudicial to the peace, good order, or security of the coastal state. In practice, this rule required submarines to navigate on the surface and to show their flag when in territorial waters, since a submerged passage could be perceived as less than innocent. No one had any problems with that in the case of three- or even six-mile territorial seas, but two hundred miles was another matter. Neither the United States nor the Soviet Union wanted its submarines to have to pop up whenever they were within two hundred miles of some other nation's coast.

There were many other uncertainties as well, and they demanded resolution. Fortunately, around this time the newly created United Nations embarked on its ambitious task of codifying international law, and the legal uncertainties of the law of the sea presented a splendid challenge. Here indeed was a situation that required clarification and that could be solved only through international cooperation. The General

Assembly accordingly requested its legal experts to prepare draft articles on the legal regime of the oceans. Seven years later they submitted four proposed conventions: one dealing with the legal status of the high seas, another focusing on the territorial sea, the third examining the continental shelf, and the last proposing measures regarding fisheries.

From February to April of 1958 delegates from eighty-six countries filed into Geneva to review these drafts and to codify them into international law. The meeting was known as the United Nations Conference on the Law of the Sea. Later, a "First" was added to the title, because more conferences would follow. But no one knew that at the time. Indeed, most delegates assumed that the meeting would do away once and for all with the uncertainties surrounding the legal status of the sea.

At the conclusion of the conference the participating nations approved four conventions, all of them along the lines of the drafts they had received. As intended, these conventions did much to clarify the legal regime of the oceans. They divided the sea into different zones over which various degrees of jurisdiction could be exercised. Coastal states, for instance, could continue to claim a good deal of control over the territorial sea. It was in fact considered part of their territory, and they could regulate it strictly, provided they respected the principle of innocent passage. In the contiguous zone, coastal states were allowed to check immigration and health provisions as well as fishery regulations. The Convention on the Continental Shelf gave coastal states sovereign rights over the resources of the continental shelf, as the Truman Proclamation had called for. And finally, the high seas remained a common zone where the freedom of the sea applied.

Unfortunately, the First Law of the Sea Conference failed to resolve some tricky questions. There was still no agreement on the width of the territorial sea, for instance, even though this was the issue that had started the entire process in the first place. Some nations stuck to three miles, others claimed four or six, and the Latin American nations continued to insist on their unilaterally declared two hundred.

There was also uncertainty about the other zones. Everyone had agreed on the meaning of such concepts as the continental shelf, but there was no consensus on how far it actually extended. The relevant convention described the shelf as the seabed adjacent to the coast "to a depth of 200 meters, or beyond that limit, to where the depth of the superjacent waters admits of the exploitation of the natural resources of the sea bed." The continental shelf, in other words, did not end where geology specified it did. Instead, it was tied to the reach of mining technology. As definitions go it was a bit of a farce, but it was the best the various participants could come up with. Besides, most of them thought that mining the sea beyond two hundred meters was out of the question for many years to come.

But it wasn't the issue of extent that caused the most problems. There were also no precise rules on how these various new ocean zones were to be divided among neighboring states. And this grew more relevant when it became clear that the ocean floor was much richer than originally expected. If anything, everyone in Geneva agreed that there was a pie, but not how large it was or how it was to be cut up.

It was in the North Sea that these questions first began to be raised in a major way. Here was one of the richest pies of all: a region surrounded by oil-starved industrial countries, all of which had been told in the mid-1960s that they might have a lot of the stuff sitting off their coasts. No wonder this led to some interesting situations.

To find out how much was known about the North Sea's oil potential at the time, I went to Norsk Hydro's operational headquarters in Sandsli near Bergen to see Eigill Nysæther, the company's chief geologist. A tall and slender man with wonderfully

As Norsk Hydro's chief geologist, Eigill Nysæther has kept an eye on North Sea oil developments for the past thirty years.

kind eyes, Eigill has been involved with the North Sea in one function or another for the last thirty years, from the first optimistic reports and disappointments to the boom years when people began to realize that there was far more oil in the North Sea than anyone could have imagined.

Quickly gathering that I am basically illiterate as far as petroleum geology is concerned, Eigill first introduces me to the world of oil exploration—a world that uses such tools as magnetometers, gravimeters, and seismographs. "I consider myself an explorer," he says, choosing his words precisely. "And like other explorers, we get to see things no one else has seen before." He then shows me one of these things, a seismic chart of the bottom of some part of the North Sea, and explains what he sees in it. To me it looks a bit fuzzy, though there are clearly a number of layers, representing the various sediments that have been deposited over the past three hundred million years. But what they are, and how deep or extensive, is anyone's guess.

Eigill's point is not to explain how to interpret these layers, but to show me what a "structure"—a potential trap for oil and gas—looks like. Actually, it is clearly visible. While most of the layers run more or less horizontally, he points to one area where they have been slanted by an enormous force, creating a cap under which oil could have collected. There are more potential structures in this particular chart, but they are either too deep or too high up. "We know that in the North Sea all source rock was laid down some 140 million years ago," Eigill explains, "so to look for anything older or younger doesn't make sense."

Next Eigill explains the importance of having the right conditions, because oil will develop only when the temperature remains between 100° and 150° for a very long time. Figuring out these conditions over geological time is tricky because the subsoil's temperature depends on depth and the type of sediments, and it will change with each successive deposit. Today, computer programs can help reconstruct the source rock's temperature, but I get the impression that the geologist's experience and interpretative skills far surpass what machines can come up with.

If there is a structure, and if it is positioned in a source-rock area that may have had the right temperatures, Eigill concludes, the geologists recommend that a well be drilled. "Drilling wells is an expensive business," he adds, "but we encourage the companies to drill because a well will provide much additional information, even when it's dry." Seismic sections provide no more than a partial picture. It is not until a well is drilled and the cuttings are retrieved or a well log is obtained that geologists can actually begin to check whether their assumptions were right.

"This is how it was in the North Sea in the mid-1960s," Eigill continues. At the time, seismic graphs showed plenty of promising structures in the North Sea, but no wells had been drilled, so no one was certain whether there was any oil. But the promise was enough to set the system in motion. Within months of the first hints of oil and gas, Great Britain, Norway, Germany, Denmark, and the Netherlands had invited the oil companies to help assess the potential of their coastal zones. But before they could get too serious about this, they had to divide the pie. Not surprisingly, that was easier said than done.

The problem was that the Geneva Convention on the Continental Shelf did not provide much guidance on how to do this. "Where the same continental shelf is adjacent to the territories of two adjacent States," it said, "the boundary of the continental shelf shall be determined by agreement between them." That wasn't much help; of course states would first try to work something out among themselves. If that didn't work, and "unless another boundary is justified by special circumstances," the line was to be drawn by "application of the principle of equidistance from the nearest points of the baselines from which the breadth of the territorial sea of each State is measured." Put more simply, the boundary was to be drawn as far from the coast of one nation as it was from the other. A similar arrangement, consisting of a "median" line, was proposed for states with opposing coasts.

For some countries these rules were sufficient. Norway and Britain agreed in 1965 on a median line to delineate their respective areas. Further south, Denmark and the Netherlands reached similar agreements with their overseas neighbor. As far as adjoining boundaries were concerned, Norway and Denmark agreed on an equidistant line in 1966, but when Denmark and the Netherlands adopted a similar course one year later, they ran into difficulties. It wasn't that they couldn't agree; the problem was that they didn't consult Germany, which was located in between.

It does not require a legal background to understand why there was a problem. To determine their common boundary up to the median line with Britain, Denmark and the Netherlands had counted on equidistant boundaries with Germany, coming to an arrangement that netted both of them a nice, big slice of the North Sea's continental shelf. But Germany realized that if it went along with the Danish-Dutch agreement, the concave form of its coast would yield it no more than a tiny fraction of the North Sea and its presumed riches. Bonn was unwilling to accept that, arguing that equidistance was not a definite rule. Like everyone else, the Germans had high hopes that there would be oil off their coast, but what Holland and Denmark were proposing would deny them the most promising areas.

Representatives from the three governments tried to work out a solution, but they did not get very far. Instead, they agreed to take the dispute to the International Court of Justice in the Hague and ask it to resolve the deadlock. Several months later the court issued its conclusion. The ruling basically agreed with the German view that equidistance was not an absolute rule. Instead, the court suggested that additional factors should be taken into account, such as the configuration of the coast and the geological structure of the continental shelf itself. The court also recommended that a certain degree of proportionality be figured in. After all, Germany was far bigger than Denmark and the Netherlands combined, and the mere fact that it had a concave coast should not prevent it from sharing in the offshore prize. The ruling was accepted, and shortly thereafter the three countries agreed on boundaries that gave Germany a larger part of the North Sea's wealth.

A few months later, at the end of 1969, the first oil was discovered in the North Sea. Several wells had been drilled by that time, but all of them turned out to be dry, and many people had begun to assume that there was no oil at all. But the core that came up from the Ekofisk area in Norway's southern sector showed that the drill had gone through two hundred meters of oil—"an unbelievable amount," as Eigill puts it. From then on things sped up quickly, with new discoveries being announced almost monthly. Fortunately, all the boundaries had been laid down. If the North Sea countries had known in advance how large a fortune they were carving up, the process might well have taken a good deal longer.

 Things did not get easier, however. The energy crises of the early 1970s did away with the era of cheap oil. Prices shot from less than a dollar a barrel to ten and later twenty times as much. As a result, the search for offshore oil became more important than ever before. Coastal nations began to realize that with a little luck, their continental shelf could turn into a veritable gold mine. Unfortunately, that turned just about every continental shelf area with oil, proven or even assumed, into a potential conflict area. The decision of the International Court of Justice did not do much to alleviate this situation. It might have worked for the North Sea, but the court's many criteria almost invited quarreling nations to pick and choose, and to apply those rules that best suited their claim for the largest possible share of the pie.

Not surprisingly, then, the problems encountered in the oil-rich North Sea reappeared elsewhere. In the South China Sea, for instance, are the Spratly Islands, a group of about thirty-three islands and four hundred reefs and atolls that no one, until recently, showed much interest in. That changed when there were hints that the continental shelf around the Spratlys looked promising in terms of oil. All of a sudden China claimed that the archipelago had been an "inalienable part" of its territory since time immemorial. Unfortunately, Taiwan and Vietnam made the same assertion. And before long Malaysia and the Philippines had staked out claims as well, not just on paper but by building up the islets so that they projected above the water at all times, and then posting troops on them.

Anything that involves conflicting claims among these countries, especially claims involving oil, is a potential source of trouble. In 1988 China and Vietnam clashed when Chinese troops landed on some "Vietnamese" islands. The ensuing action was brief, but it sank two Vietnamese patrol boats and left scores dead. China, which currently occupies about seven islands, is particularly adamant about the Spratlys, emphasizing its irrefutable claim to sovereignty time and time again. In fact, China does not even want to discuss the issue unless the other contenders accept that claim. The other countries are concerned about China's influence, but they are not about to hand over the region. Taiwan, which like China claims all of the Spratlys, occupies only one island but has been there since the 1950s. Vietnam, China's main opponent in the dispute, has troops stationed on about twenty reefs and islands but is willing to negotiate its claim with Malaysia and the Philippines, both of which have sent troops to a couple of islands as well.

Particularly interesting about the various claims are the reasons that supposedly back them up. When occupying its share of the islands, for instance, China stated that it was doing so to install meteorological instruments. Malaysia has admitted to a great interest in developing the region's tourism, an interest that naturally required it to claim some of the islands as well. The Philippines, on the other hand, is mostly interested in "conservation." So far most of these countries have managed to avoid mentioning that the region's oil potential might be playing a role too.

The oil-rich Middle East has experienced disagreements as well. The island nation of Bahrain, for instance, has its eye on the Hawar Islands, just off the coast of Qatar. But since the islands are believed to be on top of a vast oil field, Qatar is not about to hand them over. In fact, it has taken the dispute to the International Court of Justice, with a request for a judgment on the maritime boundaries between the two sheikdoms.

Further east, Abu Dhabi and Iran both claim highly productive Abu Musa in the Persian Gulf, midway between the two countries. The island had been under joint jurisdiction for many years, but Iran recently annexed the territory, deporting a good many of its inhabitants. Abu Dhabi has filed a protest, but no resolution is in sight.

In the Red Sea, meanwhile, Egypt and Sudan are at odds over a rich oil sector south of Port Sudan, a dispute directly attributable to the boundaries drawn by Britain on the map of the Middle East earlier this century. Both countries have offered concessions in the same area, though no oil companies will commit unless Egypt and Sudan resolve the conflict. Unfortunately, neither country has been willing to compromise, so the potential for conflict continues to grow.

There have also been disputes in the Americas, with Chile and Argentina arguing over the Beagle Channel (a case that was eventually mediated by the Holy See); Canada and France bickering over a small group of islands off the coast of Nova Scotia; Columbia and Venezuela disputing the delineation of the Gulf of Venezuela; and even such good friends as Canada and the United States at odds over the division of the Gulf of Maine. In most of these cases a solution was eventually reached, albeit after long negotiations. But sometimes the situation runs out of hand, as in 1982 when Argentina and Great Britain both claimed the Falkland Islands. The subsequent war was fought over more than the resources surrounding the islands, but no one will deny that they played a major role. Argentina still refuses to recognize Britain's sovereignty over the islands, and it may never do so, given the large oil reserves believed to be there.

Finally, Europe has experienced its own share of disagreements. During the early 1970s, the already poor relations between Greece and Turkey deteriorated over differences on how to split the continental shelf of the Aegean Sea. The reason was simple: almost all of the Aegean islands were Greek, which would normally give Greece control over the entire region. But this was not a normal situation. Control and ownership of the Aegean Sea had been a matter of contention for thousands of years, and the fact that both nations now believed that there might be oil did not make things easier.

The issue remains unresolved, and given the less than cordial relations between Greece and Turkey, it continues to be a potential flashpoint. As recently as 1987 there was a flareup over oil exploration rights in the northern Aegean. In fact, if Greek and Turkish newspapers were to be believed, the situation approached war fever. Fortunately, and this may well be the only saving grace, oil experts believe that there may not be enough oil in the northern Aegean to argue over.

Another potential conflict area is the Black Sea, which is believed to hold very substantial oil reserves. The former Soviet Union and Turkey agreed on a delineation of their territorial waters some time ago, but no agreements have been worked out since the map of Eastern Europe was redrawn. Given the political tensions between Russia and the Ukraine as well as Georgia, agreement may prove difficult to reach. The Ukraine will also have to work out a boundary with Romania, currently the only offshore oil producer in the region.

Norway also has one boundary yet to settle: its northern boundary with Russia, which involves a good chunk of the Barents Sea. Norway favors the equidistant line because that would give it a greater part, while Russia prefers a perpendicular line, following the meridian that runs through the border. A good deal of progress has been made on this issue, though only recently. In the days of the Soviet Union much more was at stake here than hydrocarbons. Equally important was the question of passage for the Soviet Union's White Sea Fleet, and especially its many submarines. The matter became so crucial to the Soviets that they even planted a spy in the cabinet of Norway's Jens Evensen, who was in charge of the negotiations.

Fortunately, submerged-passage rights are somewhat less important today, so the boundary issue again is mostly a matter of dividing resources. There is a massive amount of gas in the Barents Sea, some of which the two countries now intend to

Oseberg's food offerings make life in the middle of the North Sea quite bearable.

develop jointly. They also have a good deal of fish to share, over which they recently signed a fisheries agreement. It too establishes a boundary, though presumably one that will diverge somewhat from the line that will eventually cut through the northern continental shelf.

The fruits of this agreement, and of Norway's other rich waters, are on semipermanent display in Oseberg's dining hall. Lunch invariably includes heaps of smoked salmon, a salmon mousse, marinated salmon, poached salmon, and an array of lesser cousins such as cod, herring, and mackerel—smoked, steamed, pickled, fermented—you name it. Dinner includes the same, along with several choices of hot entrees and glorious desserts. Oseberg obviously takes its food seriously, I notice while making my selection and paying tribute to the catering staff's efforts.

Since there isn't a drop of alcohol to be found on the platform, there isn't much lingering over meals. Most people come in and clear out in fifteen minutes or so, presumably because they are rushing back to their jobs. But Øivind and I are not in such a hurry, so it is after our meals that we talk about boundary and other oil-related issues.

Intrigued that a country that makes so much money from oil still manages to operate at a deficit, I also inquire about that. It turns out that most of the oil revenues

The drilling tower.

Right: Oseberg Bravo, with the drilling derrick, is connected to the main platform by a bridge.

go into the country's massive welfare system and its disproportionately large bureaucracy. The benefits to Norwegians are considerable: child-care grants, free education, sickness benefits, generous (seven-month) maternity leaves, and even funeral grants. But there are also costs. After all, this is the country of the 40-kroner ($6.00) pack of cigarettes and the 40-kroner beer, the country where that universal currency gauge, the Big Mac, commands a hefty 35 kroner ($5.50). Even gas, of which Norway has so much, sells for 28 kroner ($4.50) a gallon—more than in virtually all of Europe. It makes me wonder what this country would have done without the massive oil jackpot off its coast.

It is also after lunch that I find out about some of the things that are not written up in the corporate brochures. Particularly intriguing is the case of the German submarine that bumped into Oseberg Bravo in 1988. "It just sailed into the legs and got stuck," Øivind confirms. "I guess they didn't have their charts marked up."

While speculating about the unfortunate captain's subsequent assignments, we head toward the B platform. Connected to the main platform by a 350-foot bridge, Oseberg Bravo is where the actual drilling takes place. Prior to installing the steel-jacket platform in late 1987, Norsk Hydro predrilled eight wells here, enabling the structure to come on line in a matter of months. In fact, the company projected a production start of 1 December 1988, which just about everyone in the industry thought quite impossible. "We made it with fifteen minutes to spare," Øivind tells me as we climb up many flights of stairs toward the derrick. "At 11:45 P.M. that day Oseberg Bravo produced its first oil."

Since then several more wells have been drilled. There is room for forty-two of them, of which number 12 is currently in progress. When we arrive in the drilling derrick, three roughnecks in mud-splattered overalls are wrestling with chains and steel tubulars, adding sections of pipe to the drill string. The pipes strike me as remarkably thin, but the drill string is already several miles long, pushing the drill bit through 140 million years of sediments to another corner of the field.

A few feet from the drill string is a small control cab, from which the driller and his assistants operate the various hoist and rotary controls. It is filled with strange-looking charts and controls, which the driller briefly explains. I also meet the mud engineer, who is responsible for adding a host of strange chemicals to the drilling mud. Together they are debating when to "trip" the drill string so that the worn-out drill bit can be replaced. This requires the removal of several miles of pipe—a very time-consuming process, but there isn't much they can do about it. A worn-out drill bit simply doesn't give them the precision they need.

Well number 12 is actually very complicated, Øivind explains as we move on. First, it moves at an angle away from the platform. Then, at a depth of a mile or so, it turns horizontal for several more miles toward one of the furthest reaches of the field. Horizontal wells are great, Øivind adds, because they create a pressure gradient and thus boost the field's recovery rate. They also extend the reach of a single platform by many miles. But getting the drill bit to change direction—left or right, up or down—at exactly the right spot is a tricky operation.

Since I am interested in finding out how the drillers actually achieve that level of precision, Øivind takes me to a small office near the derrick. Inside, Roland Perssom, the directional drilling supervisor, is paging though his *Navi Drill Handbook*, which must be something akin to the directional driller's Bible. Roland is Swedish but has obviously spent a good bit of time in Houston. "What we do is all a matter of experience and weight," he says with a Texas drawl. Then he explains what he means by that. I gather that there are not any "smart" drill heads yet, so the process of getting the drill string to move in a certain direction has to be directed from the surface, by adjusting the rotation and orientation of the drill string and occasionally adding weight.

The scope of what this really involves doesn't quite sink in until Roland makes an analogy. "Suppose you're a dentist," he says, "and your office is on the eighth floor,

and your patient is sitting on the first floor of the building next to yours. Now imagine being asked to fill a cavity with a tiny drill from that distance. It sounds impossible, doesn't it? And yet that's exactly what we're doing here, only on a much larger scale. Whether it's a dentist's drill or an oil drill, the principle remains the same."

I am halfway glad Roland decided on a career in oil rather than in dentistry, but it is an impressive feat nonetheless. Since he has worked on platforms all over the world, I next ask him whether there are any limits on water depths as far as offshore oil recovery is concerned. "Technologically there really aren't," he replies. "If you go over a certain depth, you would have to operate from a 'floater,' either a drilling ship or a semisubmersible rig, but it can be done. The key question is whether it can be done economically."

This is a response I often hear on Oseberg. Certain things remain impossible, of course, but in general the technology is not as much of a limiting factor as the economics. Once the money falls into place, the rest usually follows. The money, in turn, depends on the price of oil. If the price is high, companies are willing to invest more readily in new technologies. If it is low, they stick to what is already in place.

 With the price of oil increasing dramatically during the 1970s, offshore technology developed rapidly, bringing more and more of the ocean within the reach of the oil industry. Before long, several companies were drilling in depths well over two hundred meters—a depth that, just fifteen years earlier, the delegates at the First Law of the Sea Conference had thought to be at least several generations away. Yet it was not the oil industry that would trigger the changes needed in the Geneva conventions. There was a massive amount of ocean floor beyond the continental shelf, in the deep sea, and it too appeared to be rich in minerals.

The first indications of these deposits came during the late 1950s, when scientists began to lower underwater cameras in order to better their understanding of the deep sea. Their pictures revealed that vast regions of the deep-sea floor were covered by dark, potato-sized lumps, known as manganese nodules. The nodules themselves were nothing new; they had been discovered a hundred years earlier. What was new was the astonishing size of the deposits. Thousands of square miles of deep-sea floor were literally covered by them. Not only that; laboratory analyses revealed that aside from manganese, the nodules contained high concentrations of iron, nickel, copper, and cobalt. It then began to dawn that the deep sea might contain one of the largest mineral deposits on the planet.

Early reports contained glowing predictions on the potential of mining these deposits. Nodules from the Pacific Ocean, for instance, averaged 20 percent manganese, 6 to 10 percent iron, and smaller amounts of copper, cobalt, and nickel—concentrations comparable to those of high-grade land ores. In all, about 75 percent of a nodule was usable, scientists said, compared with no more than 2 percent of land-based copper and nickel ores. Moreover, some areas had reported densities of 50 to 100 kilograms of nodules per square meter. Based on these figures and a few samples, the overall quantity of manganese nodules was estimated to be in the trillion-ton range for the Pacific Basin, and perhaps twice as much worldwide. Even if only 10 percent of this quantity could be mined, one report suggested, there were sufficient supplies of metals there to last many thousands of years.

In subsequent years these enticing predictions were tempered somewhat by additional data and by a more realistic evaluation of the mining costs. Nonetheless, few people doubted that with a little luck, the deep sea could turn into a veritable Klondyke. Cobalt, copper, nickel, and manganese, all of them essential in the production of high-performance alloys, were of particular interest. It was not that any of them was scarce on land, but their principal reserves were located in third world countries and what was then the Soviet Union—places not always known for their reliability. If the resource estimates were accurate and the projected mining costs could be met, the ocean could provide a far more reliable source of these materials.

During the late 1960s several companies began to examine what it would take to mine the deep ocean. They soon realized that they faced fantastic technological problems. Not only did they have to develop a mining system that would permit nodules to be brought up in massive quantities from miles beneath the surface; they also had to come up with the technology, either at sea or on land, to extract the most valuable metals. There were some advantages to deep-sea mining: there was not any overburden to be removed, for instance, and there was no need for explosives, drilling, or construction. These were major considerations, but they did not quite outweigh the fact that the nodules were located in a place that had been visited only by a few deep-sea submersibles.

To cover the enormous costs associated with this enterprise, several companies formed consortia. Each spent millions of dollars on developing a prototype mining system. After much research and experimentation, most of them settled on a hydraulic recovery system. In principle, it worked like a giant vacuum cleaner, with a dredge head to collect the nodules on the seafloor and a pipe string to transport them to the surface. Suction was created by injecting air into the pipe, with the rising bubbles forcing the nodules to the mining ship. On a few occasions a prototype system recovered a few hundred tons of nodules, proving that it worked. It was a far cry from the millions of tons that would be needed to make deep-sea mining profitable, but it was a first step.

None of the consortia took the next step, however. What was missing was not the technology, but the right economic climate. For one thing, metals prices were not stable enough. Most mining companies had configured their revenues on the basis of prices for cobalt and nickel, which collapsed during the late 1970s. Running a profitable operation was out of the question, unless prices rose again. There was also uncertainty about how nodule recovery would affect the metals market in general. Suppose one or two companies began mining, thereby increasing the supply of metals such as cobalt and nickel. Nobody was quite sure of what that would do to prices.

Market projections were only one consideration. Just as important were the legal implications, especially questions of ownership. When the companies began their investigations in the late 1960s and early 1970s, it could have been argued that the deep sea belonged to no one, and that nodules were therefore available to anyone attempting to recover them. Alternatively, one could refer to the Geneva Convention on the Continental Shelf, which stated that the shelf extended to the point where its depth "admits of the exploitation of the natural resources of the sea bed." Did this mean that the deep sea could be claimed by coastal states once they possessed the technology to mine it? No one knew for certain.

Arvid Pardo, Malta's ambassador to the United Nations, feared that the industrialized nations would soon begin providing answers for themselves. The deep sea was obviously up for grabs, he felt, and unless something was done, the most powerful nations would claim the richest pickings, as they always had. Malta was one of the United Nations' smallest members, but the soft-spoken diplomat felt that this should not be a limitation. After all, the United Nations was not about size, he reasoned. It was about equality and strength in numbers.

In 1967 Pardo made his move. Like all delegates, he was asked to address the opening session of the General Assembly, and took the opportunity to deliver a passionate speech on what was about to happen to the last frontier on earth. There is nothing in international law, he warned, that would prevent industrialized nations from claiming the deep sea. Just look at what happened in 1946, or much earlier during colonial times. Unless something was done, the deep sea would be no different from Africa a hundred years earlier: it would be carved up by countries having the technical ability to exploit it.

To prevent this, Pardo urged his colleagues to adopt a resolution that would declare the deep sea the "common heritage of mankind." He also proposed that a treaty be formulated to ensure that nations would not unilaterally appropriate the deep sea, but that instead it would be developed in a manner consistent with the United Nations charter. If there were to be any pickings, they should be shared with the world's poorer countries. The only way to do this, in Pardo's view, was through an international agency that would assume control of the deep-sea floor as a trustee for all countries.

Pardo's unexpected speech set off a chain reaction. In December 1967, just a few months after his call for action, the General Assembly established an Ad Hoc Committee on the Peaceful Uses of the Seabed and Ocean Floor beyond the Limits of National Jurisdiction, which mercifully became known as the Seabed Committee. Its mandate was to review the various aspects of Pardo's suggestions. A year later it recommended that a permanent committee be established to study the international machinery to develop the resources of the deep sea.

Though the discussions had barely begun, it was already clear that the deep-sea question was creating a rift between the industrialized nations and the third world. Developing nations wholeheartedly endorsed the spirit of Pardo's proposal. If the deep-sea floor contained the mineral bonanza they had been led to believe in, they naturally wanted to share in the profits. They also agreed on Pardo's call for an international agency to control pricing and production, so that the economies of metal-exporting third world countries would not be disrupted by deepsea mining.

The industrialized nations, on the other hand, were wary of international entities setting the rules. But their stalling techniques did not work. In 1969 the Seabed Committee drafted a Declaration of Principles Governing the Seabed. It began by stating that the seabed and the ocean floor beyond the limits of national jurisdiction were the "common heritage of mankind," just as Arvid Pardo had declared two years earlier. Also following Pardo's suggestions, it went on to say that no state could unilaterally appropriate any part of this area or develop its resources. A year later the resolution was adopted by the General Assembly, with 108 nations voting in favor and 14 abstaining. With it, the last legal no man's land on earth had been given firm legal status. From then on it belonged to the world community at large, rather than to no one.

For the declaration to have the force of international law, a treaty was required, preferably under the United Nations umbrella. Given the many differences that had surfaced before, several member states felt that it would not be wise to draft a treaty on the legal status of one ocean area without reviewing the others. The General Assembly therefore broadened the mandate of its Seabed Committee and asked it to consider all legal aspects of the sea. That way, the entire law of the sea could be updated, if needed.

Early in 1969 the Seabed Committee accordingly resumed its meetings, this time to discuss ocean law in its entirety. Between 1970 and 1973 it held no fewer than 469 formal meetings, generating a massive pile of documents. But despite this work, the committee could not agree on a draft convention. In the years since the 1958 Geneva conference, the law of the sea had grown far more complex, and three years of preparations proved not enough to produce a draft that covered all the issues. More important, three years was not enough to settle the differences among the members of the Seabed Committee itself. Nonetheless, the General Assembly felt that sufficient groundwork had been laid, and that it was time to convene a new Law of the Sea Conference, the third in the series.

In June 1974 150 nations sent their law-of-the-sea experts out again, this time to the Venezuelan capital of Caracas. A brief organizational session had taken place in New York in December 1973, but Caracas was where the real work was to be done. At the outset it was assumed that the Third Law of the Sea Conference would follow the for-mat of its predecessors and would come to an agreement during the session, but after several weeks it became clear that there was little that any state agreed to, in whole or in part. Each of the participating countries had put forward its position on the entire range of law-of-the-sea matters, generating another formidable pile of documents, but that was about the only achievement.

As during the preparatory meetings of the Seabed Committee, the issue of deep-sea mining generated the strongest emotions. Third world countries continued to insist on the involvement of an international agency, and some of them suggested that the organization should even be directly involved in deep-sea mining. That, of course, would require richer nations to share their technology with this organization, a prospect that struck most of the other countries as insane. For one thing, they knew that they would have little or no input into the decision making of the organization, even though they would be asked to share technology developed at a cost of millions of dollars.

Not surprisingly, the Caracas meeting ended in an impasse, the only agreement being to meet again and continue the process. The Third Law of the Sea Conference thus continued its work, in no fewer than fourteen subsequent sessions alternating between New York and Geneva. It was a painstakingly slow process, with discussion drafts developing from a "single negotiating text" into a "revised single negotiating text," then into an "informal composite negotiating text" followed by a "revised informal composite negotiating text," and so on until no one, except for those involved in the discussions and the legal experts, cared about what was being discussed at all. Yet every meeting and every "text" inched a little closer to a consensus, and in 1980 a deep-sea mining compromise was finally worked out. It consisted of a parallel mining system, whereby developing and industrialized countries were guaranteed equal access to the deep sea. Whether the system would work in practice was anyone's guess, but that was not so important. The key point was that for the first time, everyone appeared willing to agree on how to exploit the deep sea.

Little seemed to stand in the way of a formal treaty, except for the timing. A few months later President Ronald Reagan took office in the United States. Committed to strengthening America's military power, the new government emphasized the importance of maintaining adequate supplies of strategic minerals. In its view the deep-sea mining provisions hammered out at the Law of the Sea Conference were unacceptable, and the American delegation was fired. Replacing it was a new group, which returned to the position that deep-sea minerals should belong to any country that had the technology to recover them.

Despite attempts to resolve the matter in subsequent meetings, the deep-sea mining issue was back at square one. With no indication that the United States would change its position anytime soon, the conference decided to proceed without American approval. When the draft treaty was presented for a vote in April 1982, the United States, along with only three other countries, voted against. Eighteen others opted to abstain, among them the United Kingdom, Germany, Japan, and most of the Eastern bloc countries. Third world countries, in contrast, voted overwhelmingly in favor. One hundred and seventeen of them signed the convention when it was opened for signature in Montego Bay, Jamaica, a few months later. One state, Fiji, even ratified the whole thing on the same day.

The 1982 Law of the Sea Convention, as the treaty became officially known, brought important changes to the legal regime of the oceans. It finally cleared up the issues that had been left unresolved by the Geneva conventions. The maximum width of the territorial sea, for instance, was set at twelve miles. The continental shelf too was given a new definition. It still had little to do with the geological concept of the shelf but at least did away with the vague exploitability criterion of its predecessor, stating that the shelf extended as far as the "outer edge of the continental margin." The problem then became one of defining the continental margin, something that was done in

Oseberg Alpha.

Dwarfed by the two platforms of the Oseberg Field Center, the *Far Sky* returns to pick up refuse and other materials that need to be transported to land.

a complex definition involving the thickness of sedimentary rocks, submarine ridges, the distance from the foot of the continental slope, and the twenty-five-hundred-meter depth line. With a bit of creative interpretation, this should allow some countries to claim areas extending well over three hundred miles from their shores.

Coastal jurisdiction was further complemented by a new concept in ocean law: the exclusive economic zone. The new zone, which extends two hundred nautical miles from shore, gave many new rights to coastal states. For instance, they received exclusive rights over all resources of the seafloor and the water above it, control over marine scientific research and marine pollution, and jurisdiction over just about everything else, as long as it did not interfere with the freedom of navigation. Most important, of course, was the clear entitlement over marine resources. Coastal states already had control over the mineral resources of their continental shelf, but the exclusive economic zone broadened that control to minerals regardless of whether they were on the shelf, as long as they were within two hundred miles of the coast. This gave countries with a narrow continental shelf a bit of a break.

The exclusive economic zone also included all living resources, giving coastal nations extended fisheries jurisdiction. Countries like Iceland that had stood up for this principle saw their efforts vindicated and given the status of international law. But exclusive economic zones were not necessarily beneficial to everyone. In fact, taken together they subtracted a massive chunk of what Arvid Pardo in 1967 had called the "common heritage of mankind." More than a third of the world ocean now fell legally under the jurisdiction of coastal states.

Whatever was left after nations finished claiming their various zones was considered "high seas." Here the traditional freedoms of the sea continued to apply, at least on the surface. The bottom of this region was given a different status. Called "the Area," it is to be managed by a new international organization, the International Seabed Authority, for the benefit of all nations.

Evening finds the *Far Sky* back near Oseberg Alpha, this time to pick up refuse and other materials that need to be brought back to shore, or "the beach," as the platform's crew refers to it. Once everything has been transferred, a basket is attached to the crane's cable so that I can take the ride down to the ship several hundred feet below.

On the bridge Ollbjørn is preparing the ship for the return trip to Mongstad. He wants to know what I thought of Oseberg, and I tell him I was impressed. Especially about the fireplace, I explain, which probably is the most expensive fireplace in the world. "Not only that," I add, "they told me it has hardly been used."

As the *Far Sky* begins to head east, I walk out onto the deck to get a better view of the Oseberg Field Center. It still looks as huge and impressive as when I first saw it. What people have managed to build and operate here, in a place that gets some of the roughest weather anywhere, is testimony to human skill and ingenuity. I no longer have any doubt that once the economics make sense, the rest of the ocean floor will be developed as well. Technology will not be the limiting factor when mining ships start heading for the deep sea.

Whether that development will take place for the benefit of humanity remains to be seen, of course, for it is not certain whether international business will follow the spirit of international law. But perhaps that is not really the point. The new law of the sea is about more than new rules and technicalities. In a very real sense it is the first major international agreement on how to deal with valuable common resources. The community of nations established an agency to develop and manage the resources of a huge area for the benefit of humanity—a concept based not on power and might, with the strongest claiming the largest share of the pie, but on equity, with all nations having an equal say. Whether or not the system works, this expression of collective will is a milestone in and of itself.

As Oseberg becomes smaller, I begin to see some parallels between the work that takes place there or anywhere at sea, for that matter, and the law of the sea. Working at sea requires preparation, cooperation, and anticipation. Without an adequate measure of these, Oseberg could not have happened, nor could it continue to function. The sea simply doesn't allow for mistakes. So too is the law of the sea about preparation, cooperation, and anticipation. Without international preparation and cooperation, there simply could not have been an agreement. And without anticipation, that agreement would soon prove worthless. Take the 1958 Geneva conventions, for instance, which were outdated before the ink had even dried. It is true that law often lags far behind technological developments, but the new Law of the Sea Convention makes an attempt to reverse this trend. To some extent this was because deep-sea mining looked far more imminent when the conference began than when it ended, but even when timetables began to slip, the participants stuck with it and continued their negotiations. As a result, the 1982 Law of the Sea Convention, unlike its predecessor, will not be hopelessly out of date by the time it enters into force.

Of course, it took a long time to get to this point. Not counting the many years of preparatory work, nearly ten years of formal negotiations were needed to revise the legal regime of the oceans, and even then this revision did not get the approval of one of the major players. No one could have foreseen this, but then again no one had figured in how much the oceans had grown in importance or how difficult it would be to get all nations of the world to agree on their future. No wonder the Third Law of the Sea Conference became the largest, longest, and most complex conference in history.

By sunset, Oseberg Alpha is no more than a tiny orange spot on the horizon. Oseberg Charlie has disappeared, as have the flares from the other fields in the vicinity. Preparation, cooperation, anticipation—this is what it takes to succeed at sea, whether on the *Far Sky* or Oseberg Alpha or anywhere else. As I gaze at the evening sky's magic cast over this still-placid North Sea, it becomes clear this is what it will take to succeed on the planet as well. The sea has been telling us this for thousands of years. Funny how it is only now that we are beginning to listen.

よこすか

横須賀

YOKOSUKA

YOKOSUKA

A Depth of Knowledge

Kayiō Centā the locals call it—the Ocean Center, though it is officially known as the Japan Marine Science and Technology Center, or simply Jamstec. Wedged between a sprawling Nissan shipping plant and the huge Sumitomo shipyard in Yokosuka, near the entrance of Tokyo Bay, Jamstec is one of the world's foremost oceanographic institutions. The center is especially known for the quality of its deep-sea research, a reputation derived in no small part from its two Shinkai submersibles. The first of these, Shinkai 2000, can reach depths of up to two thousand meters (about sixty-five hundred feet). Shinkai 6500, a more recent cousin, can handle sixty-five hundred meters (more than twenty thousand feet), making her the deepest-diving submersible in the world and the pride of Japan's deep-sea oceanographers.

During research voyages Shinkai 6500 is housed aboard her mother ship, the *Yokosuka*, which I find tied along the Jamstec quay on a hot and hazy July afternoon, a couple of hours before departing on her summer campaign. About 350 feet long, the ship looks immaculate, with a bright white hull and freshly painted decks. For the past several days the crew has been readying her for the four-week trip to Japan's northern seas. Now there is only one item left to load, the most important one of all: Shinkai 6500.

To take her precious cargo aboard, the *Yokosuka* pivots 90 degrees around the stern, so that she lies perpendicular to the quay, facing Tokyo Bay. Meanwhile, in a large hangar along the dock, Shinkai is carefully lowered onto a flatbed and driven out to the vessel. Then the ship's massive A-frame is positioned over the submersible so that she can be hoisted aboard. Once that has happened, Shinkai is secured onto her base and slid into another hangar aboard, ready for the voyage to her next encounter with the deep.

Above: The *Yokosuka* departs for Japan's northern seas, where she will spend her summer campaign.

Left: This stern view of the *Yokosuka* shows the A-frame that is used to lift and lower the submersible Shinkai 6500.

Right: Prior to the *Yokosuka's* departure, Shinkai 6500 is carefully hoisted onto the ship.

I am watching the loading from the stern. The entire procedure takes about an hour and is executed with the utmost precision. Attended by a good many uniformed crew, each one of whom knows precisely what to do, it reminds me of the preparations for a space launch, albeit on a much smaller scale. The comparison is not that farfetched. Shinkai may not have anything to do with outer space, but she ventures into the deep sea, into inner space, and works in conditions that are just as difficult. And in that type of work the Japanese are unquestionably one of the leading players.

Just as the major powers had good reasons to set their eyes on outer space, Japan has compelling grounds for its interest in inner space. For it is there, in the deep sea off Japan's coast, that three plates of the earth's crust meet. Occasionally the constant jostling among them releases a jolt strong enough to be felt by humans. In 1991 Tokyo experienced fifty of those, the strongest one registering 4.9 on the Richter scale. It interrupted life in the city for no more than half an hour, but the Japanese know that they are in for a much bigger one. And nothing concerns them more than a *chokka-gata*, a big earthquake directly under Tokyo. The last one of these occurred on 1 September 1923, killing more than 140,000 people and leveling over half a million buildings in a city that was much smaller than today's Tokyo. Trying to figure out when the next one will occur is, not surprisingly, a national priority.

The *Yokosuka's* crew is an important part of that effort, for it is clear that the deep sea holds important clues to earthquake prediction. Last year, for instance, Shinkai was diving off northern Japan, where the Japan Trench drops steeply to over twenty thousand feet, and on one of her last excursions discovered a series of fissures in the ocean floor. Since the cracks were located where one of the plates buckles to slide under another, it appeared that they had been caused by bending stresses, as if the seafloor's surface had actually been ripped open. It also appeared that this had occurred recently. Unfortunately, that summer's campaign was coming to an end, so there was not much time left to study these strange features. The *Yokosuka* will be heading to the same spot on this voyage in order to figure out their significance.

A few minutes before the departure, the loudspeakers along the quay begin belting out a scratchy rendition of "Anchors Aweigh," presumably to convey a departing mood. Jamstec's brass and some families have meanwhile gathered on the dock to wave the ship a safe and productive voyage, a gesture reciprocated from the stern.

At 15:00, precisely on schedule, the engines jump to life and the ship nudges forward. As we gradually pull away from the dock and head into Tokyo Bay, the fading naval marches remind me that this vessel too represents a component of sea power. Perhaps it is a less visible one, for few sea power analysts have bothered to include research in their assessments. But if sea power is about using and controlling the sea, then knowing how to do so must be considered an integral part of it. And to know about the sea, one has to study it.

 Learning about the sea dates back to ancient times. Greek and Roman philosophers described the sea's natural phenomena, speculating about everything from the nature of life in it to its saltiness. They also tried to map it. Restricted at first by a desire to explain the world in terms of symmetries, these attempts gradually took on realistic proportions. The maps of the Greek geographer Ptolemy, for instance, were remarkably accurate in their depiction of the Mediterranean. Drawn during the second century A.D., they contained obvious errors about the regions beyond the classical world, but even so one cannot but admire the precision of Ptolemy's rendering.

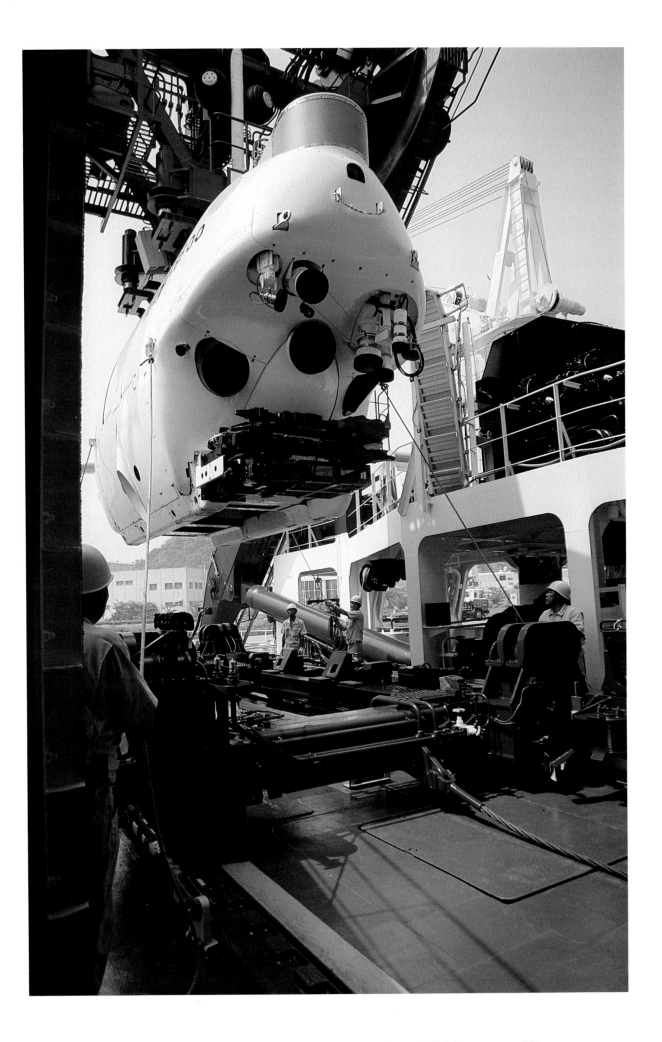

The so-called *Panel do Infante* from the set of panels attributed to the Portuguese painter Nuno Gonçalves. Saint Vincent, Portugal's patron saint, is depicted here surrounded by historical figures of the sixteenth century. Among them, his hands folded in prayer, is Henry the Navigator. (Museu Nacional de Arte Antiga, Lisbon.)

Medieval Europe ignored this information, replacing what the Greek geographers had painstakingly put together with a new religious image, the so-called *mappa mundi*. Most of these maps depicted the earth as a circular dish with a vast landmass in the center surrounded by the great Ocean Sea. Asia was usually placed at the top, divided from the West by a straight line of water. Europe and Africa too were separated by water: the Mediterranean, running as a straight line from center to bottom. As a reflection of Christian dogma the *mappa mundi* was a wonderfully simple and even elegant conception, especially if it positioned Jerusalem at the center (as many of the maps did). As a geographical representation, however, it was no more than a caricature. Unfortunately, the two were often confused at the time, leading many people to believe that this was the actual shape of the world.

The expansion of trade in the late Middle Ages brought about a change in people's perspectives on the sea. Larger ships were built, which allowed mariners to venture further out. The compass, introduced from the East sometime during the twelfth century, enabled them to do so even under cloudy skies without losing track of their direction. As a result, the sailing season lengthened, and soon ships were sailing year-round in the Mediterranean and even in northern seas.

As seamen reached less familiar waters, the need for sailing instructions became greater. A new type of map emerged: a coastal chart depicting landmarks and other information that helped pilots determine their position or alerted them to dangers ahead. These were called portolanos, or harbor guides, but they extended well beyond ports. By the middle of the fourteenth century they covered the entire Mediterranean as well as other coastal areas.

Being based on everyday observation rather than on theological speculation, portolanos were a big improvement over the *mappae mundi* of that time. Here at last were maps that showed the indentations of a coast, rather than landmasses that looked absurdly like pieces of pie and seas that resembled canals. Before long they even began to influence the *mappae mundi*. Abraham Cresques's *Catalan Atlas*, drawn in 1375 for the king of Aragon, was a *mappa mundi* in that it sought to provide an image of the world. It still placed Jerusalem near the center and included other biblical references, but aside from that, Cresques relied on the portolanos he had access to, carefully transferring their findings onto his own image of the world. The result was something of a revolution: a map that, while paying lip service to religious convention, showed a world picture based on empirical findings rather than dogma, a picture interpreted by scientists and sailors rather than bishops and the Bible.

Portolanos and compilations such as the *Catalan Atlas* were useful up to the limits of the known world. Beyond that mapmakers accepted rumor or applied a bit of imagination to fill in the gaps. In hindsight this may strike us as somewhat strange, but to medieval cartographers and mariners, as well as to medieval people in general, the line between myth and reality was not clearly drawn. In fact, myth was reality until proven otherwise.

A world in which strange and uninviting phenomena surrounded the security of what was known did not encourage exploration. European sailors had no problem sailing along the coasts of the known world, but heading into unfamiliar waters, where their charts visually reminded them of all sorts of unpleasant possibilities, was another matter. As if to confirm these premonitions, the few fools who had tried to venture that way had never been heard of again. It seemed much safer to stay put. Why venture beyond, anyway?

It would require a good answer to change that attitude, and during the fifteenth century it finally emerged. By this time several Europeans had reached the East overland, returning with tales of magnificent treasures: silks and spices, gold and diamonds, untold quantities of exotic luxuries. Along with these accounts came speculations that the East could be reached by sea. Marco Polo had already returned by sea as far as the Persian Gulf, whence it was a relatively easy trek to the ports along the eastern Mediterranean seaboard. His countryman Niccolò de' Conti, who traveled in his footsteps two hundred years later, went even further, suggesting that it might be possible to reach Cathay by sailing around Africa. This assumption ran counter to prevailing beliefs, but mapmakers included it on their maps anyway, thereby opening the sea route to the East—at least on paper.

However important that intellectual step, it would take a major effort to open that sea route physically. By the end of the fifteenth century it had been done, in large part as a result of the efforts of Dom Henrique of Portugal, better known to us as Henry the Navigator. Time has turned Henry into a mysterious figure, one who may not even have had his eye on a sea route to the Indies. But his vision and determination made that passage possible. Any discussion of the Age of Exploration must begin with this pivotal figure who propelled Portugal, and the West, into an oceanic breakout that forever altered the shape of the world.

Much of what we know about Henry comes from the writings of Gomes Eanes de Zurara, who began to chronicle Henry's life and achievements during the mid-fifteenth century. Henry was still alive at that time, so this is one of the most accurate biographies. But much has been added to Zurara's account, some of it quite doubtful. There was a desire among sixteenth- and seventeenth-century Portuguese historians to commit to posterity the great deeds of their ancestors, and their interpretations gradually became part of history itself. Invariably they elevated Henry to near-mythical status: a man who from a school of navigation at Sagres, in southwestern Portugal, orchestrated the grand scheme of world exploration, much as he is depicted on Lisbon's Monument to the Discoverers.

As always, the truth is slightly different. There never was a school of navigation at Sagres, at least not in a physical sense. Toward the end of his life Henry lived at Sagres, where he had intended to build a port—the so-called Vila do Infante—but these ambitious designs failed. Subsequent historians chose to ignore this fact. For some reason they began to associate Henry's reputation as the organizer of Portugal's early discoveries with the town he founded, and the idea simply stuck. The fact that the place looks like a natural launching site, with its two capes thrusting like spearheads into the Atlantic, probably had something to do with this.

Many historians also praised Henry's vast learning. "He was very gifted in the study of letters, mainly Astrology and Cosmography," wrote Damião de Gois in 1567, seeding another rumor that gradually came to be accepted as historical fact. There is no doubt that Henry was a shrewd man—a feudal lord who was concerned with managing his estates and went about it in a practical manner. But his reputation as a man of letters remains largely unfounded. Not that any of this should detract from his achievements. Just as he was not a navigator, Henry was not a classical scholar. But he encouraged people who were, using his position and financial resources to do so.

All accounts mention that religion played a major role in Henry's life, and there is little doubt that it did. The prince was a very religious man who lived a sober and austere life. Historians often point out he lived a life of strict celibacy, never drank, and died wearing a hair shirt—a sign of his virtue and chastity. They also report spells of mysticism and, above all, an obsession with the Moorish infidels—a result, no doubt, of his upbringing as a knight in the Portuguese court. The figure that emerges from these descriptions is hardly congenial, but it is probably closer to the truth than the navigator and classical scholar of other accounts.

In 1415 the young prince participated in Portugal's conquest of the Moorish stronghold of Ceuta. The campaign, which he helped plan, no doubt satisfied some of his crusading zeal; after all, a good many infidels were killed against only eight Portuguese. But the worldly aspects of the conquest did not go unnoticed either. As one of the terminals of the North African gold trade, Ceuta was a very rich place, providing Henry and his compatriots a tantalizing hint of the wealth that lay hidden in Africa and beyond. That image never left him, and when he returned a few years later to serve as Ceuta's governor, Henry was determined to follow up on it. He found out that the gold trade originated at a so-called River of Gold several days south of Ceuta. Going there overland, through hostile territory, was out of the question, however. The only way to get there, it seemed, was by sea.

It was accordingly from Ceuta that Henry the Navigator dispatched his first ships.

Like all the vessels that would follow, they left with a dual mandate. On the one hand there was the economic motivation. Gold was in enormous demand in Europe—no question about that. On the other hand there was the religious element. Henry was convinced that depriving the Arabs of their trade was a crusade in its own right. And perhaps curiosity played a role as well. Like all European rulers of that time, the prince was fascinated by reports of the legendary Prester John, a Christian ruler who was believed to live in Africa. Prester John, it was said, was waging his own war against the Moors. Presumably he could be counted on to join Europe in its struggle against the Infidel, provided someone could find him.

The first voyages, sent out shortly after 1420, reached Madeira and the Canary Islands and, further west, the Azores. With the exception of the Azores this could hardly be called new territory, but now, under Henry's impetus, some of the islands were colonized. These decisions speak of a shrewd business mind. All colonized territories became Henry's property, and by introducing new crops he guaranteed himself a new and steady source of revenue.

Sailing as far as the Canary Islands proved relatively easy, but beyond that things got tricky. Henry's sailors were approaching the limits of the known world, and that seemed to be as far as they were ready to go. Not only did contemporary charts and descriptions remind them of the possible doom they faced further south; they noticed that they were actually reaching unpleasant waters. Near Cape Non (now Cape Juby at the southwestern tip of Morocco), fogs often obscured their view and currents ran adversely. Getting in was easy, getting out a problem. Was this the beginning of the so-called Green Sea of Darkness they had all heard about—a region of perpetual fog inhabited by awful monsters and dominated by currents that precluded any return?

Pressured by Henry, some hardy souls inched their way beyond, but before long they too had to give up. First the sea appeared red, discolored by the sands of the desert. Sometimes the ships themselves turned red under a coating of dusty sand. Next they were met by heavy swells from the northwest, and the currents seemed to grow worse. The sea actually turned green, and the fogs grew denser. The coast, usually a reassuring sight, became desolate, even sinister. The red sandstone cliffs of Cape Bojador, some 150 miles south of Cape Non, appeared especially intimidating. Seen through the fog in the distance, they actually resembled a barrier. Crews refused to go on and forced their captains to turn back, convinced that Bojador was the gateway to the void beyond.

This fear of the unknown, so wonderfully symbolized by the forbidding cliffs of Bojador, proved to be Henry's greatest challenge. Henry did not share his sailors' belief in the Green Sea of Darkness and its horrors, but he knew that it would take more than his encouragement, financial or otherwise, to get people beyond. It would take the most advanced instruments and the best maps—the best information—and to that he now turned his attention. He made it a personal concern to finance the university at Lisbon, encouraging scientists to focus on navigational problems. Suppose sailors were to stay out of sight of land, he asked; how could they find out where they were?

The answer required a better understanding of astronomy, so some of the best astronomers were invited to Lisbon to work on practical solutions. They brought along their instruments, many of them developed by Arab astronomers, and began to adapt them for use at sea. Henry also invited prominent cartographers to Lisbon. Among them was Master Jacome de Mallorca, son of Abraham Cresques, who had compiled the revolutionary *Catalan Atlas*. It was a shrewd move, for Jacome de Mallorca was by far the most renowned cartographer of his time, and he taught the Portuguese all he knew about the intricate art of mapmaking.

Henry subsequently asked his cartographers to chart the progress of each voyage, and to draw in, piece by piece, every new bit of information. Whatever was not known was left blank, for the prince would not allow his staff to fantasize about the unknown. To assist in this effort the captains of his vessels were required to keep precise logbooks, noting everything they observed during the voyage: winds, currents, anchorages, and whatever else might be of use to their successors.

If, to use a modern-day analogy, the charts and guidebooks represented state-of-the-art software, Henry did not neglect the hardware either. At the shipyards of Lagos his shipwrights were building ships suitable to the task of exploration. At first they simply used strengthened versions of local fishing craft—sturdy single-masted ships, with one square sail. But these did not suffice, the mariners complained; it was too difficult, if not impossible, to return against adverse currents, not to mention adverse winds. So Henry got his mariners and shipwrights together and had them figure out a better design. These efforts culminated in the development of caravels—the "best ships sailing the seas," according to one of Henry's captains. Caravels had two (and later three) masts, all of them lateen-rigged so that the ship could sail closer to the wind. Crewed by hardy men and able captains, they proved a vital factor in Portugal's oceanic breakout.

Under Henry's leadership the Portuguese discoveries thus developed into the first systematic national program for advances into the unknown. It would be nice to believe that Henry did all of this out of a single place, surrounded by the best minds of the time on the lonely cape of St. Vincent at Sagres, but it is simply not true. Henry in fact spent much of his time in Lagos, whence most of the voyages departed. Zurara's account makes clear that the prince also spent a good bit of time in Lisbon and other areas of Portugal, making his coordinating role all the more remarkable.

In 1434 the feared Cape Bojador was rounded by Gil Eannes, one of Henry's squires, personally selected by him for the task. With that step taken, Henry's systematic program of exploration could begin in earnest. Just one year after his return from the Gulf of the Red Roses, Eannes left for unknown waters again, this time with Alfonso Baldaia, who commanded a second vessel. Not far south of Bojador, they found footprints—an exciting find, for it proved that these regions were inhabited. Upon hearing the news, Henry sent his two master mariners south again, urging them to capture at least one of the natives.

It was 1441 before the Portuguese were able to return with some natives. It was the work of Antão Gonçalves, who sailed some 250 miles beyond Bojador. Two people were captured, a man and a woman. Gonçalves's successor, the young knight Nuno Tristão, who went as far as Cape Blanco, brought back ten more, guessing that Henry might well be interested in people who could bring profits "by their service or ransom." He guessed correctly. His return with additional prisoners marked the beginning of the European-African slave trade. A few years later Gil Eannes, sailing with one of the first caravels, came back with no fewer than two hundred prisoners, who were sold as slaves at Lagos. Now even more revenues were flowing back to Henry, silencing those who had called his efforts a waste of time and money.

The returns allowed Henry to continue the expensive business of exploration, sending one ship after another to the south. Each captain was requested to sail one step further, effectively pushing back the limits of the known world. In 1444 Nuno Tristão, already on his third voyage, went as far as the northern side of the Senegal, finding a lush green landscape very different from the six hundred miles of barren coastline that preceded it. A year later Dinis Dias sailed as far as Cape Verde, Africa's westernmost point. Next went Alvaro Fernandes, going as far as the Cape of Masts near the Gambia River. In 1446 he sailed again, this time passing the estuary, but a fierce encounter with armed natives forced him to return. Nuno Tristão was less fortunate. On his fourth and final voyage he and nineteen of his crew were killed by natives while exploring the Gambia estuary. Only five people were left to sail the vessel back to Portugal.

Despite these setbacks, Henry's scheme of exploration was working in every respect. By now some fifty ships had set sail for Africa; they had rounded its westernmost point, and they had begun to bring back trading goods. Slaves proved the most

profitable—some 927 had been sold at Lagos—but there were also tantalizing hints that the gold fields of Africa were not very far off. Most important, every vessel brought back more information. Henry's sailors complained that they wanted larger ships so that they could bring back more slaves, but that was not the point. What Henry really wanted could be fit into the mind of one man.

Over the next several years Portuguese explorers ventured as far as Sierra Leone, more than twelve hundred miles from Bojador. But in 1460 their ventures came to a temporary halt. Back in Portugal, at the Vila do Infante in Sagres, their great sponsor died at age sixty-six. At first there was no one to fill the void left by Henry's death. Trade with West Africa continued, but there were few attempts to continue the search for the elusive passage to the Indies.

It was not until 1469 that the Portuguese court turned its attention to the West African trade again, granting Fernão Gomes, a wealthy Lisbon merchant, exclusive rights in return for a share of the profits and a commitment to explore at least three hundred miles each year over a five-year period. Aside from being an ingenious way to turn discovery into cash, the lease restarted the stalled exploration process. In fact, Gomes's men did far better than the required fifteen hundred miles. In the five years between 1469 and 1474 they covered the two thousand miles between the River Gambia and the easternmost point of the Gulf of Guinea, and then continued south for several hundred miles.

When the Gomes contract expired, King Alfonso turned the African lease over to his son John, who took the job to heart. His coronation as King John II in 1481 heralded the second great period of Portuguese exploration. This was the period of explorers like Diogo Cão, who single-handedly added 1,450 miles of African coastline to the map, a feat he achieved in two voyages between 1482 and 1486. The last took him as far as Cape Cross, fifty miles north of Walvis Bay in Namibia. Two years later the final thousand-mile stretch was covered by Bartolomeu Dias, who rounded the Cape of

Storms, as he called it, near the southernmost point of Africa. King John later renamed it the Cape of Good Hope, for the sea route to the Indies had finally been opened.

Like Henry, John II understood that accurate information was the key not only to exploration but also to the trade that would surely follow. He therefore required his mariners to survey the coast so that their findings could be used to update existing maps. He also demanded information on the secrets of the sea: winds and currents, the coast, places to provision, and anything else that would be of use to others. It was all incorporated into the guidebooks that now detailed the entire length of the West African coastline.

Efforts to improve on the science of navigation were not neglected either. Following the example of his great-uncle, John made a practice of inviting the brightest minds of that age to Portugal. Given the choice between exile and conversion to Christianity, some of Spain's greatest Jewish astronomers and mathematicians readily accepted John's invitation and moved to Lisbon, where they continued their efforts to devise practical navigational instruments and techniques. Among them was Abraham Zacuto, author of the *Almanach Perpetuum*, which described the correlation between latitude and the declination of the sun. Joining Zacuto was his student Joseph Vizinho, who is believed to have sailed on one of Diogo Cão's voyages to take measurements on the position of sun along the way. Vizinho subsequently updated Zacuto's tables and translated them from Hebrew into Latin. Along with more precise instruments to measure the altitude of the sun at noon, these tables gave Portuguese sailors a practical means of determining their latitude at sea.

Encouraged by rulers who firmly grasped that accurate information was the key to the riches of the East, later scientists developed navigation from an art into a science. Portugal had Duarte Pacheco Pereira (c. 1460–1533), for instance, whose *Esmeraldo de Situ Orbis* was one of the most comprehensive treatises on seamanship of its time. A generation later came Pedro Nunes (1502–78), one of the greatest mathematicians of the Renaissance, and Don João de Castro (1500–48), probably the leading figure to emerge from this new scientific establishment. His books—the *Tratado do Esfera* and especially his various *Roteiros*—contained everything the Portuguese had learned in the hundred years since they set sail for Africa, from the magnetic variation of the compass needle to astronomy and descriptions of various coasts and harbors. In fact, they were nothing less than a blueprint for attaining the riches of the East.

The experience gained at sea, combined with strong scientific support, allowed Portuguese mapmakers to compose a view of the world that had never been seen before. But it was not a view the Portuguese were willing to share. Already there was a lot of interest from other nations in what Portugal was doing. Dias's rounding of the Cape of Good Hope had not gone unnoticed. It was "very bad news," as the Venetian diarist Girolamo Priuli put it. Priuli's fear was confirmed when Vasco da Gama reached India ten years later and returned to Portugal, his ships loaded with spices. Within years Lisbon had replaced Venice as the major spice market in Europe.

In subsequent years Venice, whose espionage service was the envy of the world, and other contenders for the Eastern spice trade sent spies to Lisbon, in order to get their hands on one of the guidebooks that detailed the sea route to the Indies. They would have killed to obtain one of João de Castro's *Roteiros*. But John II and his successor, Manuel, were not about to let go of Portugal's hard-won information. Obtaining a chart of the voyage, not to mention a pilot book or rutter, was out of the question. Anyone caught trying to smuggle one out was executed.

For nearly a century Portugal's policy of secrecy remained quite effective. Every once in a while some information leaked out because foreign agents paid big money for anything that revealed information about the sea route to the East. But Portugal made sure that the big picture remained secret, realizing that as long as it kept this information to itself, it ruled the seas and hence much of the world.

In the end, it was not so much the spying as the development of printing that caused Portugal to lose hold of the secrets of the sea. Printing allowed for a wider and much more rapid distribution of information. The Portuguese were mortified when Dutchman Jan Huyghen van Linschoten published an account of his experiences in India. Not only did it reveal that Portugal's control of the Indies was not what Portugal would have liked others to believe; it also included sailing directions to the Orient. Here, available to not just one possible competitor but to everyone, was everything the Portuguese had so desperately tried to keep secret. Against that there was nothing they could do. Within a few years of Linschoten's work, the Portuguese had been driven out of much of the East Indies, forever losing control over the trade and the seas they had called their own.

One hour into the *Yokosuka*'s trip, chief officer Hitoshi Tanaka assembles the vessel's scientific complement in the conference room for a safety briefing. For several of the scientists this is the first trip aboard the ship, so he keeps things simple and to the point. The Japan Marine Safety Agency reports one man-overboard incident each week, he says, looking around the table to emphasize that any one of us could be next, unless we follow his instructions. We also find out how to operate the fire extinguishers, are assigned a lifeboat, and are told to keep warm clothes on in case of an emergency—all of which seems to make eminent sense.

Then comes the important part. The *Yokosuka*'s catering staff has a fine reputation, but mealtimes are disappointing: 16:20 for dinner, an hour later on dive days. Smoking and drinking—both an essential part of Japanese socializing—are briefly touched upon, as are the workings of the all-important *ōfuro*, the hot bath. Not that anyone needs an explanation. The *ōfuro* is just as much a part of Japanese daily life as are eating and sleeping.

We adjourn from the meeting in time for dinner, which in true Japanese fashion is presented exquisitely, with each dish—and there are six or seven of them—beautifully prepared and displayed. On this first evening we get a bit of tuna and squid *sashimi*, some vegetable tempura, a delicately grilled sea bream, some stewed vegetables, and the omnipresent rice and *miso-shiro*. I regret that we have to gobble it down so quickly,

The *Yokosuka*'s on-board cuisine is exquisitely presented.

and at such an uncivilized hour, but enjoy it nonetheless. Subsequent meals prove a treat as well. Only once is there a tiny disappointment, when a delicately prepared cut of meat turns out to be liver. Fortunately, most of my table mates leave their *reba* untouched as well, proving that there is a certain universality to these things.

After dinner I head up to the bridge, where Captain Hiroshi Hyōdo, or Senshō-san, as he is known here, is in command. Sensho-san turns out to be a friendly person who has spent a good deal of time at sea. From our brief conversation I gather that he started out with Nippon Suisan, one of Japan's largest fishing companies, then moved on to a variety of tankers and merchant ships. A research vessel like the *Yokosuka* is something new, but he likes it. "It's very interesting work," he confides, "and the trips aren't too long."

Senshō-san is in charge of a lot of people. There's the crew itself, twenty-seven strong and consisting of ten officers, twelve able-bodied seamen and deck hands, and a catering staff of five. Shinkai's staff, headed by Katsumi Sakakura, consists of thirteen people, including four pilots and a number of technicians. The scientific complement numbers eighteen and includes geologists, geophysicists, and biologists. It is headed by chief scientist Hiroshi Hotta, director of Jamstec's Deep Sea Department.

I get a chance to meet most of the scientists that evening, when they gather in the conference room to discuss their various projects. Dr. Hotta, who is joining Shinkai's next dive, is doing most of the talking, explaining to his colleagues what he will be looking for on the seafloor twenty thousand feet below. Seated around the table are people like Yujiro Ogawa and Hisada Kenichiro, both geologists at Tsukuba University near Tokyo; Koichi Owada, a microbiologist from Tokyo University's Ocean Research Institute; and Toshiko Kanazawa, also from Tokyo University, or Tōdai, as it is known. All have brought a few of their brightest students, who are listening to the discussion with rapt attention. Also attending is Jamstec's Yuko Kaiho, the only woman aboard, who is here to launch a number of earthquake sensors.

My mastery of Japanese being mostly limited to ordering supageti with *cram sosu* and a couple of *biiru*, I don't gather much from the meeting. But the frequency of words like *kaikō* (trench) and especially *Nihon Kaikō* (Japan Trench), along with some animated discussion over a map of the area, makes clear that the main topic of conversation is the deep-sea trench that gives Japan an occasional jolt. Hotta-san points to the detailed chart of the ocean floor in front of him, to mark the path of his dive in comparison with the dives that were made last year. From this it becomes clear that he will descend between the two spots where the fissures were observed last year, presumably to check whether they continue all the way.

Later that evening I briefly meet with Hotta-san to find out what was discussed. Seated at the desk in his stateroom, Hotta-san grabs a piece of blank paper and sketches a map of Japan. "As you know, the earth's crust is made up of a number of plates," he says while touching up the sketch, "and three or maybe four of these meet right near Japan." He then draws a line through Sagami Bay southwest of Tokyo, and another parallel to the coast of Japan's main island of Honshu. "These are the plate boundaries we are most concerned with," he continues, pointing to the divisions: "The Philippine plate to the south, the Pacific plate to the north, and the Eurasian plate, with Japan on it, to the west."

Both the Pacific and the Philippine plate are heavy oceanic plates that sink under the lighter Eurasian plate, causing the deep trenches off the coast of Japan. Using his hands to mimic the plates' motion, Hotta-san shows how the Philippine plate slides under the Eurasian plate in the Sagami Trough while the Pacific plate does so in the Japan Trench. "The subsiding plates drag down part of the continental plate," he explains, "but occasionally the continental plate rebounds, and that's when you have an earthquake. We call this a trench earthquake. The great Kantō earthquake of 1923 was caused like this."

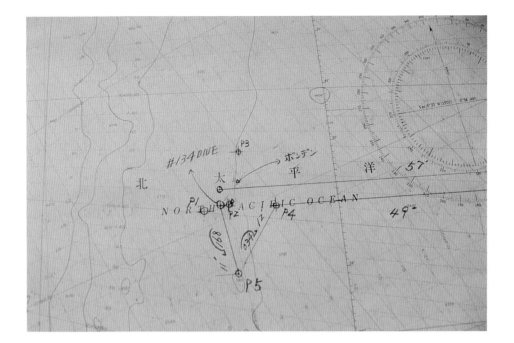

Our destination. The dive site is located near the epicenter of the 1933 Sanriku earthquake.

"There is a different type of earthquake in Japan," he goes on, "and that's the type we're studying on this trip." In 1933 there was another jolt that caused massive loss of life: the Sanriku earthquake. But this movement was caused not by the continental plate being dragged down and rebounding, but rather by a break in the bending Pacific plate itself. "In the case of the Sanriku earthquake, one part of the seafloor suddenly bolted up while the other went down," Hotta-san continues. Normally this would hardly have been felt on land, but in this case it created a massive water displacement, which started as a tiny ripple in the deep ocean but gradually gained height and momentum as it reached coastal waters. Northern Honshu, with its deeply indented coast, was devastated by the wall of water that suddenly emerged. Thousands of people never had a chance.

"Finally, we also have earthquakes caused by a normal fault, when two continental plates grind against each other. So you see, Japan is one of the most complicated areas in terms of plate dynamics," Hotta-san concludes with a shy smile. "For us geophysicists there couldn't be a more interesting area in the world to study. But you have to get used to experiencing a jolt now and then."

When asked about the upcoming dive, Hotta-san looks for the seafloor chart he was discussing with his colleagues. As he points to the various contours, it becomes clear that the seafloor does not simply bend smoothly to slide under the continental plate, but is broken up into a number of cliffs and terraces, each about a hundred meters apart. "It was here, on the terraces, especially between sixty-two hundred and sixty-three hundred meters, that we found the cracks," Hotta-san continues. "Because they have very little sedimentation, we think they are quite young. And because they are located right near the epicenter of the Sanriku earthquake and have never been seen anywhere else, we suspect they are related to it. But before we can be sure of that, we need a lot more observations."

At a steady clip of 15 knots, it doesn't take the *Yokosuka* long to reach the dive site, about 125 miles east of the coast of northern Honshu. Occasionally the ship stops to launch a number of earthquake sensors, slowing her progress somewhat, but early the second morning she is approaching the site. I climb up to the bridge, where Captain Hyōdo and second officer Masayoshi Ishiwata are directing the maneuvering. Senshō-

Even during diving operations, the *Yokosuka*'s
bridge is always manned.

san is standing in front of a monitor that shows him the ship's exact position in relation to the diving point. Ishiwata-san has taken a position by the engine telegraph, so
that he can transfer the captain's commands to the engine room.

As we begin to get closer, Senshō-san orders half speed. "Half speed, sir," Ishiwata-san echoes, shifting the telegraph. Gradually the *Yokosuka*'s speed falls by a couple of knots. Senshō-san remains close to the monitor, occasionally ordering a few
course corrections to the helmsman, but Ishiwata-san keeps scanning the horizon
through his binoculars. A few miles off the starboard bow is a large fishing vessel,
which has no clue that the white dot off her port bow is a research vessel in the
process of slowing down. So Ishiwata-san informs Senshō-san, who decides to alert
the intruder. The first two radio calls don't get a reaction, but after the third the fishing vessel's captain acknowledges, inquiring how long the *Yokosuka* plans to stay in
the area. "We'll be here from 08:00 to 17:00," Senshō-san replies. "Please give us a
two-mile berth for the duration."

Meanwhile, the *Yokosuka* has crept closer to the site, and Senshō-san orders slow
speed, and shortly thereafter stop engines. "Stop engines, sir," comes the reply, and
the ship drifts toward the intended rendezvous. Because the conversation with the
fishing vessel took a little longer than expected, Senshō-san realizes that he might
overshoot the spot, so he briefly orders engines slow astern, bringing the ship to a
stop. I glance at the monitor, which indicates that we're at 39:20.698 N and
144:36.069 E—smack on top of the diving point. I am impressed; Senshō-san obviously knows how to maneuver this ship.

Meanwhile, Ishiwata-san checks the navigation displays to confirm the ship's
exact position and walks over to the chart table. After marking our position on the
chart, he writes down "07:20," and just below that, "Dive 133." He then calls the diving staff to inform them that we have arrived. Shinkai can now be launched.

Watching the ease of this procedure, with satellites doing all the work, one cannot but feel respect for the sailors of old who had to struggle with cumbersome instruments on a moving deck to get a position fix. And for many hundreds of years latitude was all they had. Longitude— their exact position east or west from home—they never even knew. They could estimate it, of course, by guessing their average speed and throwing in adjustments for leeway, currents, and whatever else affected the ship's forward progress, but that was all. In regions where one did not have to sail out of sight of land for long, this was not too much of a problem; whenever a landmark was sighted, the sailors again knew where they were. But in regions where ships remained on the open sea for days and sometimes even weeks on end, the difference between where people thought they were and where they actually were increased with each passing day.

In retrospect it makes the achievements of the Age of Exploration even more impressive. Imagine Ferdinand Magellan in 1520, having made his way through the strait that now bears his name at the tip of South America, and finally reaching the Pacific. Ahead was the mightiest ocean on the planet, but he had no way of knowing that. The moment he left the South American coast, he had no idea where he was. More than ten thousand miles of open sea lay ahead, and more than three months of sailing without provisioning, an ordeal that turned this into one of the most appalling voyages of the Age of Exploration.

A seventeenth-century geographer, surrounded by the symbols of his trade and his times.

Magellan's successors at least had the advantage of knowing the formidable extent of this ocean, but they too never knew their longitude. After a few weeks at sea they would be lucky if they were within a hundred miles of where they thought they were. One way or another most of them managed, relying on their skill and the accuracy of their reckoning. But inevitably some did not. Claimed by uncharted reefs and islands or a lack of fresh provisions, their ships never came back. Unless the longitude puzzle could be solved, such losses were inevitable.

Solving this puzzle, in theory at least, was not very complicated. In 1530 Gemma Frisius, a German astronomer, pointed out that figuring out longitude, on land as well as at sea, required no more than an accurate clock. The reason was simple, he explained. Since the earth rotates 360 degrees in twenty-four hours, or 15 degrees an hour, people who knew the exact times at their current location and their place of departure could determine how far they had traveled east or west. All they had to do was to multiply the time difference by fifteen.

Unfortunately, that was much easier said than done, especially at sea. Finding local time was relatively easy; a determination of the sun's highest position in the sky indicated local noon. But there was no clock that could tell what time it was at that very moment at one's point of departure. Hourglasses were totally unreliable, leading to errors of hundreds of miles. So other devices were sought. In 1610 Galileo, responding to a request by the Dutch East Indies Company, proposed a clock with a pendulum to keep the time. His suggestion was followed up on by the Dutchman Christiaan Huygens, who built several pendulum clocks. But none of them did the job, because there was no way a pendulum could keep accurate time aboard a rocking ship.

For a while it appeared that a spring-driven clock, using a thin piece of coiled metal as its motive force, could provide the answer. But this did not work either. Even after a system was figured out that allowed an uncoiling spring to provide an even force, it was found that temperature changes caused the various metals in the clock to expand and contract at different rates. This was not much of a problem if the clock stayed in one place, but it made a difference on a ship moving from one region to

Without accurate techniques to measure longitude, ships were always at risk in unknown waters.

another. Even if the clock was off by no more than a minute, the ship's position could be wrong by as much as seventeen miles—more than enough to cause serious trouble.

No vessel was immune to this problem, even in familiar waters. Nothing underscored that point as much as the calamity that befell the British Gibraltar squadron, on its way home in 1707. On a dark and rainy fall night the fleet, led by Vice Admiral Cloudesley Shovel, ran aground on the rocks of the Scilly Isles, in the western approaches to the English Channel. Four ships and more than two thousand sailors perished, including the hapless admiral, who survived the grounding but was murdered ashore by robbers.

A subsequent inquiry revealed that Shovel had assumed he was on the other side of the English Channel, near Ushant, and literally ran aground more than a hundred miles off course. The disaster would never have happened, the report concluded, if his navigators had possessed the means to determine their position.

The loss of so many lives so close to home shocked public opinion. There were calls for action—for something, anything practical, that would finally enable mariners to figure out their longitude at sea. In response, the British Parliament in 1714 promised a reward for "such Person or Persons as shall Discover the Longitude at Sea." "Nothing is so much wanted and desired at Sea, as the Discovery of the Longitude, for the Safety and Quickness of Voyages, the Preservation of Ships and the Lives of Men," the preamble stated. But that was not all: "Such a Discovery would be of particular Advantage to the Trade of Great Britain, and very much for the Honour of this Kingdom."

This was one of the central problems of the time, and the reward proposed was commensurate with the difficulties: £20,000 for any "generally practical and useful method" of finding longitude at sea within thirty miles after a six-week voyage—a stupendous amount of money for that time. And to avoid discouraging less precise methods, smaller rewards were offered for less accurate means: £15,000 for errors within forty miles, and £10,000 for errors within sixty miles.

To supervise the competition, Parliament appointed a Board of Longitude, consisting of sailors as well as scholars. Its most prominent member was Isaac Newton, then president of the Royal Society, who summarized the scope of the problem. Various methods existed, he stated, all of which were "difficult to execute." First on the list was a watch that would "keep time exactly." But, he added, "by reason of the Motion of a Ship, the Variation of Heat and Cold, Wet and Dry, and the Difference of Gravity in different latitudes, such a Watch Hath not yet been made." He didn't think it ever would.

Newton also mentioned several methods using astronomical observations, including one based on the assumption that if the motion of the moon is known, it is possible to derive tables forecasting its angular momentum from the sun and certain fixed stars as observed on a standard meridian. This method basically used the night sky as a giant clock, with the moon serving as a single hand and the stars and planets as the digits. In 1752 Tobias Mayer, a German astronomer, succeeded in compiling these tables after many years of observations. They turned out to be very accurate, provided one took precise measurements, but it took several hours of complicated calculations to obtain a fix. Naval ships, which had professional navigators aboard, could afford to take that time, but these skills could hardly be expected aboard a simple merchant carrier. The Board of Longitude accordingly rejected Mayer's method. Accurate it was, but "generally practicable and useful" it simply was not.

That left only the watch, and it took an extraordinary man to construct it. That man was John Harrison, a carpenter turned clockmaker from Barrow-on-Humber in Lincolnshire. Harrison took on the problem as his mission and devoted nearly all of his life to constructing not one but five clocks and watches that met the board's requirements.

John Harrison's first timekeeper—a little bulky and cumbersome, but it seems to have done the job. It still runs accurately at the National Maritime Museum in Greenwich, England.

By the time Harrison began his efforts around 1720, clocks had become quite accurate. Both Christiaan Huygens in Holland and Robert Hook in England had made clocks with a balance wheel, a device that oscillated back and forth at intervals determined by the torsion of a spring. The combination of a mainspring for motive power and a balance spring as a regulator provided the needed periodic movement to tick off constant units of time.

On land these clocks proved quite sufficient, but on a ship there were still the problems caused by motion and temperature changes. Harrison solved the latter problem by using an alloy of brass and steel, two metals whose expansion or contraction rates basically canceled each other out. He also developed an escapement that never required oiling, and with these two original inventions he proceeded to construct the most accurate clocks ever built, unaffected by motion, temperature, humidity, or any of the other factors Newton had summed up. Of his fourth device, a watch, Harrison exclaimed, "I think I may make bold to say there is neither any Mechanical or Mathematical thing in the World that is more beautiful or curious in texture than this, my watch or Timekeeper."

That opinion was not necessarily shared by his competitors, but Harrison was close to the truth. The search for an accurate seagoing clock had been one of the central problems of his time, and he had cracked it with little, if any, help from the scientific establishment. Nonetheless, Britain was unbelievably slow to acknowledge its debt to the clockmaker. For the first three clocks, which took forty years to construct, Harrison received an advance, though nothing close to the reward. When the number 4 watch was tested in 1761 on a voyage from England to Jamaica, it proved to be off by no more than five seconds, well within the award conditions laid down by the Board of Longitude nearly fifty years earlier. Harrison accordingly requested the money but was ignored. On a repeat voyage to the West Indies a year later the watch performed as impressively, but still the board showed no signs of paying. Another ten years passed before Harrison finally got his prize, and even then it took the personal intervention of King George III. Harrison did not live much longer to enjoy it. Three years later, in 1776, he died at age eighty-three.

Concerned that the intricate mechanism of the number 4 chronometer would die with its inventor, the Board of Longitude required the old watchmaker to dissect and explain his work. Harrison agreed, and he took the watch apart in his house in the presence of the watchmaker Larcum Kendall, who later made a copy of it.

The Kendall replica was sent to Plymouth in 1772 and packed aboard HMS *Resolution*, a Whitby collier that was being readied for James Cook's second Pacific voyage. As in the voyages of earlier times, the *Resolution*'s objective was to seek new lands, in particular Terra Australis Incognita, the mysterious southern continent that England hoped to claim or at least to use as a trading base. With most of the globe now explored, Terra Australis had taken on mythical significance, with many people believing it to be a fabulously wealthy territory. One influential geographer, Alexander Dalrymple, even claimed that the scraps from its table "would be sufficient to maintain the power, dominion, and sovereignty of Britain by employing all its manufacturers and ships." No wonder Cook was told to press as far south as possible and find it. He was also asked to survey as much of the Pacific and Antarctic oceans as possible and to test a number of chronometers, including the number 4 replica, in the process.

Initially Cook relied on the time-consuming lunar method of determining longitude, but the never-faltering performance of the Harrison chronometer did much to change his mind. During the voyage Cook spent 117 days out of sight of land, and the chronometer never failed. Soon there were references in his logbooks to "our never-failing guide" and "our trusted friend, the Watch." In a letter to the Admiralty Cook wrote that the Harrison replica "has exceeded the expectations of its most zealous advocate and by being now and then corrected by lunar observations has been our faithful guide through all the vicissitudes of climates." Harrison could not have hoped for higher praise.

Though Cook never found the mysterious southern continent, the three-year voyage was a major success. First and foremost, Cook disproved the myth of the riches that were thought to exist in the southern seas. Given the appalling conditions he encountered, he could claim with some certainty that if there was a continent there, it most likely would not be a promising colony or even trading base. In addition, Cook surveyed the Pacific as no one had ever done before, using the chronometer to pinpoint every island he encountered.

Britain did well in the process; among its new acquisitions were New Caledonia, the South Sandwich Islands, South Georgia, and several others, all of them appropriately surveyed and claimed on behalf of the crown. The voyage also confirmed the practical advantages of the chronometer, and not just for determining a position at sea. By solving the riddle of longitude, Harrison had given Britain a major lead, not only in the science of navigation but also in the art of mastering the sea, and hence the world. It was something the country proceeded to do with great skill during the next hundred years.

Shinkai 6500 resembles a beehive this morning, with technicians from the diving staff crawling all over the submersible. The manipulators are tested, lights are switched on and off, batteries are checked; it seems that every moving part is checked at least twice. To the casual observer it may look a bit disorganized, but like bees in a hive, every member of the diving staff knows precisely what to do during the predive checking process.

Shortly before eight Hiroshi Hotta arrives in Shinkai's hangar and briefly walks around the submersible. Dressed in a light green sweat suit, he looks cheerful, joking with the technicians as he passes. This is his seventh dive in Shinkai 6500, and as always, he is looking forward to it. "There's simply nothing like seeing for yourself what happens down there," he told me earlier. "Even the most precise sonar equipment could never have picked up the cracks that were discovered last year. For that, there's nothing like sharp eyes and a trained mind to interpret what they're seeing."

At precisely 08:00 Hotta-san boards the pressure hull, followed by Masahiko Ida, Shinkai's chief pilot, and Katsufumi Akazawa, his co-pilot. A bag with snacks and drinks is handed down as well, and the hatch is closed. Attended by the diving staff, Shinkai is then slid out onto the aft deck, where the A-frame has been readied to hoist the submersible into the water.

I am watching the launch from the aft bridge, high above the deck, where chief officer Hitoshi Tanaka is in command. "Down cables," he commands, and down come the cables that fasten Shinkai to the A-frame. Below, the deck crew is unlashing the lines that hold the submersible to the deck. "Up," Tanaka-san orders, and slowly Shinkai ascends a few feet from the deck. For a moment the submersible is dangling in midair, looking ever so much like the armored deep-sea creatures she will soon join. Next the A-frame swivels about 120 degrees, bringing Shinkai directly above the water. "Teishi," Tanaka-san instructs, "Stop," and the A-frame halts.

Tanaka-san waits so that the inflatable with divers can pull up, and then orders Shinkai lowered until just the top and the tail fin remain above the water. While the divers are unlocking the cables, the submersible is bobbing up and down; given the cramped conditions in the pressure hull, it looks mighty uncomfortable. But finally everything is unfastened, and the pilots are told they are cleared to dive. For an instant Shinkai seems to hesitate, but then she blows her ballast tanks, sending a stream of bubbles alongside, and begins to sink.

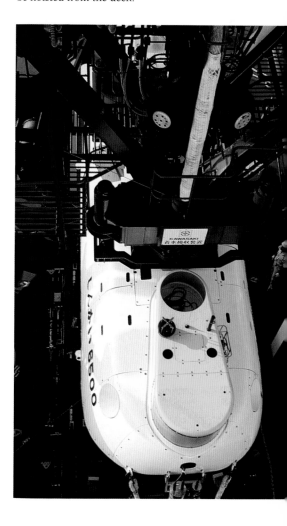

Hooked onto the cables, Shinkai is ready to be hoisted from the deck.

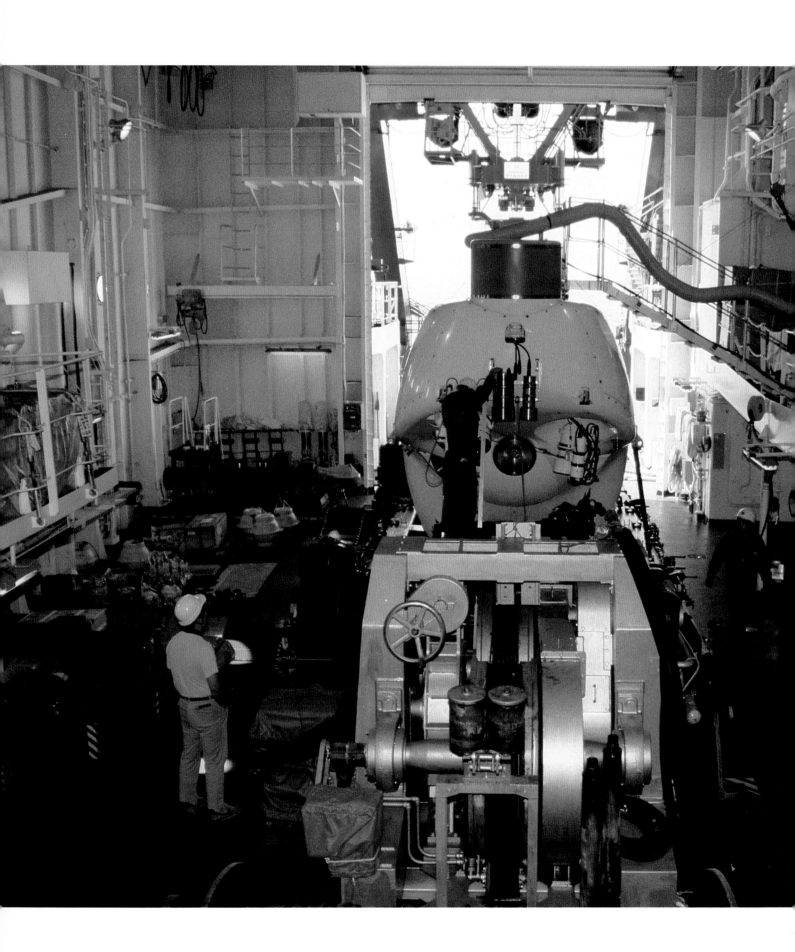

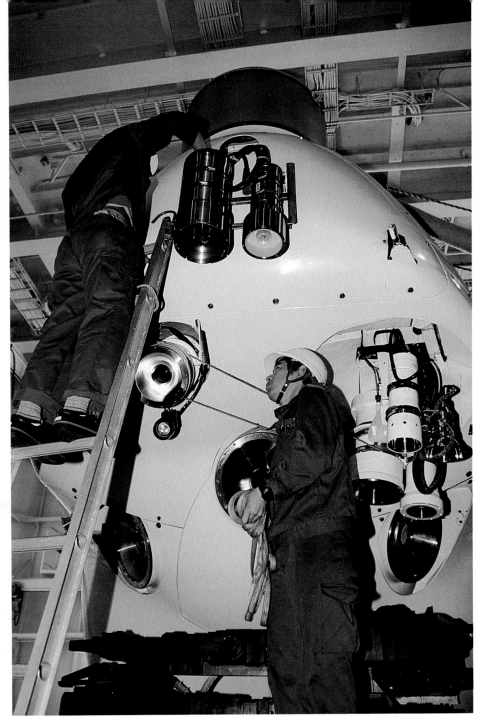

Above: Prior to the dive, Shinkai gets a final examination. There is no room for error here. The deep sea does not allow for any.

Left: Inside the *Yokosuka*'s hangar, Shinkai is constantly attended to and maintained.

Far left: Dangling from the A-frame, Shinkai looks ever so much like the strange deep-sea creatures she will soon join.

Left: Once Shinkai has been spotted, the inflatable heads out so that divers can connect the submersible.

Below: Shortly after emerging from the deep, Shinkai is immediately attended to by the divers.

I catch a distorted glimpse of Shinkai's white hull, but in a few seconds she disappears, embraced by the deep blue underneath. For a while I stare at the spot where the submersible just vanished, trying to imagine her descent through a hundred shades of blue. I guess I'm a bit envious of Shinkai's crew, but I'm not the only one. Everyone on the scientific staff would have jumped at the opportunity to go along and discover what lies far below the surface.

Before submersibles allowed us to make these excursions, there were few ways of finding out what was hidden in the deep sea. Nonetheless, during the nineteenth century people began to take a real interest in doing so. At that time there were still a few uncertainties about the distribution of landmasses in the oceans, but for all practical purposes their extent had been mapped and most of the pickings had been claimed. Now it was time to refocus the quest for ocean knowledge and begin to investigate what these great bodies of water hid underneath.

This shift in focus did not originate at a national level, however. In the grand scheme of sea power, nations had only been interested in knowing what was on the surface and how they could get there. What lay below seemed irrelevant. So it was up to individuals to shift attention to the deep. Working with primitive tools and instru-

With the lines connected, Shinkai can be hoisted onto the *Yokosuka*'s deck again.

ments, they began to probe the ocean depths, discovering things that captured the public imagination. People soon became interested in finding out what the deep sea contained and, more important, what it had to do with them.

One of the most popular and charismatic of these early deep-sea explorers was Edward Forbes, who grew up on the Isle of Man in the middle of the Irish Sea. Forbes was apparently bitten by the natural-history bug very early. In 1827, barely twelve years old, he began writing "A Manual of British Natural History in All Its Departments." He did not quite get to all the departments, but the attempt gave a clear indication of what was yet to come.

At eighteen Forbes entered Edinburgh University's Medical School. But medicine was not his calling; natural history was. He spent as much time as possible near the shore collecting marine organisms. Summers were spent on the Isle of Man, where he joined fishermen and began collecting animals from deeper waters, using small dredges. No one had ever done this before, certainly not on this scale, and before long young Forbes had collected hundreds of animals new to science. All of them were preserved, described, and classified according to the depth at which he had found them.

Forbes never got his medical degree; he simply did not show up for the final exams. The decision freed him to devote his time to studying marine animals, though there were such inconveniences as making a living. To get by, he delivered lectures describing his findings. They were sparsely attended but enabled him to eke out an existence. Working from a small room in Edinburgh, he spent the next several years researching and writing a monograph on British starfishes. When published in 1841 it drew superb reviews. Not only was it the most complete work of its kind; it also contained hundreds of meticulous drawings, all done by Forbes himself, and was extremely well written. Virtually overnight it elevated him to the ranks of Europe's most respected naturalists. Forbes was just twenty-six at the time.

The next ten years were the most productive of his life. Forbes joined several expeditions, expanded his collecting domain to include the Mediterranean, and published a general work on life in the sea, in which he classified all marine animals according to eight depth zones. He also perfected the collecting dredge so that it could be used in deeper water, at one point reaching a depth of 230 fathoms—almost a quarter of a mile. From these observations he drew two conclusions. Life in the sea was just as complex as life on land, he said—which was right. But he was mistaken in speculating that the lack of light and motion, as well as the huge pressures, prevented life from existing in the deep sea. He called this the azoic, or lifeless, zone and postulated that it began at a depth of three hundred fathoms.

Forbes was now at the height of his career. He was elected a fellow of the Royal Society and president of the Geographical Society. In 1854 he was invited to fill the chair of natural history at his alma mater. This time, students and scientists as well as the general public flocked to hear him speak. They were fascinated by what he had to say, especially the bit about the lifeless zone in the ocean depths. His enthusiasm encouraged a new generation of scientists to turn to the sea, a generation that would eventually prove his azoic concept wrong. But Forbes did not live to see that day. The many years of collecting at sea, often in awful conditions, had begun to take their toll. Within a year he was dead, at barely thirty-nine years of age.

In the years following Forbes's death, interest in the deep sea continued to grow. The exact extent of the azoic zone in particular remained a topic of considerable discussion, motivating scientists to build better dredges so that they could retrieve samples from deeper waters. It was not long before they passed Forbes's three-hundred-fathom mark, making clear that life did not cease to exist there. In fact, each time the dredge went deeper, the limit of life in the sea was pushed back a bit. Even so, most naturalists were convinced that there had to be a lifeless zone somewhere in the darkness of the abyss. After all, it was difficult to imagine how anything could survive the appalling pressures that existed so far below.

During the 1860s this theory was finally refuted. Better dredges allowed scientists to reach what were then thought to be the deepest parts of the ocean. The resulting bottom samples should have been lifeless, but they still showed plenty of animals. It then became clear that Forbes had been wrong; there simply was no such thing as an azoic zone. More than that, many of the organisms retrieved from greater depths looked positively strange. Some naturalists began to refer to these archaic life forms as living fossils, in line with what Charles Darwin had postulated in his controversial *On the Origin of Species* (1859).Darwin's theories actually seemed to fit this assumption quite well. If, as his work contended, each of the earth's living organisms was constantly adapting to the demands imposed by the environment, then it could be argued that the rate of evolution should be slower in the sea than on land, because seasons and climates change much more rapidly on land. And from there it was a small step to suggest that deep-sea organisms would have changed at the slowest rate of all. It was in the deepest parts of the ocean, in other words, that one would have to look for ancient life forms, or perhaps even the famous missing link.

In order to assess these intriguing possibilities, some living fossils would have to be collected from the ocean depths. This required more than coastal dredging, however. A major expedition was called for, one that would actually seek out the deepest reaches of the ocean and retrieve some sign of what went on there. Since this kind of effort might easily take a couple of years, it could no longer be handled at the individual or institutional level. It would require government assistance.

By this time governments had begun to show a bit more interest in undersea studies. Scientists had demonstrated that there were pragmatic sides to their investigations. In the United States, for instance, Matthew Fontaine Maury's surveys had facilitated the laying of the first transatlantic cable. Other nations too had begun to send out expeditions to collect ocean information. Depth soundings in particular appeared useful, if not essential, for the safety of navigation. Large-scale oceanic features, such as the Gulf Stream, also appeared worthy of investigation. After all, using the Gulf Stream wisely could take days off a transatlantic crossing.

Deep-sea research, however, was a bit more difficult to justify in terms of the national interest. Searching the deep sea for answers to the mysteries of life was fascinating work, no doubt, but it did not seem to have any practical benefits. Britain had already sponsored a number of small-scale dredging trips in the late 1860s, but a voyage that would seek out the deepest parts of the world ocean was a different matter. Even in a country that had a tradition of supporting science for the sake of science, support for an undertaking of that nature demanded a very good reason.

William B. Carpenter, the vice president of Britain's Royal Society, came up with that reason. Carpenter desperately wanted Britain to take the lead in this deep-sea expedition, and in an 1871 lecture to the society he called on the government not to allow Britain's edge in the marine sciences to vanish. "Having shown other nations the way to the treasures of knowledge which lie hid in the recess of the ocean, we are falling from the van into the rear, and leaving our rivals to gather everything up," he stated with a bit of calculated exaggeration. "Is this creditable to the Power which claims to be mistress of the Sea?"

It was a brilliant move. Though Britain was not about to lose its lead in the field, putting marine research into a political context and playing the national-pride card proved decisive. The government agreed with Carpenter that this type of expedition called for British initiative, and requested the Admiralty to provide a suitable ship and crew. In little more than a year the expedition was approved, organized, and ready to go. The ship selected for this mission was the twenty-three-hundred-ton naval corvette *Challenger*, commanded by Captain G. S. Nares, a man with extensive surveying and hydrographic experience. The scientific staff was appointed by the Royal

HMS *Challenger*. Her three-and-a-half year navigation, and especially the lengthy follow-up, marked the birth of modern oceanography.

Society. Carpenter, whose groundwork had made the expedition a reality, decided not to go along. The society selected instead his friend and colleague C. Wyville Thomson of Edinburgh to head the team. Joining him were chemist John Young Buchanan and three naturalists: Henry Nottidge Moseley, John Murray, and Rudulf von Willemoes-Suhm. The final member of the civilian staff was James John Wild, the expedition's artist and secretary.

On 21 December 1872 the *Challenger* left Portsmouth, beating her way against a strong wind down the English Channel toward the Atlantic Ocean. The ship and the 240 men aboard were embarked on a 68,930-mile voyage, charged with finding out as much as possible about "the conditions of the Deep Sea throughout the Great Oceanic Basins." During the three-and-a-half-year voyage, hundreds of sea-bottom samples were collected from all oceans. The first times the dredge clattered aboard from its mile-long trip, the scientists, officers, and crew crowded around it to gape at what had been brought up. But the novelty of this noisy procedure quickly wore off, and soon the crowds around the dredge thinned until only the scientific staff was left to inspect the haul. Bored with the monotonous routine of taking countless bottom and water samples, more than sixty sailors eventually deserted.

In May 1876 the *Challenger* returned to England with hundreds of seafloor deposits, 1,441 water samples from all depths and almost all latitudes, and approximately 13,000 kinds of plants and animals from a total of 362 collecting stations. Its dredges had reached a depth of nearly forty-five hundred fathoms (twenty-seven thousand feet), far deeper than anyone had expected the oceans to be, and still they retrieved traces of life.

For some of the scientists the three and a half years aboard were just the beginning of the work. For the next twenty years they sorted and described the expedition's vast collection. Hundreds of bottles and jars were distributed among the world's marine specialists. Germany's Ernst Haeckel wrote a report on radiolarians; France's Alexandre Guillaume Leopold, better known as the Marquis de Folin, examined the snails; Norway's Georg Sars, son of the naturalist Michael Sars, studied several crustaceans; and in the United States, Harvard zoologist Alexander Agassiz set out to describe the hundreds of sea urchins and brittle stars the *Challenger* had collected, a task that caused him to wish that the entire race would become extinct so that he would never have to face another echinoderm.

The *Challenger* collected marine plants and animals from 362 dredging stations, reaching a depth of nearly twenty-seven thousand feet. The mysterious "missing link" was never found, however.

Buchanan, meanwhile, examined the specific gravity of the water samples he had collected, while the German chemist William Dittmar investigated their composition. In the process Dittmar concluded that the ratio among the dozen or so major chemical elements dissolved in seawater is constant, regardless of salinity or location. Finally, the deep-sea bottom sediments were examined and described by John Murray. His classification was so precise that it is still largely in use today.

The results and conclusions of this work were published between 1880 and 1895 in fifty bulky volumes, known collectively as the *Challenger Report*. Though its 29,552 pages were heavily weighted in favor of zoological observations, the work did not neglect the other findings of the expedition. There was a description of the general form of the major ocean basins; a report on the distribution of deep-sea sediments; a classification of marine life, along with descriptions of more than four thousand new species; and novel theories on oceanic circulation and geology. The *Challenger Report*, in short, summarized everything then known about the ocean. For this reason the expedition, and especially its lengthy follow-up, came to be identified with the birth of modern oceanography.

Despite this achievement, there was regret that the Challenger had not confirmed the speculations on the origins of life it had set out to prove. If anything, it had dispelled most of these notions. Many of the organisms brought back to England had never been seen before, but none qualified as a missing link in the great zoological family tree. On the other hand, there was a wealth of new information. Most of it reflected science in its purest form—science for the sake of understanding the sea rather than for the sake of using it. As far as marine research was concerned, this was an important shift, brought about in no small part by the public's growing curiosity. But the British treasury was not impressed. It was so astonished at its own generosity in footing the £170,000 cost of the *Challenger* expedition that nearly half a century passed before another investment in science of that scale was made.

The scientific success of the *Challenger* expedition gave a major boost to oceanography in other countries. Within several years major expeditions had been sent out by Russia, Germany, and Italy. Shorter cruises were undertaken by French and Norwegian vessels. Even in the United States, where research traditionally had to be tied to pragmatic results, the mood changed. This allowed people like Alexander Agassiz to organize expeditions of their own, to fill in "the grand outlines laid down by the great English expedition."

It was not only well-established maritime powers that got involved. One of the most enthusiastic proponents of the new science of oceanography was Prince Albert of Monaco, heir to the throne of one of the tiniest nations on earth. In 1873, at age twenty-three, Albert purchased a schooner, named her the *Hirondelle*, and set off to explore the coastal waters of Europe. Initially these trips were nothing more than an excuse to get away from Monaco, but as they continued Albert became more interested in the sea itself. Before long the *Hirondelle* had been turned into a research vessel, and in 1885 she was ready for her first serious oceanographic cruise.

Albert's goal on this trip was to demonstrate that the Gulf Stream actually crossed the Atlantic, something a number of scientists still doubted. To do so he released hundreds of bottles, each containing a message requesting information on where the bottle was retrieved. Enough of these were returned over the next few years to prove that the current indeed flowed all the way across the Atlantic.

In subsequent years Albert expanded his interests from ocean currents to just about everything that had to do with the sea. Questions about marine life in the middle depths particularly fascinated him, because many scientists believed that there was little if any marine life in intermediate waters. Albert disproved that assumption by devising ingenious new traps that could be dangled beneath the ship in deep water and later retrieved. The results made clear that all of the ocean, including its intermediate layers, was inhabited by life.

With a vast amount of time and money at his disposal to pursue these activities, Albert regretted little about his professional interest in the sea, except perhaps one thing. He too had read Jules Verne's *Twenty Thousand Leagues under the Sea* when it was published in 1870, and had been captivated by its descriptions of the deep. Yet unlike Aronnax and his companions, Albert would never see any of this for himself. The best he could do was to retrieve deep-sea life from a trap or a dredge, or even from the stomachs of whales.

Of course, everyone was limited by these tools. Dredges and traps were fine for a while, but they yielded no more than a few random samples from which it was impossible to paint a broad picture. Describing the deep sea on the basis of these samples was like trying to describe the surface of the earth from a balloon at night, high above the clouds, using a bucket and a line. Sometimes the bucket would scoop up some water, other times some soil, but the observer would have a hard time deducing what the earth below was really like. Albert and his contemporaries knew just as little about the deep sea, with no more than a few dredge furrows on the seafloor to show for it.

Nearly sixty years after Verne depicted an imaginary deep-sea world, William Beebe finally saw the real thing. An ornithologist turned marine biologist, Beebe was director of the Department of Tropical Research of the New York Zoological Society. The job allowed him to join a number of oceanographic cruises during the 1920s, and it was there that he realized how inadequate deep-sea observation methods were. After all, most specimens did not survive the collecting trip to the surface, losing their colors and natural form, and yet it was on this basis that undersea life was being studied and described.

There had to be a better way, so Beebe began to think about means of getting into the water himself to observe marine life in its natural setting. At first he focused on shallow-water observations, using a hard helmet to make hundreds of dives in tropical waters. The equipment was simple: a tall copper helmet with vertical panes of glass and a hose that sent air down from a surface boat. Clad in a swimsuit, with the helmet on his head and sneakers on his feet, Beebe would venture down and begin his observations.

Beebe was not the first man to dive like this, but he was the first trained naturalist to do so and write about it. His book *Beneath Tropic Seas* for the first time introduced the public to this "realm of gorgeous life and color," as he called it. But these were more than colorful descriptions of life underwater. We spring from "far distant aquatic ancestors," Beebe wrote in the book, implying that in a very real sense his ventures were a return to a familiar setting. Like Forbes's first steps into the deep, Beebe's adventures addressed deeper questions about our existence, and they found a receptive audience.

Beebe's true interests lay far deeper than these excursions, however. His tethered equipment enabled him to explore depths of fifty or at most seventy-five feet—shallow water, really, into which none of the denizens of the deep ever ventured. Yet those were what Beebe wanted to see, so he began to explore ways of getting deeper. A submarine of sorts was needed, though not the kind that was already roaming the seas. It would need observation windows, and it would have to be able to go far deeper than anything had ever gone before.

It did not take long for Beebe to figure out that he needed a spherical observation chamber to handle the immense external pressures exerted by the deep. Beebe decided on a cylindrical shape, but in 1928 Otis Barton, a young New England engineer, convinced him that a sphere would be far better. Beebe was impressed with his explanation, and Barton's subsequent offer to finance construction sealed the deal. The young engineer completed the "tank," as he called it, in late 1929. It consisted of a steel ball four feet nine inches in diameter, with four short legs at the bottom and a cable attachment at the top.

In the spring of 1930 the tank, by now better known as the bathysphere, was brought to Bermuda, where Beebe and Barton had planned to make a number of dives. First the tank was lowered progressively deeper without anyone inside it, to check whether it would hold. This turned out to be a good idea, because on several occasions the cable got tangled, making recovery a very slow process. Once these problems had been ironed out, Beebe and Barton descended, first to eight hundred feet, then to a thousand, and finally to over fourteen hundred.

The experience had a profound effect on Beebe. He realized that he was the first person ever to see the animals that paraded in front of his observation window in their natural setting. "From here down, for two billion years there had been no day, no night, no summer, no winter, no passing of time until we came to record it," he wrote in *Beneath Tropic Seas*. He finally felt some of his goals achieved.

Beebe and Barton returned with their bathysphere in 1932, this time going as far as twenty-two hundred feet, an achievement shared via radio broadcast with an audience of millions in America and England. At this depth there was no longer any light, just "black, black, black," as Beebe put it. But in this blackness the creatures of the deep themselves were lit, using luminescence to tell of their presence. Beebe and Barton were bewildered by the abundance and variety of life at these depths—proof once more that nets and dredges were poor means of figuring out what really existed in the deep.

Finally, in August 1934 the men reached 3,028 feet, an achievement described in Beebe's appropriately titled *Half a Mile Down*. The success of the book, as well as support from the National Geographic Society, made Beebe a major media figure. But that exposure did not sit well with his scientific colleagues. They objected to his generalizations and occasional exaggerations, and particularly to the certainty with which he assigned new species names on the basis of a few glimpses of a strange animal. Science was not supposed to work that way.

Criticizing Beebe's scientific methodology was beside the point. Beebe was first and foremost a pioneer, the first man to go into the deep and return to tell about it. Aside from opening the undersea world to millions of people, his endeavors set the stage for his successors. In 1948 the Swiss scientist August Picard directed an untethered bathyscaphe to a depth of forty-six hundred feet. A few years later he built the *Trieste*, a sturdier version of the bathyscaphe, and took it down with his son Jacques

William Beebe and his bathysphere. This steel contraption allowed him and his friend Otis Barton to penetrate the deep sea as far as half a mile down.

to a depth of 10,400 feet. In 1953 two French navy divers bettered that record by taking their submersible to 13,287 feet off the West African coast. The final stage was set seven years later when the *Trieste*, crewed by Jacques Picard and U.S. Navy Lieutenant Don Walsh, reached the bottom of the Mariana Trench—at 36,198 feet the deepest point on earth. Beebe lived to hear about that feat, but not much longer. He died in Trinidad two years later, at eighty-four.

"*Yokosuka* . . . Shinkai. Happyaku meta," the intercom crackles. It is Shinkai calling the mother ship, reporting a depth of eight hundred meters—just about half a mile down. In the *Yokosuka*'s central control room a technician records the time and depth in a logbook. Next to him, in front of the large instrument panel, two of his colleagues monitor the submersible's position. Behind them is a graphics plotter, which updates Shinkai's progress every sixteen seconds. And behind the plotter is another row of instruments, including a Multi Narrow Beam Echosounder, which shows what the seafloor below looks like.

Katsumi Sakakura, head of Jamstec's diving operations, supervises the dive

Checking the plotter's printout is director of diving operations Katsumi Sakakura, who gives me a brief explanation of the various instruments in mission control. "Most of this equipment is acoustically controlled," he explains. "The Multi Narrow Beam Echosounder, for instance, sends a 12-kilohertz signal down to the seafloor and then graphically displays the returns, showing us the seafloor's topography." Shinkai's navigational equipment also relies on acoustics; the submersible can use the mother ship as a reference point or can update her own position independently. Communications naturally depend on acoustics as well, with signals shooting back and forth at fifteen hundred meters per second, the speed of sound underwater. "That means that at her deepest and furthest point it may take six or seven seconds before Shinkai's communications reach us," Sakakura-san concludes.

Meanwhile, the descent proceeds uneventfully, with chief pilot Masahiko Ida reporting Shinkai's depth every two hundred meters. "Ni-sen meta," he radios. Two thousand meters; another forty-five hundred to go. Descending at a rate of about fifty meters per minute, it should take another hour and a half to reach the seafloor. Inside the pressure hull, conditions are cramped. Only two meters in diameter and crammed with instruments, it offers little room to move, especially with a crew of three. "I always bring some classical music, usually some Mozart," Hiroshi Hotta told me when I asked him what he does during the descent. "And we talk about all kinds of things. The key is to relax during the descent, because you don't want to miss a thing for the two and a half hours Shinkai spends near the bottom."

By 11:00 A.M. Shinkai is reaching the six-thousand-meter mark, and the submersible begins to slow her descent. Just before 11:30 she reaches the bottom and switches on her lights. "*Yokosuka* . . . Shinkai. Rok-sen yonhyaku ni-ju san meta," Ida-san reports from far below; 6,423 meters. After mission control acknowledges, Shinkai sets off on her exploration, heading due east, roughly perpendicular to the Japan Trench axis.

Communications back and forth are kept to a minimum, but we can follow Shinkai's exploration on the "Shinkai 6500 video shistemu," developed for Jamstec by one of Japan's largest electronics firms. Located in front of a small sitting area in the control room, the system receives a 20-kilohertz signal sent up by Shinkai and converts it into a video image. It is not full-motion video; every few seconds the monitor screen scans to reveal another image of the seafloor, providing a slightly interrupted rendition of what Shinkai is recording far below. The images are fascinating nonetheless, especially since there are no cables connecting the submersible to the mother ship. So far the *Yokosuka* is the only ship in the world equipped with the system.

It doesn't take long for the sitting area to fill with the *Yokosuka*'s scientific staff, all of them eager to watch what Shinkai is recording and to be among the first to know whether the fissures extend this far. Their patience is being tested. Everyone is glued to the screen, but one hour expires and then another, and still there are no cracks. What we see instead is a relatively smooth surface, with a few rocks and boulders, that to me at least looks remarkably like the images beamed down from the moon by Apollo 11 in the late 1960s. Sometimes Shinkai ascends along a cliff wall to move toward the next terrace, but of the mysterious cracks there is nothing to be seen.

People are a bit disappointed, for Shinkai has just one hour left in her dive, and the absence of fissures in this region may require them to reevaluate their theories. But just before 13:30, I hear a relieved "Arimashita" from the sitting area—"There it is." Yuko Kaiho, who never stopped watching the monitor, is the first to see it: a deep fissure filling up the screen. Eight seconds pass before another image fills the screen, revealing another one, and even more on the next scans. The room is filled with excited chatter. Yujiro Ogawa, who will join Shinkai's next dive, is rapidly taking notes while watching. The others congregate around the plotter, to check Shinkai's exact position and thus the location of this new set of fissures.

Shortly after 14:00, after floating over two terraces with a considerable number of cracks, it is time for Shinkai to return. Compressed air is released into the ballast tanks, and the submersible begins the two-and-a-half-hour ascent. In the control room, the depth display on the instrument panel returns to less intimidating figures. Every few minutes Ida-san's voice can be heard over the radio: "*Yokosuka . . . Shinkai. Go-sen meta.*" Five thousand meters. Three miles below us, in the eternal "black, black, black" of the abyss, Shinkai is slowly rising, a Mozart piano concerto filling the tiny pressure hull.

Submersibles like Shinkai have come a long way since Beebe's bathysphere plunged into the clear waters off Bermuda sixty years ago. But it was not only the pursuit of science and the thrill of discovery that made these advances possible. A few years after Beebe's last excursion, World War II engulfed the world. Suddenly, nations like the United States were confronted with a very real need to know as much about the sea as possible. Within a matter of months a massive effort had been implemented to collect unprecedented amounts of information about the sea. Yanked out of its leisurely childhood, oceanography would never be quite the same.

The reason for this activity was simple: submarines. Germany's submarines posed a terrible threat to the Allied war effort, but finding and destroying those submarines was much easier said than done. Light fades quickly underwater, making submarines practically invisible. Radar, then still in its infancy, was useless as well because its waves did not penetrate water. There was only one way to find submarines: by listening for them.

There were two ways of doing this. The first simply involved listening for the noise made by the submarine itself, a process called passive sonar. The second consisted of emitting pulses of acoustic energy (the so-called pings) and then listening for their echoes. Known as active sonar, this method was considered to be the most effective. By the time the war started, high-frequency transmitters had been developed, allowing

The threat posed by German submarines, and the consequent need to find and destroy them, boosted the need for sea information. Oceanography would never be the same.

sonar operators to produce a sharp beam of sound and aim it in a variety of directions, much like the light cone of a flashlight. If the beam struck an object and echoes were returned, chances were there was something below that should not be there.

Listening for submarines turned out to be a complicated affair, because there are many ways in which the ocean distorts sound. It soon became clear, for instance, that the speed of sound in water depends on depth as well as temperature, which was a problem since the ocean has different temperature layers. More important, sometimes the sound waves bounced off the boundary between these layers. The seafloor's topography and composition also played a role, with various substrates reflecting sound in different ways. A flat, firm sandy bottom tended to reflect sound without much distortion; rocks, on the other hand, caused sound to bounce back and forth in confusing patterns, making it impossible to pinpoint the target. And if that were not enough, there were also natural noises that had to be contended with, sounds produced by anything from snapping shrimp to whales.

Here, then, was a deceptively simple problem with mind-boggling complications. In fact, figuring out how sound propagated in the sea to pinpoint a submarine, required an understanding of the physical and biological characteristics of the water, as well as of the seafloor underneath. The best minds were brought together to develop means not only of collecting the needed information but also of interpreting it. Places like sleepy Woods Hole, Massachusetts, and La Jolla, California, sites of the Woods Hole Oceanographic Institution and the Scripps Institution of Oceanography, became veritable beehives.

This massive harnessing of resources led to the development of many new instruments and techniques. Among them was the bathythermograph, a device that measured the temperature of the sea from the surface to a depth of several hundred feet. The device proved essential, for it allowed sonar operators to determine where the various layers of water, which played tricks with their echo returns, were located. U.S. submarines as well as destroyers were equipped with them, the first so that they could hide, the second so that they could chase.

American scientists also provided information on seafloor sediments and their impact on sound propagation, and on the bewildering variety of sounds in the sea. In the end, this information gave American sonar operators a decisive advantage. As the war progressed, increasing numbers of German submarines were sent to the bottom of the Atlantic, breaking their stranglehold on Britain. Meanwhile, on the other side of the globe, U.S. submarines now had access to information that gave them a fighting chance against Japanese submarine hunters. Temperature readouts and charts told them where to expect water layers under which they could hide. Sediment charts too proved extremely valuable, providing information on how the seafloor would interfere with sonar or whether, as a last resort, it could be used as a safe hiding place.

Not surprisingly, this massive research effort had profound effects on the development of oceanography. An immense amount of information had been collected, much of it with instruments and technologies specifically designed to address wartime needs. Priorities had been reoriented as well, with physical studies taking precedence over biological research. And finally, a far closer relationship between government funding and research had been established. This was good news for oceanographers, who no longer had to beg for funding to support their work. But it was bad news in that they no longer decided which studies would be pursued; often the government determined the priorities.

After the war the U.S. military continued its reliance on oceanography. Germany no longer posed a threat, but its place had been taken by a new contender for global supremacy, the Soviet Union. A formidable terrestrial power, the Soviet military command decided to concentrate its naval efforts on sea denial, a policy designed to pre-

The development of ever-quieter submarines, this time with nuclear weapons, intensified the cat-and-mouse game between submarines and their hunters.

vent the West from using its vast naval superiority. For that task the Soviets wisely decided to rely on submarines—hundreds of them.

The undersea cat-and-mouse game between submarines and their hunters continued. Backing it up was a continued scientific effort to perfect acoustical techniques and make the search for submarines less of a guessing game. A great deal of progress was made, though much of it was canceled out by advances in the technology of the submarines themselves. They grew quieter, for instance, becoming far more difficult to detect. Their capabilities also increased. Better engines allowed them to stay submerged longer, stronger hulls allowed them to go beyond the four-hundred-foot maximum depth of most wartime submarines, and the introduction of nuclear technology enabled them to stay submerged as long as their crews could handle it.

But nuclear technology did more than extend the range of submarines. When the first nuclear-tipped missiles appeared aboard submarines during the late 1950s, anti-submarine warfare (ASW) changed from a military issue to a national priority. Here indeed was a platform that could conceivably sneak up to the coast and launch a barrage of nuclear devastation far inland. A few years later both superpowers installed ballistic nuclear missiles on their submarines, enabling missiles to be launched from thousands of miles out at sea. Nuclear strategies had to be adapted, for this was a new and unassailable component in the uneasy game of nuclear deterrence. Land-based missiles could be pinpointed and destroyed, and bombers with nuclear payloads could be downed while under way. But it was almost impossible to find a submarine, especially if its only job was to hide.

Finding and keeping track of these submarines became a top priority—especially in the United States, where a research effort was initiated the likes of which had never been seen in peacetime. The stakes were high. If either side succeeded in finding the other's submarines, it would possess naval and possibly global superiority. Of course, it had to find all of them. If one slipped through the net, it could lay waste to dozens of cities.

For much of the cold war the United States maintained a sizable lead in acoustic technology. Not only was the country building much quieter submarines; it also had far more sophisticated detection techniques. Passive listening devices were placed in areas through which Soviet submarines had to pass on their way to open seas, so that they could be tracked from the moment they left port. Surface ships, attack submarines, and aircraft were equipped with the most advanced listening technology, all of it far ahead of Soviet counterparts. And a remarkably choreographed ASW system was developed, whereby all elements of the fleet cooperated to keep track of the prey.

Accompanying this deployment of hardware was the most advanced acoustic technology in existence. U.S. scientists developed computer programs that sifted through the bewildering variety of sounds in the seas and then zeroed in on frequencies that corresponded with submarine noises. Using data on water temperatures, currents, and everything else affecting sound propagation in the sea, the programs then tried to determine where this signal came from.

Aiding these efforts was the fact that Soviet submarines were quite noisy. A U.S. attack submarine cruising at low speed made less noise than a car passing on a highway. Trying to pick that sound up amid the cacophony of sounds in the ocean posed problems for even the best sonar systems. Soviet submarines, in contrast, seemed to clang and bang their way through the oceans, making them relatively easy to track. In 1980, for instance, the Soviets introduced a new *Alfa*-class attack submarine. It appeared to be a formidable adversary, capable of diving much deeper (three thousand feet) and moving much faster (42 knots) than its American *Los Angeles* class counterpart. But it was noisy. It was so noisy, in fact, that on its first test run off the Norwegian coast, U.S. sonars picked it up as far away as Bermuda—a distance of more than four thousand miles.

During the early 1980s the Soviets began to bridge the acoustical gap. First, the secrets passed on to them by the Walker spy ring made them realize how far behind they really were and what they had to do to alleviate some of the problems. A second blow to American ASW efforts came in 1984, when the Soviets acquired the machinery to cut super-smooth propellers, doing away with much of the cavitation noise that had consistently given their submarines away. The result was a quieter Soviet submarine, one that was much harder to pick up and trace.

In response to these developments, American scientists intensified their efforts. Sonars were improved, allowing quieter targets to be picked up. Computers and satellites were harnessed to collect and process far greater amounts of data on ocean conditions. Along with better signal-processing programs, this enabled U.S. sonar operators to determine where even the faintest signals were coming from.

Most of this information—including the best database on the oceans anywhere in the world—was, and still is, kept very secret. After all, it makes little sense to develop such technology to share it with the other side. In that sense American ASW efforts were no different from Portugal's efforts in the sixteenth century to keep its sea route to the Indies secret, or Britain's attempts to safeguard its technology three hundred years later. And as those countries did at the time, the United States allocated a massive amount of resources. In fact, year after year the U.S. Navy spent more money on ASW than on any other mission. Clearly, control of the sea was once more seen as the key to global power.

There are no claims to secrecy about the information Shinkai brings back to the surface. Hiroshi Hotta and his colleagues are eager to disseminate their findings. Japan would certainly benefit from a better understanding of plate tectonics, but so would many other countries. These efforts benefit the world at large, rather than just one nation.

Shortly after dinner the scientific staff gathers in one of the ship's laboratories to view Shinkai's tapes and to discuss what the new observations reveal. This is the first time all of us get to see the tape in full motion, rather than as a string of individual images spaced several seconds apart, and it is beautiful. As we observed in the control room, the deepest part of the trench looks relatively smooth, but once Shinkai climbs up a few cliffs and reaches a depth of sixty-two hundred meters, the cracks begin to show up. It is difficult to estimate how deep they are. "I would have liked to descend if we had found one large enough," Hotta-san explains, "but none of them would have fit the submersible." Besides, the pilots might not have been too keen on the idea.

The discussion turns to the significance of these fissures. It is clear now that they are a large-scale phenomenon, extending along a large portion of the buckling Pacific plate. It is also clear that they are relatively young, because the level of sedimentation inside the cracks is smaller than that of the surrounding area. But no one can say with certainty whether the fissures are related to the great Sanriku earthquake of 1933. They appear to have been formed by a horizontal stretching of the superficial crust, Yujiro Ogawa later tells me. "So they could have been caused by a great earthquake, or possibly by the shallow micro-earthquakes that often occur in this region."

Discovering the cracks is one thing, but figuring out their significance will require far more observations. "First we have to map the entire area," Hotta-san explains, "so we can study whether there are any changes from one year to the next. And one way or another, we should try to measure whether the cracks are growing. Only then can we begin thinking of meaningful conclusions. At this point everything we say is speculation."

Speculation or not, there is excitement aboard the *Yokosuka*. Perhaps no one will admit it directly, but Hotta-san and his colleagues seem to feel that they are on to something important—something that could provide further insight into the Pacific plate's behavior and, perhaps, into its next moves. The cracks seem to be an essential piece of the earthquake puzzle, though no one is quite sure where it fits.

The presentation over, someone gets a couple of beers and gradually the talk changes from scientific matters to other topics. While walking from the lab to the officers' mess, Hotta-san keeps stretching his shoulders. "I'm still sore from spending nine hours crouched in Shinkai," he confides. In response, I tell him how struck I was by the similarity between the images sent up by Shinkai and those beamed down by Apollo 11. "One could be forgiven for confusing that yellowish image of the seafloor with the surface of the moon," I insist. But Hotta-san is not convinced. "They may look somewhat alike on a television screen," he replies, "but the bottom of the sea is full of life. The moon, in contrast, is dead."

Hotta-san's response explains better than anything else why it is so important to continue our ventures into inner space. Studying the sea is about life and how this vast body of water affects the planet. With global change a very real concern, this work is more important than ever because of the ocean's critical role in the workings of the planet. How much carbon dioxide can we continue to spew out without affecting global climate? We will never know unless we figure out how much of it is being absorbed by the ocean and what happens to it afterward.

There are many other ways in which the ocean plays a buffering role. It redistributes heat around the globe, for instance, reducing the temperature differences that would otherwise exist. It also tempers the effects of our actions by redistributing, and

in large part neutralizing, what we put into it. In that sense the sea is the planet's lifeblood, a vast filter that keeps us and the planet healthy.

Much progress has been made in our attempts to understand the sea. Computers and satellites have revolutionized our ability to measure what it is doing at any one time. The quality and extent of marine research have improved greatly as well, with vast international programs now examining some of the ocean's most important features in the way this sort of work should be done: on a global scale. And now that the race between rival naval technologies has lost some of its urgency, perhaps that data can be opened up as well. Some of the most sophisticated information on the oceans is held in military computers. Making it available in order to seek a global understanding of the oceans, rather than to detect enemy submarines, is just one way in which sea power can assume a broader mandate. In fact, sea power can no longer remain a matter of merely using and controlling the sea. It must also begin to include the ability to understand and protect the sea, and to do so for the benefit of the world at large, rather than just those who want to control it. Today, at the close of the twentieth century, we cannot afford anything less.

Bibliography and Selected Readings

Chapter 1

Bailey, James. *The God Kings and the Titans: The New World Ascendancy in Ancient Times.* New York: St. Martin's Press, 1973.

Bass, George F. *A History of Seafaring.* New York: Walker, 1972.

Bunge, Frederica M., ed. *Cyprus: A Country Study.* Washington, D.C.: American University, 1980.

Casson, Lionel. *The Ancient Mariners.* New York: Minerva Press, 1959.

Chelminski, R. *Superwreck: Amoco Cadiz, the Shipwreck That Had to Happen.* New York: William Morrow, 1987.

Culican, William. *The Ancient Levant in History and Commerce.* New York: McGraw-Hill, 1966.

Davidson, Art. *In the Wake of the Exxon Valdez.* San Francisco: Sierra Club Books, 1990.

Diepraam, J., et al. *Met Olie op de Golven. 100 Jaar Tankvaart.* Rotterdam: Maritiem Museum Prins Hendrik, 1986.

Garnsey, P., et al. *Trade in the Ancient Economy.* Berkeley and Los Angeles: University of California Press, 1983.

Hagg, Robin, and Nanno Marinatos, eds. *The Minoan Thalassocracy: Myth and Reality.* Stockholm: Acta Instituti Atheniensis Regni Sueciae, 1984.

Hill, George. *A History of Cyprus.* Cambridge: Cambridge University Press, 1940.

Los, Matheos. *Ages of the Sea: A Brief History of the Greek Merchant Marine.* Athens: Akritas, 1988.

———. *Post-war Greek Shipping.* Athens: Akritas, 1991.

Mostert, Noel. *Supership.* New York: Alfred A. Knopf, 1974.

National Research Council. *Tanker Spills: Prevention by Design.* Washington, D.C.: National Academy Press, 1991.

Ratcliffe, Mike. *Liquid Gold Ships: A History of the Tanker, 1859–1984.* London: Lloyd's of London Press, 1985.

Sandars, N. K. *The Sea Peoples: Warriors of the Ancient Mediterranean.* London: Thames and Hudson, 1987.

Stopford, Martin. *Maritime Economics.* London: Unwin Hyman, 1988.

Thubron, Colin. *The Ancient Mariners.* Alexandria, Va.: Time-Life Books, 1981.

Yergin, Daniel. *The Prize.* New York: Simon and Schuster, 1991.

Chapter 2

Boxer, C. R. *Jan Compagnie in Japan, 1600–1850.* The Hague: Martinus Nijhoff, 1950.

————. *The Portuguese Seaborne Empire.* New York: Alfred A. Knopf, 1969.

Conners, Michael, and Alice King. *CY Tung: His Vision and Legacy.* Hong Kong: Seawise Foundation, 1984.

Corlett, Ewan. *The Ship: The Revolution in Merchant Shipping.* London: Her Majesty's Stationery Office, 1980.

Craig, Robin. *The Ship: Steam Tramps and Cargo Liners.* London: Her Majesty's Stationery Office, 1980.

Facey, William, *Oman: A Seafaring Nation.* Muscat: Ministry of Information and Culture, Sultanate of Oman, 1979.

Furber, Holden. *Rival Empires of Trade in the Orient, 1600–1800.* Minneapolis: University of Minnesota Press, 1986.

Gardner, Brian. *The East India Company.* New York: Dorset Press, 1971.

Gold, Edgar. *Maritime Transport.* Lexington, Mass.: Lexington Books, 1981.

Graham, M. G., and D. O. Hughes. *Containerization in the Eighties.* London: Lloyd's of London Press, 1985.

Greenhill, Basil. *The Ship: The Life and Death of the Merchant Sailing Ship.* London: Her Majesty's Stationery Office, 1980.

Greenhill, Basil, and Dennis Stonham. *Seafaring under Sail: The Life of the Merchant Seaman.* Annapolis: Naval Institute Press, 1981.

Hale, J. R. *Renaissance Exploration.* New York: W. W. Norton, 1958.

Hourani, George F. *Arab Seafaring in the Indian Ocean in Ancient and Early Medieval Times.* New York: Octagon Books, 1975.

Howarth, David. *Dhows.* London: Quartet Books, 1977.

Hyma, Albert. *A History of the Dutch in the Far East.* Ann Arbor: George Wahr, 1953.

Kemp, Peter. *The History of Ships.* London: Orbis, 1978.

Kummerman, H., and R. Jacquinet, eds. *Ships' Cargo, Cargo Ships.* Hong Kong: Mandarin, 1979.

Lyon, David. *The Ship: Steam, Steel, and Torpedoes.* London: Her Majesty's Stationery Office, 1980.

McGowan, Alan. *The Ship: The Century before Steam.* London: Her Majesty's Stationery Office, 1980.

MacGregor, David R. *Clipper Ships.* Watford: Argus Books, 1979.

————. *The Clippers: Their History and Development, 1833–1875.* Annapolis: Naval Institute Press, 1983.

Marriot, John. *Disaster at Sea.* New York: Hippocrene Books, 1987.

Martin, Esmond B., and Chryssee P. Martin. *Cargoes of the East: The Ports, Trade, and Culture of the Arabian Seas and Western Indian Ocean.* London: Elm Tree Books, 1969.

Masselman, George. *The Cradle of Colonialism.* New Haven: Yale University Press, 1963.

Miller, Russell. *The East Indiamen.* Alexandria, Va.: Time-Life Books, 1981.

Muller, Gerhardt. *Intermodal Freight Transportation.* Westport, Conn.: Eno Foundation for Transportation, 1989.

The Periplus of the Erythraean Sea. Translated and annotated by W. H. Schoff. New York: Longmans, Green, 1912.

Samhaber, Ernest. *Merchants Make History.* New York: John Day, 1964.

Unger, Richard W. *The Ship in the Medieval Economy, 600–1600.* London: Croom Helm, 1980.

Van Gelder, R., and L. Wagenaar. *Sporen van de Compagnie. De VoC in Nederland.* Amsterdam: De Bataafsche Leeuw, 1988.

Villiers, Alan. *Monsoon Seas: The Story of the Indian Ocean.* New York: McGraw-Hill, 1947.

————. *Sons of Sinbad.* New York: Charles Scribner's Sons, 1939.

Chapter 3

Ardman, Harvey. *Normandie: Her Life and Times.* New York: Ardman, 1985.

Beaver, Patrick. *The Big Ship.* London: Bibliophile Book, 1987.

Bixby, W. *South Street: New York's Seaport Museum.* New York: David McKay, 1972.

Braynard, Frank Osborn. *Fifty Famous Liners.* Cambridge: P. Stephens, 1982.

Chen, Jack. *The Chinese of America.* San Francisco: Harper and Row, 1980

Dumpleton, B., and M. Miller. *Brunel's Three Ships.* Toronto: Colin Venton, 1975.

Fitchett, T. K. *The Great Liners.* Adelaide: Rigby, 1972.

Jones, M. *Destination America.* New York: Holt, Rinehart, and Winston, 1976.

Maber, John M. *The Ship: Channel Packets and Ocean Liners.* London: Her Majesty's Stationery Office, 1980.

Maddocks, Melvin. *The Great Liners.* Alexandria, Va.: Time-Life Books, 1978.

Miller, Byron S. *Sail, Steam, and Splendour.* New York: New York Times Books, 1977.

Miller, William H. *S.S. United States: The Story of America's Greatest Ocean Liner.* New York: W. W. Norton, 1991.

Reynolds, E. *Stand the Storm: A History of the Atlantic Slave Trade.* London: Allison and Busby, 1985.

Rowland, K. T. *Steam at Sea: A History of Steam Navigation.* New York: Praeger, 1970.

Shih-Shan, Henry T. *The Chinese Experience in America.* Bloomington and Indianapolis: Indiana University Press, 1986.

Stern, Gail, ed. *Freedom's Doors: Immigrant Ports of Entry to the United States.* Philadelphia: Balch Institute for Ethnic Studies, 1992.

Winchester, S. *Pacific Rising.* New York: Prentice-Hall, 1991.

Woodham-Smith, Cecil. *The Great Hunger.* New York: Old Town Books, 1962.

Chapter 4

Boxer, C. R. *The Anglo-Dutch Wars of the Seventeenth Century.* London: Her Majesty's Stationery Office, 1974.

Brett, Bernard. *History of World Seapower.* New York: Military Press, 1985.

———. *Modern Seapower.* New York: Exeter Books, 1986.

Catton, Bruce. *The Civil War.* New York: American Heritage/Bonanza Books, 1960.

Chant, Christopher. *Naval Forces of the World.* London: William Collins Sons, 1984.

Clark, Gregory. *Britain's Naval Heritage.* London: Her Majesty's Stationery Office, 1981.

Compton-Hall, Richard. *Submarine versus Submarine.* New York: Orion Books, 1988.

Crane, Jonathan. *Submarine.* London: British Broadcasting Corporation, 1984.

Frere-Cook, Gervis, and Kenneth Macksey. *The Guinness History of Sea Warfare.* London: Guinness Superlatives, 1973.

Friedman, Norman. *The Postwar Naval Revolution.* Annapolis: Naval Institute Press, 1986.

———. *Submarine Design and Development.* Annapolis: Naval Institute Press, 1984.

Gray, Colin S., and Roger W. Barnett, eds. *Seapower and Strategy.* Annapolis: Naval Institute Press, 1989.

Hart-Davis, Duff. *Armada.* London: Bantam Press, 1988.

Hough, Richard. *A History of Fighting Ships.* London: Octopus Books, 1975.

Howarth, David. *The Dreadnoughts.* Alexandria, Va.: Time-Life Books, 1979.

———. *The Voyage of the Armada.* New York: Viking Press, 1981.

Kirsch, Richard. *Bismarck.* East Sussex: Wayland, 1976.

Lambert, Andrew. *Warrior: Restoring the World's First Ironclad.* London: Conway Maritime Press, 1987.

Lehman, John F. *Command of the Seas.* New York: Charles Scribner's Sons, 1988.

Livezey, William E. *Mahan on Sea Power.* Norman: University of Oklahoma Press, 1986.

Mahan, Alfred Thayer. *The Influence of Sea Power upon History, 1660–1783.* Englewood Cliffs: Prentice-Hall, 1980.

Marrin, Albert. *Victory in the Pacific.* Toronto: McClelland and Stewart, 1983.

Mattingly, Garrett. *The Armada.* Boston: Houghton Mifflin, 1959.

Miller, David, and John Jordan. *Modern Submarine Warfare.* New York: Military Press, 1987.

Moore, J. E., and Richard Compton-Hall. *Submarine Warfare: Today and Tomorrow.* London: Michael Joseph, 1986.

Morris, James M. *History of the U.S. Navy.* New York: Exeter Books, 1984.

Morrison, J. S., and J. F. Coates. *The Athenian Trireme.* Cambridge: Cambridge University Press, 1986.

Nitze, Paul H., and Leonard Sullivan, Jr. *Securing the Seas.* Boulder: Westview Press, 1979.

Office of the Chief of Naval Operations. *Understanding Soviet Naval Developments.* Washington, D.C.: U.S. Government Printing Office, January 1981.

Pemsel, Helmut. *Atlas of Naval Warfare.* London: Arms and Armour Press, 1977.

Polmar, Norman, and Norman Friedman. *Warships.* Hong Kong: Mandarin, 1981.

Potter, E. B., ed. *Sea Power.* Annapolis: Naval Institute Press, 1981.

Prange, Gordon W. *Miracle at Midway.* New York: McGraw-Hill, 1982.

Preston, Antony. *The Ship: Dreadnought to Nuclear Submarine*. London: Her Majesty's Stationery Office, 1980.

Reynolds, Clark G. *History and the Sea: Essays on Maritime Strategies*. Columbia: University of South Carolina Press, 1989.

Stokesbury, James L. *Navy and Empire*. New York: William Morrow, 1983.

Tute, Warren. *The True Glory*. London: MacDonald, 1983.

Van der Vat, Dan. *The Atlantic Campaign: World War II's Great Struggle at Sea*. New York: Harper and Row, 1988.

Walker, Paul F. "Smart Weapons in Naval Warfare." *Scientific American* 248, no. 5 (1983): 53–61.

Watkins, Admiral James D. *The Maritime Strategy*. Annapolis: U.S. Naval Institute, January 1986.

Wells, John. *The Immortal Warrior*. Emsworth, Hampshire: Kenneth Mason, 1987.

Winton, John. *Warrior: The First and the Last*. Liskeard, Cornwall: Maritime Books, 1987.

Chapter 5

Anand, R. P. *Origin and Development of the Law of the Sea*. Boston: Martinus Nyhoff, 1982.

Broadus, James M. "Seabed Materials." *Science* 235 (1987): 853–60.

———. *Testimony Concerning: Ocean Minerals Program*. Woods Hole, Mass., October 24, 1985.

Brooks, Douglas L. *America Looks to the Sea*. Woods Hole, Mass.: Jones and Bartlett, 1983.

Cuyvers, Luc. *Ocean Uses and Their Regulation*. New York: John Wiley and Sons, 1984.

Duxbury, A., and A. Duxbury. *The World's Oceans*. Reading, Mass.: Addison-Wesley, 1984.

Earney, Fillmore C. *Marine Mineral Resources*. London: Routledge, 1990.

Fincham, Charles, and William Van Rensburg. *Bread upon the Waters: The Developing Law of the Sea*. Forest Grove, Ore.: Turtledove, 1980.

Glassner, Martin I. *Neptune's Domain: A Political Geography of the Sea*. Boston: Unwin Hyman, 1990.

Kvendseth, Stig S. *Giant Discovery: A History of Ekofisk through the First Twenty Years*. Oslo: Phillips Norway Group, 1988.

Mangone, Gerard J. *Marine Policy for America*. Lexington, Mass.: Lexington Books, 1988.

———, ed. *The Future of Gas and Oil from the Sea*. New York: Van Nostrand Reinhold, 1983.

Mero, J. L. *The Mineral Resources of the Sea*. Amsterdam: Elsevier, 1965.

Open University. *Case Studies in Oceanography and Marine Affairs*. Oxford: Pergamon Press, 1991.

United Nations. *The Law of the Sea*. New York: United Nations, 1983.

U.S. Congress, Office of Technology Assessment, *Marine Minerals: Exploring Our New Ocean Frontier*. Washington, D.C.: U.S. Government Printing Office, 1987.

U.S. Department of the Interior/Geological Survey. *Success at Oil Creek*. Washington, D.C.: U.S. Government Printing Office, 1980.

Watt, Donald Cameron. "First Steps in the Enclosure of the Oceans." *Marine Policy* (July 1979): 211-24.

Whipple, A. B. C. *The Whalers*. Alexandria, Va.: Time-Life Books, 1979.

Chapter 6

Beebe, William. *The Arcturus Adventure*. New York: G. P. Putnam's Sons, 1926.

———. *Half a Mile Down*. New York: Harcourt, Brace, 1934.

Berthon, Simon, and Andrew Robinson. *The Shape of the World*. Chicago: Rand McNally, 1991.

Boorstin, Daniel J. *The Discoverers*. New York: Vintage Books, 1985.

Boxer, C. R. *The Portuguese Seaborne Empire*. New York: Alfred A. Knopf, 1969.

Deacon, M. *Scientists and the Sea, 1650–1900*. London: Academic Press, 1971.

Garcia, Josè Manuel. *Sagres*. Vila do Bispo: Vila do Bispo Municipal Council, 1990.

Guedes, M. J., and G. Lombardi, eds. *Portugal–Brazil: The Age of Atlantic Discoveries*. New York: Brazilian Cultural Foundation, 1990.

Kaharl, Victoria A. *Water Baby*. New York: Oxford University Press, 1990.

Newby, Eric. *The World Atlas of Exploration*. New York: Crescent Books, 1985.

Parry, J. H. *The Discovery of the Sea*. New York: Dial Press, 1974.

Penrose, B. *Travel and Discovery in the Renaissance*. Cambridge, Mass.: Harvard University Press, 1952.

Polmar, Norman. *Strategic Weapons: An Introduction.* New York: Crane, Russak, 1975.

Preston, Antony. *Submarines.* New York: Gallery Books, n.d.

Quill, Humphrey. *John Harrison: The Man Who Found Longitude.* New York: Humanities Press, 1966.

Rowe, Gilbert T., ed. *Deep Sea Biology.* New York: John Wiley and Sons, 1991.

Schlee, S. *The Edge of an Unfamiliar World: A History of Oceanography.* New York: E. P. Dutton, 1973.

Tooley, R. V. *Maps and Map Makers.* New York: Dorset Press, 1987.

Tucker, Jonathan B. "Cold War in the Ocean Depths." *High Technology,* July 1985, pp. 29–38.

Photographic Credits

About the Author

Luc Cuyvers is a writer, photographer, and film producer specializing in marine issues. He has produced and directed several films about the ocean, including "The Blue Revolution," an eight-part television series on man's relationship with the sea, broadcast in more than seventy countries.

In addition to his duties as series editor for Maryland Public Television's international co-production of "Sea Power," he produced the final program in the series and created the text and photographs for this companion volume. Future television plans include a maritime history project and a series on Vasco Da Gama and the discovery of the sea route to the East.

A native of Antwerp, Belgium, Luc Cuyvers has published his articles and photographs in a wide variety of European and American publications. This is his fifth book on ocean issues. Now a resident of Annapolis, Maryland, he holds a Ph.D. in marine studies from the University of Delaware.

The Naval Institute Press is the book-publishing arm of the U.S. Naval Institute, a private, non-profit society for sea service professionals and others who share an interest in naval and maritime affairs. Established in 1873 at the U.S. Naval Academy in Annapolis, Maryland, where its offices remain, today the Naval Institute has more than 100,000 members worldwide.

Members of the Naval Institute receive the influential monthly magazine *Proceedings* and discounts on fine nautical prints, ship and aircraft photos, and subscriptions to the quarterly *Naval History* magazine. They also have access to the transcripts of the Institute's Oral History Program and get discounted admission to any of the Institute-sponsored seminars offered around the country.

The Naval Institute's book-publishing program, begun in 1898 with basic guides to naval practices, has broadened its scope in recent years to include books of more general interest. Now the Naval Institute Press publishes more than sixty titles each year, ranging from how-to books on boating and navigation to battle histories, biographies, ship and aircraft guides, and novels. Institute members receive discounts on the Press's nearly 400 books in print.

Full-time students are eligible for special half-price membership rates. Life memberships are also available.

For a free catalog describing Naval Institute Press books currently available, and for further information about U.S. Naval Institute membership, please write to:

Membership & Communications Department
U.S. Naval Institute
118 Maryland Avenue
Annapolis, Maryland 21402-5035

Or call, toll-free, (800) 233-USNI.

THE NAVAL INSTITUTE PRESS

SEA POWER
A Global Journey

Designed by Karen L. White

Set in Berkeley Old Style on a Macintosh IIci
and output by Artech Graphics II, Inc.
Baltimore, Maryland

Printed on 70-lb. Westvaco Sterling Web Dull
and bound in Holliston Kingston Natural
by R.R. Donnelley & Sons
Willard, Ohio